MIXED REALITIES

Contemporary Approaches to Film and Media Series

A complete listing of the books in this series can
be found online at wsupress.wayne.edu.

GENERAL EDITOR

Barry Keith Grant
Brock University

MIXED REALITIES

GENDER AND EMERGENT MEDIA

SARAH ATKINSON AND VICKI CALLAHAN

WAYNE STATE UNIVERSITY PRESS
DETROIT

ISBN 9780814342794 (paperback)
ISBN 9780814352038 (hardcover)
ISBN 9780814342787 (ebook)

Library of Congress Control Number: 2024939542

On cover: *Goliath: Playing with Reality*, an animated VR experience, 25 minutes. 2021. Anagram. Cover design by Michel Vrana.

Published with the assistance of a fund established by Thelma Gray James of Wayne State University for the publication of folklore and English studies.

Wayne State University Press rests on Waawiyaataanong, also referred to as Detroit, the ancestral and contemporary homeland of the Three Fires Confederacy. These sovereign lands were granted by the Ojibwe, Odawa, Potawatomi, and Wyandot Nations, in 1807, through the Treaty of Detroit. Wayne State University Press affirms Indigenous sovereignty and honors all tribes with a connection to Detroit. With our Native neighbors, the press works to advance educational equity and promote a better future for the earth and all people.

Wayne State University Press
Leonard N. Simons Building
4809 Woodward Avenue
Detroit, Michigan 48201-1309

Visit us online at wsupress.wayne.edu.

Contents

Preface   vii

Acknowledgments   xi

1. Introduction: Gender and Emergent Media   1

2. Profiles: Innovators and Trailblazers   21

3. People: Contributions, Careers, and Communities   51

4. Platform: Transitional Media Moments   91

5. Place: Legacies, Resilience, and Resistances   121

6. Process: Cash Flow, Workflow, Free Flow   152

7. Production: Aesthetics and Ethics in Emergent Media   180

8. Conclusion   228

Appendix 1: Projects   241
Appendix 2: Participant Biographies   245
Glossary   269
Notes   279
Selected Bibliography   307
Index   315

Preface

We first met online in 2011 via SP-ARK—the Sally Potter Archive initiative, a project based on the principles of open access and collaborative scholarship.[1] We ran a focus group conducted via Skype with students from Vicki's Digital Media Tools and Tactics graduate seminar at the University of Southern California (USC). This was one of several focus groups that Sarah led and which resulted in a number of reports and outputs.[2] We first met in person in 2012 when we co-convened a panel—"Archive as Alphabet: Writing with Video"—at the Besides the Screen conference in London.[3] Alongside our colleagues Virginia Kuhn and Paul Gerhardt, Sarah talked about the work that she had been undertaking with SP-ARK, and Vicki presented on her work with USC's Scalar—an open source, web-based publishing software.

It was through these initial exchanges that we found a shared set of interests in digital archives, feminist creative practice, and transmedia. Over the course of several subsequent conversations, we ran a transmedia workshop together at the Society for Cinema and Media Studies conference in Seattle in 2014[4] to raise questions and share the challenges that we faced, and to trial some of our ideas about the archiving of transmedia. We collectively hatched the idea for a "transmedia database" (TMDb) as a way to archive, document, and appraise transmedia projects that prove so hard to teach and research due to their ephemeral nature. We subsequently presented it to the transmedia professional community at a Conducttr conference in London to a welcome and enthusiastic response.[5] We went a significant way in creating a working prototype using TimelineJS[6] and continued to make a number of contributions to the field of transmedia studies through a range of individual publications.[7] After an unsuccessful application for an American Council of Learned Societies research grant in 2014, and at about the same time when the MIT Docubase launched (in late 2013), we resigned ourselves to the fact that without substantial funding, we could not access the scale of expertise, resources, and significant institutional backing necessary to succeed in the realization of our ambitious TMDb endeavor.

We then saw the opportunity of applying for a small grant from Refiguring Innovation in Games (ReFig), a Social Sciences and Humanities Research Council of Canada five-year funded research project, as a way to pursue our continued interests. We were successfully awarded funds in 2015 to undertake a Women in Transmedia project. Through our individual and joint research endeavors to that date, we had recognized that there was a notable number of high-profile, highly visible, and in some cases internationally recognized women practitioners, creatives, and thought leaders in the transmedia industry. The aim of our project was to examine the scope of gender-diverse representation in transmedia and to develop understandings behind why it was seemingly a more representative sector in terms of gender in comparison to the games industry. We undertook more than 20 semi-structured interviews with many of the individuals whom we had identified.[8] We explored their career trajectories and questioned the conditions of the transmedia industry in comparison to the games industry to understand what made it a more attractive and conducive environment for them to advance and develop.

With recommendations of other interviewees beginning to snowball, we saw the opportunity to grow and expand the research beyond the original field. Through the award of a student research fellowship in 2016, we were able to undertake further interviews.[9] Having tracked the progress of many of our participants from transmedia into virtual reality (VR), we proposed to undertake a Women in VR project by applying for further ReFig funding in 2017. We saw this as an opportunity to capture what was happening at the point of the commercialization of the technology—at the time, there were significant levels of investment—including the high-profile acquisition of Oculus Rift by Facebook in 2014; Disney's multimillion-dollar investment into the Jaunt VR start-up in 2015, and the release of the PlayStation VR in 2016. What were once experimental, innovative, creative spaces were already being subsumed into the mainstream working cultures of the dominant media industries. VR was also being adopted into sports viewing, music concerts, tourism applications, museums, education, manufacturing, courtroom visualizations, NASA training, and the health care industry. At the time the VR sector presented an outwardly positive picture in terms of inclusion and gender diversity, and there were many high-profile women working at the leading edges of VR. This was a period when there were also numerous advocacy groups supporting and enabling women's participation. However, given the rise of commercialization of VR, there was a high risk of sectors of this industry being negatively impacted through its assimilation into sections of the dominant film and games industries. Collaborating with Catherine Allen and Helen W. Kennedy, we co-delivered a two-day workshop that brought together key women practitioners working in VR in the United Kingdom. This event resulted in the Vision for Women in Virtual Reality (VWVR) initiative.[10]

In 2019 we were able to extend this work through the resources made available as part of a Mitacs scholarship.[11] In 2022 we returned to our original interviewees from 2015—initially we wanted to revisit conversations with 10 of our prior participants to understand the key changes that had taken place over the preceding years in both their own careers and within their sectors. In particular, we were keen to understand the impacts of the COVID-19 pandemic. The number of interviews then snowballed, as the immersive experience economy had at that time exploded; the hype around VR had already shifted to augmented reality (AR), to mixed reality, and to extended reality (XR); and new conversations around the metaverse had begun to take hold, where we yet again saw a surge of women leading and innovating in the space. We ended up undertaking 54 interviews between us during this final period. This volume is the culmination of over 150 hours of interview material. It has not been an easy task to distill these varied and rich accounts into one book. We have so much material and regret that not all could be included in this particular volume. But we hope to take forward what we have had to leave out here in future publications and other forms of dissemination.

The six-year period from 2016 to 2022 has seen seismic change in both the advancement of computational technologies and tools and their creative application in the entertainment industries and the art world. In what follows, we present to you the many and varied mixed realities across three key periods of creative technological transformation (2016, 2019, and 2022).

Acknowledgments

We must first thank our funders—the Refiguring Innovation in Games (ReFig) project (funded by the Social Science and Humanities Research Council) led by Jen Jenson at York University, Canada (2015–2019) and the University of British Columbia (from 2019). The funding was essential to our project, enabling many of the interviews to take place while also providing a supportive platform to share our work and to learn from others at their wonderful annual conference. We would not have conceived of this project without being prompted to do so by the first 2015 ReFig funding call, so a huge thank-you.

A heartfelt thanks to all our generous, erudite, and luminary participants—many of whom are identified in the biographies at the end of the book—but some of whom wished to remain anonymous. We thank you all for your time, insight, hard work, and tenacity. You are an inspiration to us all and all of those who will now be able to follow in your footsteps because of the pathways that you have forged. We sincerely appreciate those who have spent time carefully reviewing and editing transcripts and those who have generously and willingly shared images of their projects for inclusion in this book. We also thank those we approached who were not able to contribute but who provided recommendations of others to speak to, gave us valuable advice, and shared important points of reference.

Thank you to our wonderful research assistants who undertook many of the interviews on our behalf: Viola Lasmana from the University of Southern California (USC), Rose Doherty and Simona Spinelli from King's College London (KCL), and Daniel Harley from York University, Toronto. Thanks also to Lisa Müller-Trede from USC who provided research assistance in the project. Thank you to the KCL Undergraduate Research Fellowship scheme and to Mitacs for funding Rose and Daniel's time and travel, respectively. Thank you also to John Callahan for technical assistance.

Thank you to the Arts & Humanities Research Institute Play Festival 2016 at KCL for providing an early venue for the dissemination of this research.

Thank you to Helen W. Kennedy and Catherine Allen and all of the Vision for Women in Virtual Reality participants and collaborators.

Thank you to those who have kindly reviewed early drafts of the book and provided invaluable feedback: Brenda Laurel and Helen W. Kennedy.

1
Introduction

Gender and Emergent Media

This book examines women / gender nonbinary / genderqueer experiences of creative production using emergent digital technologies. The book is about the lived experiences of those individuals who have been creating new works, leading and shaping their uses and applications, and innovating in both artistic and industrial contexts. We have been particularly focused on understanding what a moment of technological transition entails and enables for these individuals. The questions that have been the driving force behind this book are as follows: Where and what are the spaces of digital creativity that women / gender nonbinary / genderqueer have sought out and how do they compare to mainstream media domains? What challenges have women / gender nonbinary / genderqueer individuals faced within these spaces? How have these spaces been supportive and inclusive of a diverse range of participants? What are the characteristics of these spaces and what creative opportunities do they afford? Our current media landscape, which careens from one technological marvel to the next from virtual reality (VR) to the metaverse to artificial intelligence (AI), is indicative of the increasingly rapid hot/ cool cycle of tech hyperbole we repeatedly face. The narrative around these technologies has almost exclusively focused on the platform, the profit, and the singular visionary (usually white and male) behind the "product." The default ethos is too often narrowly defined around instrumentalist and corporate values, where "sustainability" has more to do with financial margins than life forms. It is a story of power that uncritically reproduces a rigid and limited sense of how we might engage with technology, the workplace, the environment, and one another. The power dynamics are frequently veiled by the erasure of the human hands at work behind the technology. Kate Crawford's 2021 *The Atlas of AI* provides the instructive reminder—one that is applicable to any investigation of technology—that "AI is neither artificial nor intelligent. Rather, artificial intelligence is both embodied and material, made from natural resources, fuel, human labor, infrastructures, logistics, histories, and classifications."[1]

Looking at emergent technologies through the lens of gender offers an alternative and expansive lens to open up this current narrative to different social and cultural experiences with which to inform and reshape our ethical framework. The glaring need to develop a more diverse and inclusive media ecology has been called for in the last decade, especially through the noteworthy interventions of the MIT Documentary Lab, Sundance New Frontier initiatives, and Kamal Sinclair's groundbreaking online series of essays on equity issues in emerging media, *Making a New Reality*, and its companion book/toolkit assembled by Sinclair, Jessica Clark, and Carrie McLaren.[2] As media historians, we have seen how both early cinema and early computing were founded on the critical contributions by women practitioners and businesspeople, but these contributions are rarely recorded or too often are overlooked or marginalized. With early cinema scholarship, it was a very thin slice of the filmmaking that was acknowledged, valued, and archived until the pathbreaking work on gender and sexuality by the Women Film Pioneers project and Women and Film History International and the work on African American cinema, through the work of the Oscar Micheaux Society.[3] The value from these and kindred interventions was that new storytelling forms, expressions, cultures and identities were recognized and honored. The emergent media sector has been equally dependent on the labor, across all types of work, from diverse groups, and the history of the art and technology written to date has been, as in the past, equally skewed to white, male, heteronormative profiles. This history limits not only our past understanding but our present and future possibilities. Our goal with this book is to expand the forms of knowledge produced by the stories we tell of its diverse contributors.

Shifting Contexts

We are using the terms "mixed realities" and "emergent media" to encompass a range of converged and immersive technology spaces that we identified during the course of our study (2016–22), including transmedia and cross-platform production, virtual reality (VR), augmented reality (AR), and interactive and immersive media.[4] "Mixed reality" captures these multiple forms since the contexts of their creation, production, and exhibition sit at various industrial intersections—between, for example, film, television, theater, gaming, technology, and computing—and as such, are situated within many different disciplinary contexts. The key defining feature of the domains that we have identified and focus on is that they are emergent or newly available—although it is important to acknowledge that some of the underpinning technologies already have long and established histories. Some were developed and used in military training contexts many decades ago; for example, VR was being used by NASA in the 1970s, and early precursors to AR can be traced back to aircraft pilot "head up" displays which were developed in the 1960s.[5] Our research has been focused on the moment when these technologies become more widely available and accessible for creative exploration and artistic experimentation. Given the breadth of technological contexts that our participants have engaged with, it is not possible to provide full histories of each different technology or platform, as each has its own specific historical trajectory and associated antecedents.

Since the book is focused on the lived experiences of women / gender nonbinary / genderqueer individuals—the term "mixed realities" is primarily adopted to capture the diverse range of experiences within these spaces as gender identity intersects with race, ethnicity, age, socioeconomic background, disability, and caring status. The term also captures the different identities and subjectivities that our participants expressed that they were required to inhabit in order to succeed and advance within their sectors.

The research was undertaken against the backdrop of the emergence and resulting impacts of the #MeToo movement, which occurred during our interview process in 2017. In a series of harassment claims within the media and tech industries from Uber, Amazon, UploadVR, and, of course, the Weinstein Company, we saw that personal wrongdoing, criminal acts, and structural oppression are still foundational elements of our cultural landscape. The implications are profound for how underrepresented communities are portrayed and how these communities are seeing and creating a space for themselves in these emergent media economies. As Safiya Umoja Noble notes in her book, *Algorithms of Oppression*, digital technologies often hide racism and sexism behind a facade of neutrality.[6] If we are to build systemic change for gender equality and inclusivity to accompany the social protest of the #MeToo movement within the media industry, it is imperative to understand the inner workings of labor and ideology as it develops within these emergent sectors. It is against this challenging cultural backdrop that our participants relayed their own individual accounts of the challenges that they have faced—as well as the successes they have achieved, many of which are still unrecognized and undocumented. This book is based on the insights generated by 140 one-on-one in-depth semi-structured interviews with women / gender nonbinary / genderqueer media makers, content creators, artists, curators, producers, technicians, designers, digital specialists, start-up founders, industry professionals, and CEOs. By thematizing, summarizing, and presenting their accounts, we seek to redress the balance of extant media histories, to reintroduce women / gender nonbinary / genderqueer and marginalized individuals into the story where they may have previously been absent.

First and foremost, this has been a project driven by the voices and perspectives of our participants. In one of our interviews—Char Davies, an artist at the vanguard of immersive space creation posed a pointed question that chimed with our own investigation: "Can artists overcome the inherent biases of the technology and the profit-imperative of the giant corporations gathering behind it, to create meaningful, relevant work?"[7] This is a question that we hope this book offers a collective response to, at least as it applies to the 2016–22 period under examination.

Media Technologies and Gender

Considerable work has already been undertaken that examines the history of women's participation and representation in the traditional media industries—including the film industry and the ongoing problem of gender diversity in the kinds of roles and the recognition of labor where women are predominantly employed.[8] There have been numerous industry and public-sector commissioned reports in recent years that have revealed the ongoing lack of diversity in the media industry workforce (including, in the United Kingdom, by the British Film Institute [BFI], Arts Council England, Creative Industries Federation,

Directors UK, and, in the United States, by UCLA, USC's Annenberg Inclusion Initiative, and the Women's Media Center).[9] To date, there are no reports that explicitly examine representation in the sectors identified within our research to the same extent, there is an XR inclusion report,[10] but the reach and scope of the data are limited. The reports listed above, without exception, all provide compelling data pointing to significant gaps in achieving equal gender representation and a diverse range of racial and ethnic groups. Crucially, the report findings all tend to be based on organization-level data, which does not capture the independent, freelance, and pre-start-up sectors, which, as we shall see through the evidence garnered from our interviews, are sites of considerable innovation and experimentation in the emergent creative technology sectors. Other reports have drawn from qualitatively generated data, including extensive roundtable discussions with sector specialists and stakeholders, which have led to recommendations and action plans (including by the All-Party Parliamentary Group [APPG] for Creative Diversity in the United Kingdom).[11]

Many of these studies have been taken up by various scholarly research projects that have interrogated and questioned the findings in further detail. They include assessing the impact and success of the interventions made by the BFI Diversity Standards within the film industry, the implications of diversity documentation, the impact of diversity initiatives, and unionization.[12] The data from reports such as those listed above have galvanized a wealth of research into patterns of disadvantage and exclusion across race, gender, and caring status lines, as previously outlined in Bridget Conor, Rosalind Gill, and Stephanie Taylor's 2015 "Gender and Creative Labour" article, and which evidently still continue to persist.[13] These studies underscore the intransigence of gender discrimination and harassment throughout media in front of and behind the camera. Whether it is the woeful numbers for diversity in the higher profile occupations of upper management and creative leads or the attendant problem of "invisible labor" in more organizational and manual tasks (e.g., continuity, production assistance, and costume and set work), gender discrimination continues to be a dominant feature. Film and television production has been persistently troubled by stark demarcations of well-paid and prestigious versus "feminized" labor where the "feminization" of key areas of creative and organization labor leaves work undervalued, mislabeled, or erased.[14] Research has suggested that there is still an unyielding "glass ceiling" or limited ability of women and minorities to move up the ranks to more powerful or well-paid posts, what Brooke Erin Duffy calls "vertical segregation," which is consistent throughout all sectors of the media industry.[15] But there is, Duffy notes, also "horizontal segregation" of work or essentially areas of labor in "gender clusters."[16] As she points out, numerous studies over the last decade have shown repeatedly that "while men dominate more prestigious creative roles as well as technical and craft fields, women are concentrated in marketing, communications, and service roles. The high ratio of women working in public relations—estimates range from 73 to 85 percent—has led to its designation as a 'pink ghetto.'"[17] *Mixed Realities* contributes to this growing body of literature through a qualitative and longitudinal analysis. Through our interviews, we sought to question if and how emergent and transitional technology spaces may have presented a more inclusive work culture.

The high-tech sector has struggled with these diversity and inclusion questions quite openly in the last few years, with scandals from Gamergate and James Damore's Google Manifesto standing out as two of the most blatant instances of sexism across the field.[18] Noble argues in *Algorithms of Oppression* that Silicon Valley's mythology of postracialism and meritocracy displaces racial and gender inequities as a "pipeline issue," placing the burden on the individual to navigate bias throughout a systematic structure from educational settings to media stereotypes to workplace culture.[19] As Noble states, given the structural oppression throughout the industry: "The very notion that technologies are neutral must be directly challenged as a misnomer."[20] The systematic forces that Noble outlines, and the stereotypes in childhood gifts and games to teenage "geek culture" has indelibly come to define the [male] programmer and tech culture of today from college to Silicon Valley.[21] Emily Chang's *Brotopia* carefully documents the building of this androcentric culture from 1960s tests, skewed to predominantly male participants, that profiled a loner "ideal personality" for the computer industry to 1990s-era tech efforts to attract workers through "sexy" women recruiters to contemporary "work" lunches held at strip clubs.[22] The ideology of a visionary individual rising solely through meritocracy was a constant refrain throughout the industry, although as Chang tracks, the key power brokers were individuals who knew each other from university through several start-up endeavors—in other words, a fairly small and consistent network. In particular, the impact of Peter Thiel and the "PayPal mafia" on the tech world and their long-standing antipathy to issues of racial or gender difference provides insight into the ongoing struggles for diversity in this sector.[23] As Joy Lisi Rankin argues in *A People's History of Computing in the United States*, the Silicon Valley narrative "by focusing on the few, has obliterated the history of the many: the many people across the United States and around the world who have been computing in different ways for decades."[24]

It is also a history that is indicative of a recurring pattern within the evolution of creative media technologies, which we discuss below. This one-sided history circumscribes how we engage with computers as consumers rather than producers, in singular rather than collaborative activities, and through private rather than public access.[25] This historical narrative puts technology and profits before our collective well-being and agency. The focus is on exceptional individuals and unlimited growth rather than sustainability and shared histories. We hope the voices and visions relayed in this book can shift that limited and outdated narrative.

Previously Hidden Histories and Recursive Patterns

> Consumer VR was born in Las Vegas this winter, and it's a boy.
> —Joanna Alexander and Mark Long, "Nintendo's New Baby Boy"

We situate our research within the history of the gendering of media technologies, particularly during their nascent and emergent phases. The quote above originates from the context of the first commercial wave of VR in the 1990s, which, while short lived, was swiftly codified by gender. We have identified a recurring historical continuum: at the advent of any technological transitionary moment, women and those with marginalized identities can be found at the forefront as lead experimenters and innovators—flourishing in spaces where technology and creativity collide. This is always at the point at which technologies are in their nascent and emergent stages, with techniques, processes, and formal qualities yet to be established, and this is evidenced even more vividly by our own study.

It is often the case that market conditions enable women's permissible participation at these points of transition and emergence (i.e., a new manual workforce with feminized skills is needed—skills that are characteristically drawn from underpaid and undervalued vocations). However, when the subsequent documentation and histories have been written about these innovations, women's contributions are often absent. Through the publication of recently excavated histories, we can point to a number of these instances that, when presented in chronological order, reveal a recursive pattern, whereby at the point of either the commercialization of a technology or the professionalization of an associated role to a recognized level, women's histories become increasingly hidden and erased as narratives of male "pioneers" very often dominate. We can here reveal a confluence of social, technological, and cultural factors that lead to this pattern, underpinned by the forces of capitalism and the commodification process (figure 1.1).

Each of the five circles in figure 1.1 represents a transitional moment of creative experimentation or artistic practice brought about by the advancement of a particular technology. The lower section of each circle indicates what that technology was (e.g., film editing machines,

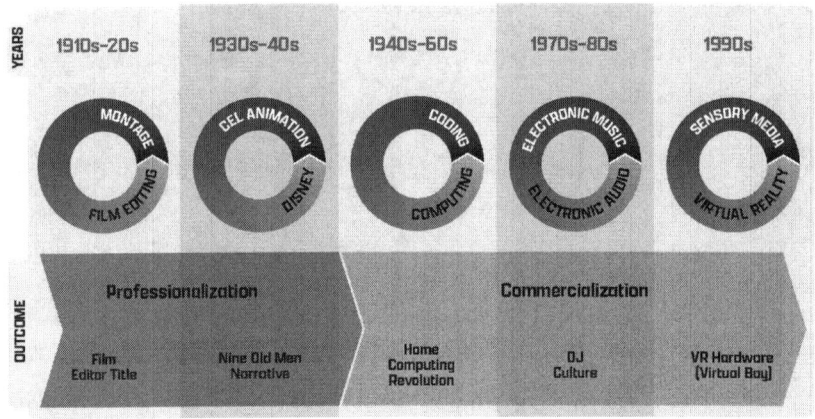

Figure 1.1. Cycles of innovation model (1910s–90s). The model reveals moments of women's experimentation with different creative technological mediums throughout history before they become commercialized or professionalized. Graphic design by Bullet Creative.

production-line animation, computing, electronic audio, and virtual reality). The upper section of each circle shows the artistic practice that it enabled through the groundbreaking experimentation of leading women artists (e.g., montage, cel animation, coding, electronic music, and sensory media). The lower third of the diagram shows the eventual outcome of these experimentations and discoveries, whether they be professionalization or commercialization; in each case, a clear argument can be made that each outcome has a gendered dimension, which negatively impacted women's future participation in these fields.

The establishment of this model became possible by later interventions that challenged the dominant histories of these innovations. Only recently, for example, have we discovered the significant contributions made by women to film editing in the early decades of the twentieth century. Not only were they the predominant gender in the workforce—a result of the need for women skilled in equipment operation similar to that required for industrial-scale machine sewing—but the contributions they made to film form and style were significant. The establishment of conventional narrative editing techniques in the context of Hollywood filmmaking is evident in such influential figures as Margaret Booth (the first person to be given the title of film editor) and Dede Allen (dubbed "film editing doctor"), while the more experimental art form of remixing within Soviet Montage can be found in the work of Esfir Shub and Elizaveta Svilova (wife of Dziga Vertov, aka Denis Kaufman).[26] Both Shub and Svilova established new techniques and conventions that would remain key principles of filmmaking to this day. Shub invented what has been referred to as the "compilation documentary," and Svilova made possible "rapid montage"—an aesthetic principle attributed to Vertov in most historical accounts. In the early 1940s many women worked as animators at Disney[27]—making key aesthetic contributions to early feature-length animated classics, including *Fantasia* (1940), *Dumbo* (1941), and *Bambi* (1942). Their ability to creatively participate in the film industry was enabled by a campaign led by Walt Disney himself to train women in order to recruit them to the workforce during a time when men were being conscripted for war. These women's artistic and creative contributions were latterly overwritten in the more popular historical accounts put forward by Disney and the more pervasive framing of "Disney's Nine Old Men."

During this same period, the Electronic Numerical Integrator and Computer—the first programmable, electronic, general-purpose digital computer—was being created, with six women central to its development. The significance of their contribution has recently been uncovered by Kathy Kleiman, and of women's participation in the field of computer coding more generally, by Mar Hicks.[28] The history of women's contribution to computing has also reached wider visibility through popular media channels, including the Hollywood film *Hidden Figures* (2016, dir.: Theodore Melfi), which tells the story of three African American women employed by NASA in the early 1960s. The three women, referred to as "human computers," were responsible for the safe orbit and return of John Glenn, an American astronaut, the first American to orbit Earth, circling it three times in 1962 during the infamous "space race." Key women coders included Grace Hopper, Jean E. Sammet, and Fran Allen, who were responsible for creating and developing programming language during the 1940s to 1960s.[29] It was at this point that women came to be seen as ideally suited for programming work given its seemingly rote, secretarial nature that called for little more than data entry. As Clive Thompson has documented, the numbers of women in coding significantly dropped to near-absent levels in the 1980s with the advent of the commercialization of the home computer. Accompanying this consumer trend were inflexible assumptions regarding gender and technology, which meant boys were more likely than girls to be exposed to computing technologies in domestic settings, and in turn, they were more likely to enter the field as young men.[30]

In the 1970s and 1980s women continued to make interventions in creative practice through their participation in the electronic music scene. Their significant contributions have only recently come to light through the 2020 documentary *Sisters with Transistors* (2020, dir.: Lisa Rovner), which maps a revised history of electronic music through the various women who were responsible for shaping the field.[31] Due to the subsequent mainstreaming and commercialization of electronic music, the stories of these original innovators had become lost.

In the 1990s consumer-level VR technologies became available. One of our participants, Char Davies was at the leading edge of innovation—experimenting with the sensory, participatory, and haptic possibilities of the form. The commercialization of consumer VR hardware was led by Nintendo and the launch of their "Virtual Boy" console. This was promoted through a high-profile advertising campaign in mainstream media outlets instilling into the public consciousness that VR was a technology for boys—as the opening quotation of this section shows. We will bring to light the important contributions that our participants made to VR and virtual world creation that were critical to the technologies' subsequent evolution in chapter 4.

For the purposes of this book, we are able to showcase only a small number of individuals who played a prominent role in key moments of technological transition. There are of course many, many more, and, indeed, those women who participated across multiple domains of expertise during the silent film era continue to be revealed by the ongoing Women Film Pioneers Project. Key to our purpose is disrupting the common (mis)understandings of how the tech fields have been shaped, and by whom. The contributions of women, at first overlooked because of the perceived feminine nature of their work and then hidden as the work became professionalized and the technologies became commercialized, were further subsumed into the success narratives of larger commercial organizations, which privileged male entrepreneurs.

By calling attention to this pattern and by recording the contributions and contexts of innovation—capturing the history as it emerges—our work will render these moments (and those past and future) more visible and durable so that they retain their place in history as touchstone moments of women's participation and contribution. Our intent here is to correct historiographical errors and oversights and also to draw on lessons from gender and cultural studies more broadly. When we attend to questions of gender, we must concurrently open issues of inclusion that range across a spectrum of areas of difference. This is not to minimize or erase social and cultural differences across these areas but to begin a conversation on exclusionary practices from the beginnings of media and technology. We see our work as but one contribution of many that have been and will be made on the questions of who can access and contribute to knowledge production that shapes the understandings of our past, present, and futures.

Approach and Process

At the start of our research process in 2015–16, we began identifying women who were actively working in transmedia and multiplatform production, initially in the United States and the United Kingdom. These individuals recommended to us others in the allied sectors of VR, AR, and interactive and immersive media, and as a result our participant pool rapidly expanded. We undertook semi-structured interviews, both in person and using video-conferencing software, with 140 different individuals. The interviews typically lasted between 45 and 70 minutes. We both worked from the same set of guiding questions, which focused on working experiences, professional practices, and career challenges and opportunities. These were sufficiently open-ended questions to enable open and exploratory conversations. The interviews took place over the following three time periods: 2016–17: 64 interviews; 2018–19: 22 interviews; and 2021–2022: 54 interviews. We interviewed nine of our participants twice across two of these timeframes, and one participant three times, in order to provide a temporal oversight of the shifts and changes that have occurred within both their own careers and within the wider sector within which they are based.[32] We attempted to ensure a diverse range of nationalities, ethnicities, job roles, and working contexts. Figures 1.2, 1.3, and 1.4 show how representation across these key areas was distributed.

Despite a focus on US and UK contexts (our initial chosen sites of study were London and Los Angeles—centers where emergent media technology take up was evidently high), figures 1.2–1.4 illustrate the heterogeneity of the individuals within our study. With over 32% people of color, our study is more ethnically representative than many. Although we did not collect data on other protected characteristics, including, age, socioeconomic status, disability, and religion, many of our participants reflect deeply on how their gender identities intersect with other aspects of their identity.

We engaged with some individuals whose career trajectories spanned several decades. Their interviews opened up further insights into the working conditions and experiences beyond our original 2000–2010s focus. We were struck by our own lack of awareness of the work that had previously been undertaken by these individuals and which had not yet featured in extant published histories. We take the opportunity in

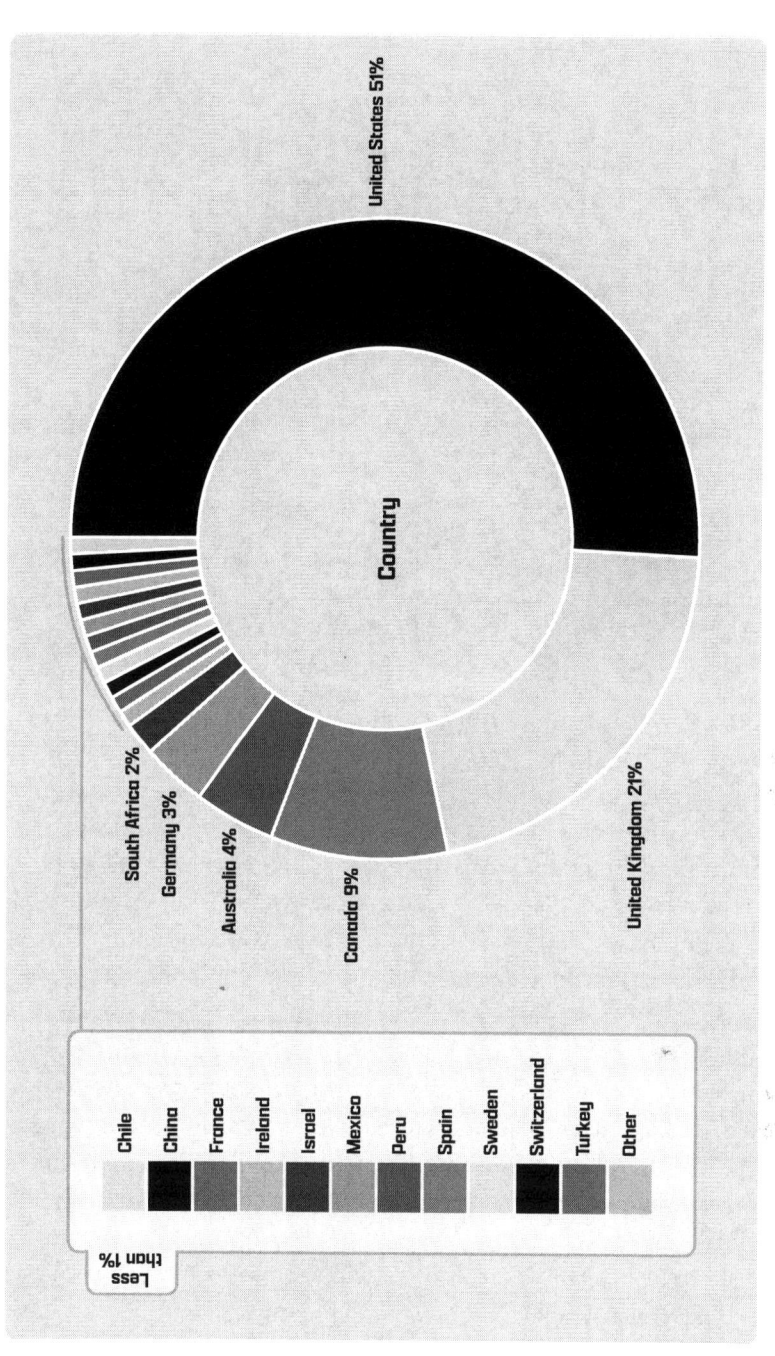

Figure 1.2. Participants by country of domicile. Graphic design by Bullet Creative.

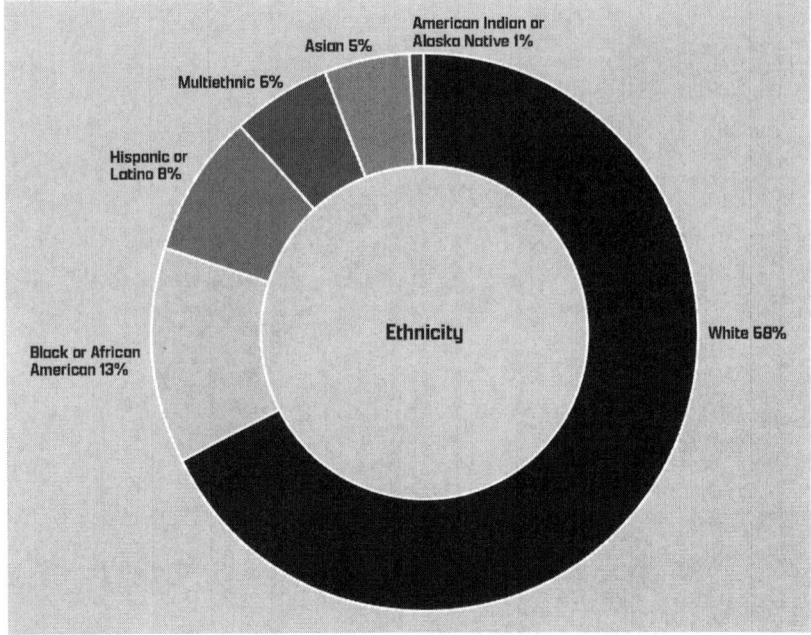

Figure 1.3. Participants by ethnicity. Graphic design by Bullet Creative.

chapter 2 to foreground four key individuals who made significant contributions for which they received limited acknowledgment elsewhere. While we do also include established voices who have received some renown, we cannot claim to have included everyone equally worthy of such exposure. We note there are many more who could have been included in this book and regret that time and resources were limiting factors. We had not sought to undertake or present a comprehensive historical account of all contributions to the fields under study. Where possible, we have attempted to identify participants who had not previously been given platforms to discuss their work. We are acutely aware that despite our best efforts to be as inclusive as possible and to amplify historically underrepresented voices, there remain many more stories that need to be heard. We are also conscious of our own positionalities as white cisgender women academics and the impact that this may have had on the responses that we received, particularly given that we are situated outside the sectors that we study. As feminist media historians,

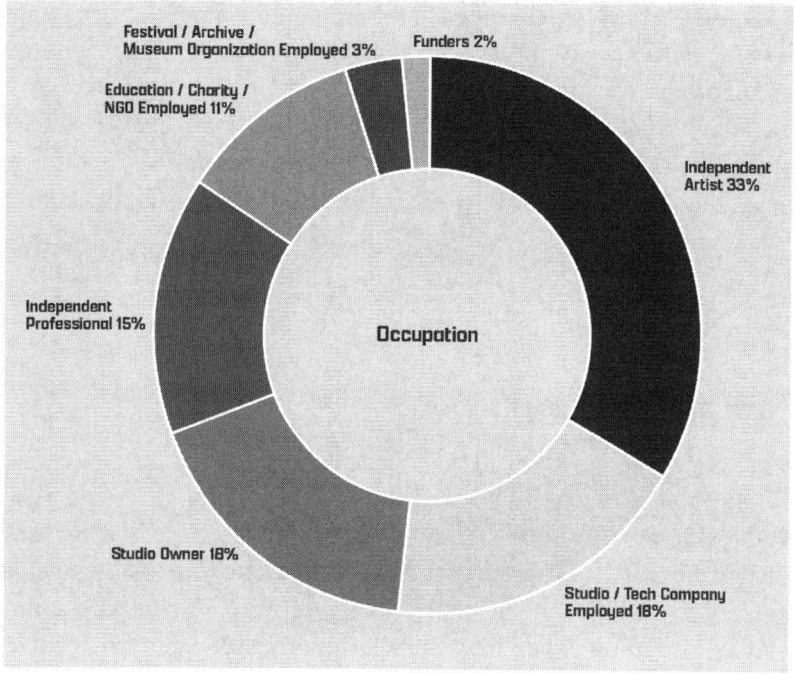

Festival / Archive /
Museum Organization Employed 3%

Funders 2%

Education / Charity /
NGO Employed 11%

Independent
Artist 33%

Independent
Professional 15%

Occupation

Studio Owner 18%

Studio / Tech Company
Employed 18%

Figure 1.4. Participants by occupation. Graphic design by Bullet Creative.

we are committed to work toward corrective histories that address elisions and marginalization of innovative voices in the field. We contacted numerous participants who do not feature in the book—some did not respond, some were unavailable during the timeframe of our research, and some preferred not to go on the record. For those we have missed, and for the important accounts that we have not been able to include, we hope that others will take up the mantle to continue the important work of uncovering the histories that have yet to be written and giving voice to those who have not had the opportunity to share their experiences and their work. Some of our more established participants working in the field of digital art feature in Judy Malloy's important anthology: *Women, Art and Technology*, which serves specifically to amplify women's contributions at the turn of the twenty-first century.[33] During this time Christiane Paul's seminal 2003 *Digital Art* was also first published and includes some of our more established participants.[34]

Paul's 2016 anthology, *A Companion to Digital Art*, is also an invaluable resource.[35] Donna Cox, Ellen Sandor, and Janine Fron's more recent *New Media Futures: The Rise of Women in the Digital Arts* (2018) profiles a number of key women figures in the United States who are clustered in the "Silicon Prairie," the Midwest centers of arts/technology innovation; these include the School of the Art Institute of Chicago and the University of Illinois National Center for Supercomputing Applications.[36] Our own work therefore makes a timely and contemporary contribution to augment the initial important research that has preceded it.

Organization and Presentation

In our endeavor to be as inclusive and representative as possible, we have chosen to include extensive verbatim quotation from our participants. We provide framing, context, and foreground key issues that garnered collective expression from our participants. Participants were asked to openly share their experiences about their career and their professional practice and to reflect on how they felt their gender identity impacted their experiences, opportunities, work, and their ability to advance in their fields as well as to influence and change them. The interviews enabled us to develop understandings of how gender, identity, precarity, and new models of work and collaboration intersect within moments of technological transition. Exploring developing sectors through the lens of gender offers an opportunity to see how women / gender nonbinary / genderqueer media makers and professionals have forged new and alternative employment categories, ways of working, and strategies of engagement within and outside mainstream industries as well as encountering the tenuous qualities of each of these areas. Our interviews revealed both rich opportunities and strategies to support gender diversity alongside some obdurate and intransigent roadblocks to change and inclusion.

Given that this is *not* a volume about technology per se but rather our participants' experiences, we have avoided any detailed descriptions of technological terms in the main text itself, although some may feature in our participant responses. We have therefore provided a comprehensive glossary so that whenever an unfamiliar term, technology, brand name, or acronym, is encountered, a corresponding summary definition can be accessed in the glossary. We also signpost other research that has already covered these areas in the notes and references. Histories of technologies have invariably been temporally organized and prioritize the characteristics of the fully formed technologies at the expense of the accounts of experimentations that have advanced and informed their development. It can often be their application in scientific and medical domains that is foregrounded, as opposed to their experimentations in artistic and entertainment contexts. It is within these creative nascent spaces where the technologies are in a process of becoming that we always place our lens.

Due to the six-year timeframe of this project and the precarious nature of the industries and sectors with which we contend, as well as the impact of the COVID-19 pandemic, many of our participants have changed roles, organizations, and employment status numerous times. When we introduce a speaker for the first time, we detail the role they held and their organizational affiliation at the time of the interview as the context from which they speak. We also identify the year in which their interview was held via endnote; for those interviewed more than once, we include the year of their interviews parenthetically in the text. In addition, we provide a short biography for each of our participants in appendix 2. Not all our participants will have a biography included—some have opted to remain either anonymous or partially identifiable (by job title) in accordance with the options set out within our research ethics framework. We have not been able to include a direct quotation from every participant. Instead, we have selected the most illustrative quotes that are indicative of a wider issue, and one expressed by numerous participants.

Chapter Outlines

The interviews, richly informative exchanges, were systematically analyzed and have shaped the structure of this book, which presents our in-depth examination of five different thematized dimensions: people, platform, place, process, and productions. Each chapter is focused on one of these areas and has been structured by the most frequently referenced themes and issues by our participants.

While the book's explicit focus is on the contemporaneous experiences of our participants during 2016–22, we have taken the opportunity to include historical accounts from four of our participants with sustained careers spanning the past five decades. In chapter 2, we have included these in the format of the detailed profiles of Rebecca Allen, Char Davies, Tamiko Thiel, and Nonny de la Peña. Chapter 3 focuses on people and examines how the roles within the media industry are being rewritten and redefined as emergent forms evolve. We track the different roles needed within the emergent media space to make a viable industry. We consider how these positions are themselves unstable or precarious and a function of the media industry's long-standing reliance on unacknowledged and underpaid "soft skills" of listening, synthesizing, and collaborating, typically gendered or "feminized." The need for "soft skills" across the production process has led to many of our participants in the evolving industry wearing multiple hats or taking on a "producer" role, an essential yet often undervalued post. Due to this peculiar and variable status, many of our participants have sought alternative organizational structures for creativity, funding, networking, and support. Recent, counter, and corrective film histories have revealed women / gender nonbinary / gender media makers as leaders and primary labor force in early stages of the industry, followed by their exclusion, deemed insignificance, and invisibility from received history as the industry developed. Similar patterns are found in the tech sector today, although funding alternatives, redesigned roles, and new storytelling forms have appeared. It is clear we are at a tipping point in terms of media structures and representations, but less certain is the direction we will take in terms of equity/diversity or consolidation/homogeneity.

In chapter 4, we adopt the term "platform" in its broadest terminological sense—as a site on which content is delivered. We first interrogate the idea of working across platforms and using multiplatforms—an approach sometimes referred to as transmedia. We explore the definition and application of transmedia within different industry contexts as a set of work practices, principles, and values. We also propose the use of the term "transmedia" as shorthand for *transitional* media which we then apply to subsequent moments of creative technological transition—such as VR. We propose the "cycles of innovation" model as a central argument within this chapter, which illustrates the recurrent characteristics of transitional media moments. We examine the second wave of commercial VR in 2012 as a transitional media moment and foreground the key women who amplified the potential of this technology and the creatives who were leading innovation. We look at earlier virtual world creation (of the mid-1990s) as a precursor to "stereo" VR and the impact and influence of documentary practice on women's participation. We then examine the increasing proprietary and limiting nature of VR, revealing the challenges of access and the barriers and gendering of technologies. We chart a shift toward social VR as a platform that emerged during the COVID-19 pandemic, with some of our participants leading the way in its use and application and raising critical awareness of its development.

In chapter 5, "place" refers to a wide range of locations, from places of work and production to places of consumption, exhibition, and promotion. Our participants have worked across a wide spectrum of places and contexts: from large commercial tech entities to cultural organizations and festivals to independent production companies. In this chapter, we set up a series of "dualities," which all comprise a negative dimension—in which our participants may have faced an exclusionary domain (e.g., a workplace setting, a conference, or industry forum)—and a secondary positive dimension—in which our participant's responses to that particular domain result in the establishment of an inclusionary context or initiative (e.g., an online community space, an alternative forum or networking space). We look at women's work cultures—in which our participants experiences ranged from everyday microaggressions and exclusions to extreme forms of harassment—and we examine the ways in which our participants either sought out alternative working cultures or set up their own work environments in response. We consider the industry conference as a microcosm of women's experiences within the broader industry context, and the challenges and exclusions that our participants have experienced within these forums. We then look at the alternative forums that they have either sought out or established. Finally, we look at institutionally led diversity initiatives and how grassroots support venues have been established and sustained in response.

Chapter 6 is concerned with "process"—how projects and productions are financed, made and managed. We cover different industry workflows and processes, from funding to sharing best practices. We look at how funding can be a barrier for women to access, progress, and secure investment but also reveal how our participants prioritized different dimensions beyond commercialization—in many cases our participants no longer pursue funding, as they see no chance of success. We examine how workflows and workloads can be characteristically heavier and more intense across a range of creative technology sector contexts: ranging across independent, artistic, and commercial domains. We look at the numerous emergent working practices that respond to the challenges faced by our participants in order to circumvent, avoid, and overcome the barriers that are often characterized by volunteer labor. Mentorship and allies are incredibly important for the advancement and success of our participants in these spaces of innovation as well as self-support (through self-teaching activities), support of one another, and a drive to proactively share best practices.

Chapter 7 explores production—that is, some of the key aesthetic issues and strategies undertaken alongside the desired outcomes and ethical challenges considered by our participants in their creative work. We note the challenges practitioners face in emergent media, beginning with the fragile or underdeveloped status of any digital artwork in the institutional art world. That uneasy status provides room for experimentation but also lives beside the ongoing threat of intercession by forces less attached to expressive, connective, or reflective goals and more to monetization and commodity culture. We look at several artists and projects that help us reimagine the boundaries of how we define not only art but also storytelling, participation, and social impact. We consider the provenance and imagined futures of production and who has access to the making, viewing, engaging, and sharing of media. This leads us to the much-discussed question of empathy with these platforms, especially VR. Almost everyone we spoke with had a weariness with the term and suggested new ways to imagine interaction from the physical or mechanical strategies employed in the user experience to a realistic assessment of outcomes achieved. We end the chapter with our participants' visions of well-being and hope.

In chapter 8, we summarize the key findings and insights generated by our research before concluding with a summary of the current state of the field. At the time of writing, in July 2022, and at the conclusion of our interviews, we found ourselves at another transitional media moment—the ascendant hype of the metaverse and Web 3.0—phenomena that many of our participants discussed in their responses. We conclude with their final thoughts and insights into these emergent spaces.

2
Profiles

Innovators and Trailblazers

We first turn our attention to an in-depth look at the people behind this research, beginning with four individual profiles of leading and influential figures and following with detailed case studies of our research participants.

During the course of our interviews, particularly with those women who have had longer careers that began in the 1970s and 1980s, we made several discoveries that related to their involvement in early groundbreaking work. Although their contributions have gone on to profoundly influence the design of creative and immersive technologies and the establishment of enduring techniques and practice in the decades that followed, these individuals have received little credit. In historical accounts that have charted key developments in creative technologies, their work has gone largely unreferenced. In the few instances where their work has been noted, it has been significantly underplayed and uncelebrated, obscured by the work of another.

Here we profile four of our participants and the key contributions that they have made. These include the 3D animation of the first computational female figure and early experiments in haptic interaction (Rebecca Allen); the advancement of creative computer design and virtual world creation (Tamiko Thiel); early innovation of headset-based embodied VR (Char Davies); and the introduction of mobile VR technology (Nonny de la Peña). While we will not claim that these individuals were the "first" to make these discoveries—as we have learned, there may well be many other hidden histories yet to be surfaced, but what we will reveal is that their contributions have often preceded that which has been claimed by another. We will also not claim that these omissions have been deliberate acts of obfuscation by those accounts that supersede theirs, something our participants were keen to point out. Rather, we argue, this happens as a result of systemic and repeated gendered norms, a pattern that has continued throughout the history of the evolution of creative technologies—as we argued in chapter 1—via our cycles of innovation model.

These are important accounts that need to be heard. Through them, we evidence an enduring pattern: women's creative contributions to the evolution of emerging technologies, practice, and designs being rendered invisible at the point of their mass commercialization.

Rebecca Allen

Rebecca Allen's artistic career spans over 40 years, and from the outset she has been at the vanguard of creatively advancing two key areas that are essential to the creation of the virtual worlds and immersive experiences of today: 3D animation and haptic interaction.

In 1980, after achieving degrees from Rhode Island School of Design and MIT, Allen joined the Computer Graphics Lab at the New York Institute of Technology, which at the time Allen said, "was the foremost place to invent a lot of the software we use today, 3D modeling, animation, [and] rendering textures."[1] Here she created the first animations of the female form (figure 2.1) and a dancing computer-generated character who played the role of St. Catherine in Twyla Tharp's 90-minute video dance piece, *The Catherine Wheel* (1982), with music by David Byrne. This is one of the first and most intricate examples of 3D computer-generated human motion and the first to be aired on television (figure 2.2). "That was the first time the public saw a computer-generated character on TV—a 3D model of a character in motion, and it was shown all over Europe and the US," said Allen, adding, "though few people knew what they were seeing back then—because nothing was very well known at that point about computers and art."[2] (For more on Allen's pioneering contribution to the 3D animation of the female form, see chapter 4.)

A special news feature on CBS in 1983 titled "The Computers Are Coming—Man or Machine" included an excerpt from *The Catherine Wheel*, and Allen was interviewed on the role of computers in society. "We need to have people from psychology and education and art and music able to work on these machines and help define the machine's personality," she said.[3] Such statements have now become a common refrain

Figure 2.1. *Swimmer,* computer animation. 1981. Rebecca Allen. Video still.

within contemporary discussions of AI, but Allen here demonstrates her exceptional vision and intuition, having proclaimed this 40 years prior.

When music video channels like MTV appeared, Allen saw this as an opportunity to create short-form video art as music videos that could be seen by a large audience. In 1986 she created the video for Kraftwerk's "Musique Non Stop" in addition to all the visual material for their album *Electric Café.* This involved the development of state-of-the-art facial animation software in order to bring the virtual mannequins of the band to life. Allen referred to her intention to create a "visual digital aesthetic" that would capture the personalities of Kraftwerk and complement their digital sound with a new form of art using computers. It was aired frequently on MTV, VH1, and other international music video programs well into the mid-1990s and was also exhibited internationally in galleries and museums. But at the time of the production, Allen explained, "no one knew who did it. Since Kraftwerk are very private and didn't mention me, I think people thought Kraftwerk did it. . . . [P]art of the arrangement

Figure 2.2. 3D animation of St. Catherine for *The Catherine Wheel*. 1982. Rebecca Allen. Video still.

Kraftwerk had was the record company didn't have any involvement in the making of this. But then the downside is they didn't know what's involved. . . . [T]hat was such a hard piece to do, simulating my voice in the style of Florian Schneider—whilst also simulating their images."[4] This work has since been acknowledged for its unique aesthetic from both fine art institutions and popular culture venues, and Rebecca was very recently credited for the work by Kraftwerk themselves: "Rebecca's video, which she and her team worked on for two years, is regarded as a milestone in 3D computer graphics. It won a number of awards and was shown on the music channels up until the mid-nineties. The ad campaign for the album was also based entirely on Rebecca's work."[5]

The commercial application and exploitation of Allen's expertise and ideas—which had thus far evolved through the conception and production of critically acclaimed and award-winning works at the cutting edge of 3D animation—came when she worked for Virgin Interactive in the early

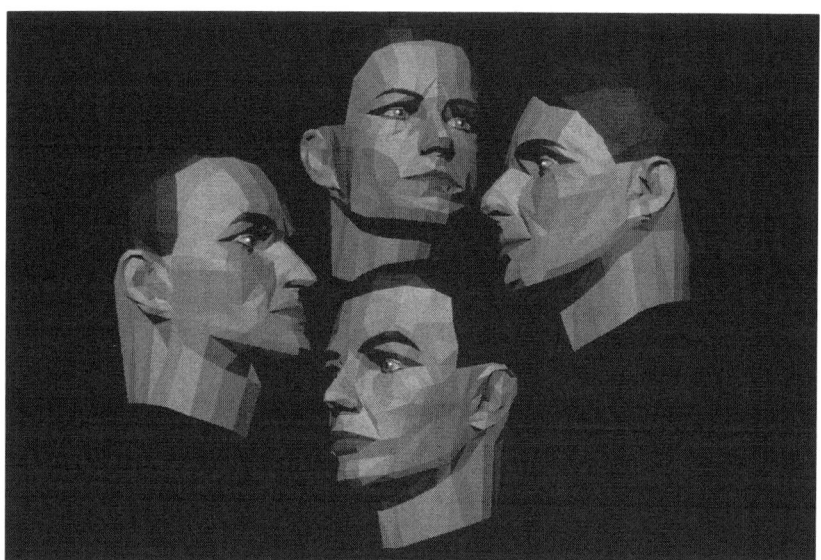

Figure 2.3. Kraftwerk portrait. 1986. Rebecca Allen.

1990s. "I did that because I wanted to learn about interactivity in games," she said. "My title was '3D visionary.' They wanted me to apply my 3D animation expertise as they were trying to move from 2D to 3D games for all the new 3D game machines coming out such as Sony PlayStation and Nintendo 64. I was helping them think about experiences using three dimensions as well as developing new game interfaces and ways to put games together."[6] From this point, Allen started to make very early interventions into haptic interaction through a series of three works called *The Bush Soul* (1997–99). Recounting her motivation, she said, "Knowing that we're going to be more and more in virtual reality and virtual worlds, I was thinking about what we are going to be doing with our bodies. Where are our bodies in virtual reality? In cyberpunk science fiction, the body was called meat and you jack directly into your brain. But as a woman, I wanted to consider the presence of a body and not discard it."[7]

Within *The Bush Soul* series, we see the very early use of haptics to create simultaneous sensation using a "force feedback" joystick, a now ubiquitous technology that first entered game controllers in the late 1990s. Allen explained:

Figure 2.4. *The Bush Soul (#3)*, immersive VR with haptic interaction. 1999. Rebecca Allen. Video still.

> In *The Bush Soul* experience, a force-feedback joystick provides both navigation and tactile sensations. It serves as a connection between your physical body and virtual soul. Many cultures believe that certain places have a special kind of energy. And in this world, you can identify these places through touch. Through vibrations in the joystick, you can feel the "energy" of the environment. Or you can feel an emotional energy during certain interactions with creatures who inhabit this world. It took three years to finally complete the whole underlying technology, a system called "Emergence."[8]

Allen took this particular work forward to collaborate with researchers at USC on pain distraction and VR. This is work that has been cited in medical journals and has paved the way for further clinical studies and research, which has resulted in the release of new VR pain distraction applications in recent years.[9]

Allen extended her sensory experimentations in 2001 through an AR piece called *Coexistence*. This was a very early example of AR—to put this in perspective, Pokémon Go wasn't released until 2016. *Coexistence* enables users to interact through their breath with a modified force feedback game pad (figure 2.5). Allen explained:

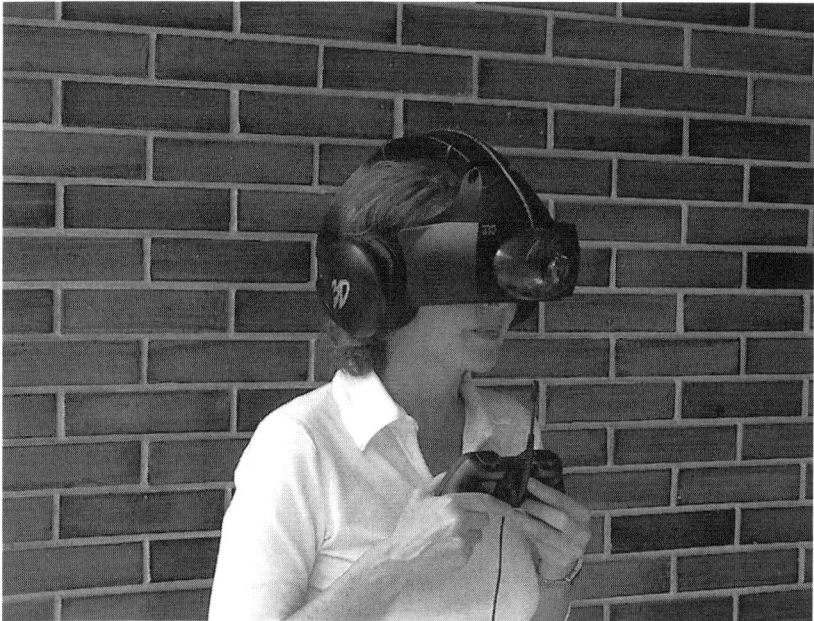

Figure 2.5. *Coexistence*, AR with breath interface and haptic interaction. 2001. Rebecca Allen. Photograph. Allen with the headsets/camera, holding the controller and breath sensor.

Interaction occurs through breath. When blowing into the sensor you see your breath visualized as a stream of digital particles that can move and affect the virtual objects. Each time your collaborator blows into the sensor you can feel their breath as vibrations in the hand-held device. You can feel each other's breath as tactile feedback. Breathing and touching are the ultimate expression of our physicality. Breath and tactile sensations connect us to another person while connecting our body to a mixed reality that blends human presence, virtual form, and physical space.[10]

AR eye wear experimentation went even further when Allen joined Media Lab Europe and created *MyoPhone* in 2003, an intimate interface using an electromyographic (EMG) sensor.

Working with an early model of AR eyeglasses, *MyoPhone* demonstrates an intimate interface using a peripheral display and EMG sensor to facilitate unobtrusive, simultaneous coexistence in physical and virtual realities. By using subtle muscle contractions, *MyoPhone* can answer and respond to a call without disrupting activities in your physical environment. Incoming calls flash discreetly in one's peripheral vision and caller identities are displayed, equally discreetly, on the lens of a pair of glasses.

She continued: "Sergey [Brin] and Larry [Page] came by the lab, and I gave them a demo of *MyoPhone* [see figure 2.6]. The guy who invented the glasses we were using went on to head the optics part of Google Glass and said it was that demonstration that sparked their interest in thinking about eyeglass displays."[11]

Figure 2.6. *MyoPhone* demonstration. 2003. Rebecca Allen. Photograph. Google founders Larry Page and Sergey Brin. Brin is wearing the eyeglass display during Allen's demonstration of *MyoPhone*.

This account clearly evidences the direct impact that Allen's explorations have had on the commercialization of mainstream digital technologies and platforms, but we also see through the other examples of her groundbreaking work the influence that she has since had on health care, gaming, art, and culture. The world has learned much from Allen despite the fact that her discoveries and innovations have been hidden from view by more dominant institutional narratives. By recovering the myriad contributions she has made, we could stand to learn a lot more. "For many years," Allen said, "I always felt like the ideas were way ahead of the technology. More recently, I feel the technology is ahead of the ideas. I think it's moving so quickly, that people aren't even taking the time to reflect on the powerful impact technologies are having. It's still being led by the same narrow group of people, without much diversity of thought."[12]

Tamiko Thiel

Tamiko Thiel has been at the forefront of virtual world creation, using both VR and AR from the very first moment that it was possible to work with these media. She has had significant influence on computer design, which is a lesser known aspect of her portfolio as a leading contemporary digital artist.

After achieving her bachelor of science in product design engineering at Stanford and a master of science in mechanical engineering at MIT, Thiel joined the Thinking Machines Corporation in 1983 where she was responsible for the group designing the physical and visual form of the Connection Machine.[13] The Connection Machine "massively parallel supercomputer" project was led by Danny Hillis, a PhD student in the MIT Artificial Intelligence Lab under Marvin Minsky, "one of the grandfathers of artificial intelligence."[14] The conceptual design of the supercomputer's form drew on Nobel physicist Richard Feynman's design for the internal routing network in the shape of a 12D hypercube, as best exemplified by the logo that Thiel designed. Thiel recounted the story:

> When it came to designing the first T-shirt for the company—Danny [Hillis] said, "I think of the machine as being this cube of cubes structure. But inside it has these fuzzy connections that are the software that can be connected independently of the hardware

structure." So this is the logo I came up with and Feynman loved it and wore it very often. Come the '90s, way after he had already died, the company had gone bankrupt, everyone had declared that artificial intelligence was a completely hare-brained idea and would never become a reliable technology that could actually be useful for anything—Apple brought out their "Think Different" campaign and lo and behold, one of the images was Richard Feynman wearing my T-shirt [figure 2.7]. I always say this is the only supercomputer designed after a T-shirt logo which is actually the best description of the functionality.[15]

Feynman went on to use the Connection Machine to run the first simulations of his idea of quantum computing. The Thinking Machines Corporation went bankrupt in 1996, and "people declared that artificial intelligence was completely useless," said Thiel. "That's when the so-called 'AI Winter' started, which only ended in 2012."[16]

Thiel has since maintained her own archive of materials documenting the Connection Machine and its legacies—including how it informed Google's search algorithm and English language searching. Thiel also became responsible for bringing the Connection Machine into public view in 2015–16 when AI was resurfacing in the public eye, promising to revolutionize our way of life. She approached the Museum of Modern Art (MoMA) and shared with us the two factors that piqued their interests:

> Google had bought the bots technology from Danny [Hillis]. Google's AI was highly structured by both the hardware ideas and the software ideas that Danny and the other scientists at Thinking Machines had come up with. . . . My ace with MoMA was my response to their question—"we understand that the machine is technologically important, but did it have any effect on design?"— and I said, "Talk to my friend Joanna Hoffman." There's actually a film about Steve Jobs where she plays a very important role.[17]

Here, Thiel refers to *Steve Jobs* (2015, Dir: Danny Boyle), in which Kate Winslet plays the character of Joanna Hoffman. Hoffman joined Apple in 1980 to work on the product marketing of the first Mac computer.

Figure 2.7. Tamiko Thiel standing in front of Apple's Richard Feynman's "Think Different" poster, San Francisco, 1998. Photo credit: Lew Tucker. Feynman is wearing the CM-1 T-shirt that Thiel designed in 1983 at Thinking Machines Corp. while they were working on the Connection Machine CM-1.

She then joined Jobs at his own software business NeXT, which was later acquired by Apple. Thiel explained:

> Joanna [Hoffman] had told me a few years after I had left Thinking Machines—but years before this came up—that when the Connection Machine came out, she was working directly with Steve Jobs at NeXT and he saw a photo of the machine and said, "Bring me that designer. I want them to design my next cube," and Joanna said, "I'm sorry, Tamiko went to Europe to become an arts student and she has no email and I have no idea where she is." All of which was true. But now, at least 30 years later, it was confirmed that the machine *had* influenced Steve Jobs sense of design.[18]

MoMA's acquisition of the Connection Machine in 2015, Thiel said, "was the breakthrough that I needed for my career to really be taken seriously" (figure 2.8).[19]

After leaving Thinking Machines, Thiel pursued her interest in virtual world creation, made possible by the release of the OpenGL standard, which enabled VR—real-time 3D creativity—from 1992 onward via standard PCs as opposed to cumbersome and expensive workstations. Worlds, Inc., founded to create online virtual worlds, launched "Worlds Chat" in 1995—one of the first PC-based online 3D virtual worlds. (We will further outline Thiel's achievements at this key moment of transition in chapter 4—through her creation of Starbright World in 1994, the first 3D online interactive virtual world for children.) In 2000, using text-based Virtual Reality Modeling Language, Thiel produced her first interactive large-scale monoscopic VR projection—*Beyond Manzanar*—with Zara Houshmand. "It's very similar to HTML," she said. "I literally typed in *Beyond Manzanar* by hand, I did not build it in a 3D program." Navigated by a simple joystick, it was one of the first VR artworks to be acquired by a US art museum—Silicon Valley's San Jose Museum of Art in 2002 (figure 2.9).

Thiel went on to create many influential works in the first decade of the 2000s, including *In the Land of Babari-an* (2006), a live dance improvisation with a real-time 3D stage set—paving the way for virtual production technologies and techniques to emerge more than a decade later. In 2008 she created *Virtuelle Mauer / ReConstructing the Wall* with Teresa

Figure 2.8. Tamiko Thiel with Connection Machine CM-2 (1987) in the Museum of Modern Art, New York, during the exhibit *Programmed*, 2017.

Reuter—an immersive, interactive 3D VR large-projection art installation depicting the Berlin Wall "Death Strip" through the dual perspective of the East and West Berlin neighborhoods. The environment was navigated through a simple joystick, and the users' decisions and actions were treated differently depending on their perspective. From the viewpoint of West Berlin, participants enjoyed freely partaking in graffiti tourism, but from an East Berlin perspective they were arrested and interrogated.

Figure 2.9. *Beyond Manzanar,* interactive VR large-screen projection. 2000. Tamiko Thiel and Zara Houshmand. Installation photo at Tokyo Metropolitan Museum of Photography, video game war scene.

Thiel was also leading on early AR innovation and experimentation—well in advance of Pokémon Go being released in July 2016—using the medium as a form of political protest and climate change activism. In 2010 she co-created *We AR in MoMA* in geolocative AR. It was an "uninvited guerrilla" AR intervention virtually situating artworks within the GPS location of MoMA in New York without the museum's permission. She cofounded the AR artist group Manifest.AR, going on to stage a Venice Biennale Intervention in 2011, titled *Shades of Absence: Public Voids* in Piazza San Marco. Here, the "erased" silhouettes of artists with censored public artworks threatened by arrest or physical violence (e.g., Ai Weiwei) were virtually overlaid on the physical environment. Thiel created another geolocative AR entitled *Reign of Gold* in 2011 for Occupy Wall Street—whereby the viewer was surrounded by a rain of $50 US golden eagle coins. It could be viewed all over the world in front of appropriate objects of protest.

Figure 2.10. *Reign of Gold*, AR installation. 2011. Tamiko Thiel. Installation view in front of the New York Stock Exchange.

Beginning in the mid-2010s, Thiel created numerous VR and AR works focused on climate change, combining powerful and poetic concepts and the affordances of the technologies to reveal and overlay humankinds' detrimental impacts on their natural environment. These included *Gardens of the Anthropocene* in 2016, an AR installation staged in numerous US cities in which native plants with absurd sci-fi mutations evolved to survive climate change. In *Unexpected Growth* (2008) an AR installation viewable on iPads, the more people who viewed the animated corals, the more the corals became bleached. *Evolution of Fish* (2019) placed viewers in the middle of a large AR projection that enabled them to guide swarms of fish—but their interventions would turn the fish into plastic waste. In the 2020 *Sponge Space Trash Takeover*—an intervention within a Mozilla Hubs conference space—Thiel populated a beautiful, restful underwater environment with plastic waste, including masks and gloves used during the COVID-19 pandemic. In *Atmos*

Figure 2.11. *Evolution of Fish*, AR livestream large projection. 2019. Tamiko Thiel and /p. Projection onto a house facade at Alys Beach, Florida, USA, for the Digital Graffiti Festival.

Sphaerae (2021) Thiel created a 360-degree VR time-based experience that revealed the changing nature of Earth's atmosphere.

In 2020 Thiel returned to AI as a tool for making art, using AI face recognition software and deepfake AI technology. In *Lend Me Your Face!* (2020)—a participatory deepfake AI video installation—a neural network animated a single photo of each participating visitor's face to match "driving videos" of leading public figures. The deepfakes were displayed in large projections surrounding the public. The visitor was confronted with a very personal encounter of how the most intimate and yet public part of the self—the face and the emotions it expresses—can easily be manipulated and placed in contexts out of their control.

Thiel is not just a prolific artist who has made significant contributions to the evolution of VR and AR art making; she is also an activist bringing the major issues of the time into stark and compelling focus. Furthermore, she is a dedicated curator, collector, and archivist. It is

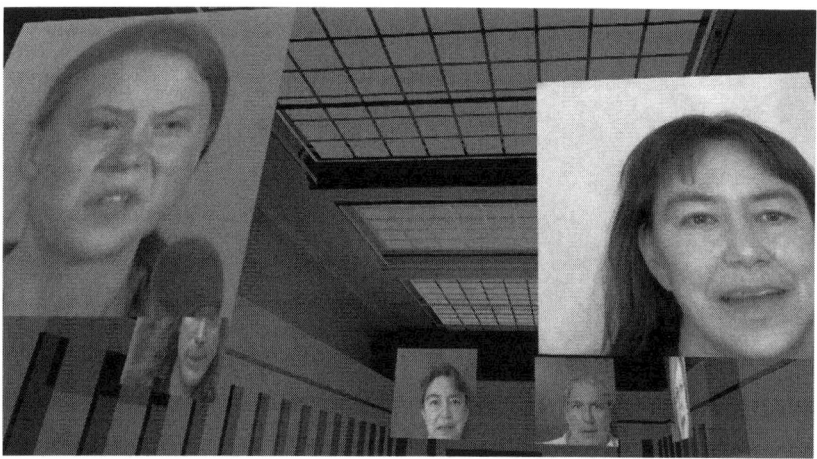

Figure 2.12. *Lend Me Your Face!*, participatory deepfake artificial intelligence video installation. 2020. Tamiko Thiel and /p. Rendering of Greta Thunberg deepfakes in *Götzendämmerung*, Artists Association in Haus der Kunst, Munich.

through the labor of her own fastidious documenting that has ensured that both her own legacy and those of others can be resurfaced, recognized, and celebrated.

Char Davies

Char Davies has made a hugely significant contribution to the creation of immersive virtual spaces both through her own works in the 1990s and through her involvement in the early development of 3D authoring and design software in the 1980s. The first aspect of her contribution is relatively well known and documented in both academic and art-based literature, as well as in her own as yet unpublished doctoral dissertation.[20] During the first commercial "wave" of VR in the 1990s, Davies created the first ever immersive artwork for a VR stereoscopic head-mounted display in 1995. The piece, titled *Osmose*, uses motion-tracking breath and balance sensors through a "sensor vest" and spatialized sound (figure 2.13). Davies pioneered the creation of semi-transparent textures enabling the viewer to navigate through luminous digital forest landscapes.

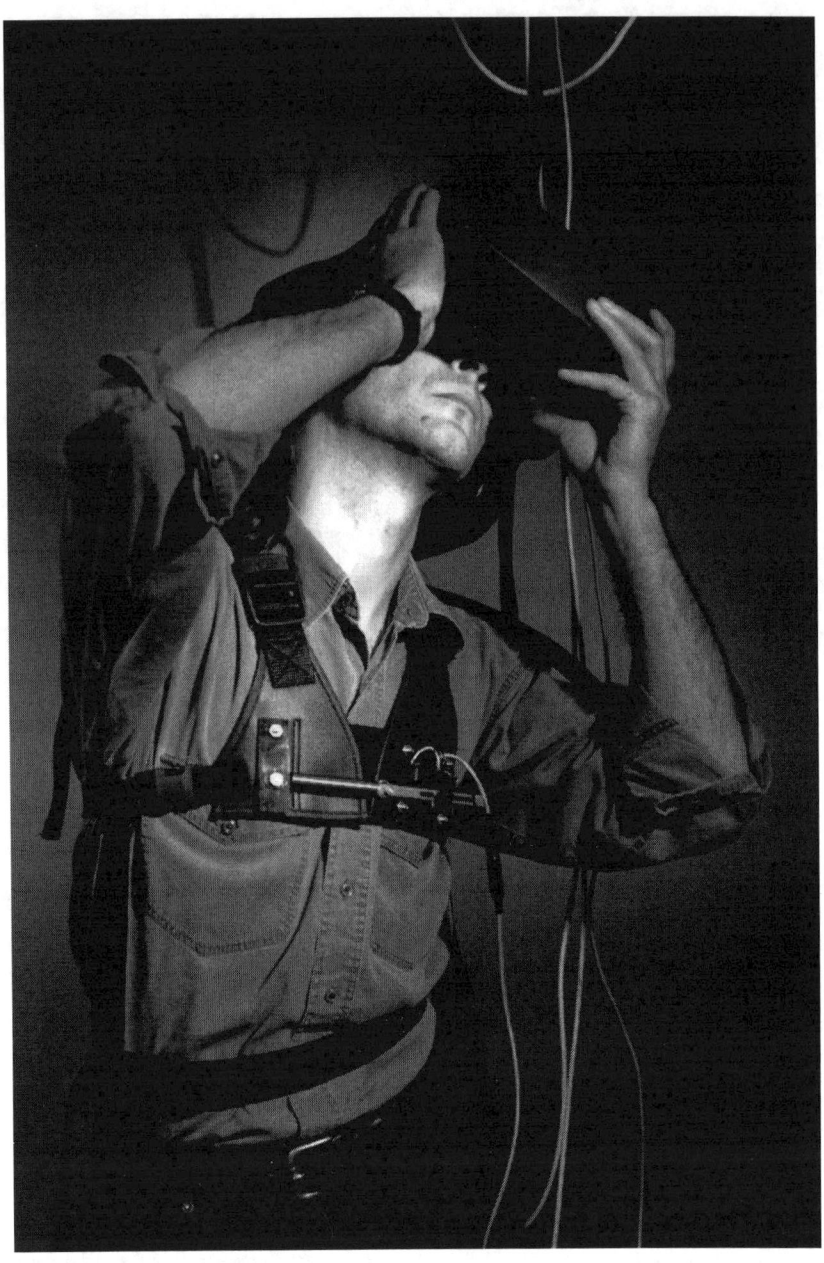

Figure 2.13. Immersant wearing a stereoscopic head-mounted display and breathing/balance interface vest. 1995. Char Davies.

Figure 2.14. *Ephémère*. 1998. Char Davies. Immersant seen through shadow screen during live performance of immersive virtual environment at the Australian Centre for the Moving Image, 2003.

Davies's use of sensor-based interactivity was groundbreaking, and she explained the deliberate choice to take away the use of hands in this way: "I wanted to shift the experience away from conventional instrumental/ dominating behavior (i.e., *do* this *to* that) to one of receptivity and even awe, amplified by the use of breath to float and balance around one's body-core."[21]

In *Osmose* there are a dozen realms to explore—the pacing and experience of which is unique to each viewer and is controlled through their breath and balance (as well as gaze, in *Ephémère*). Davies went on to create *Ephémère* in 1998, which used the same technologies, principles, and aesthetics. Both works are recognized as touchstones in the evolution of digital art and have been exhibited around the world—however, in the latest wave of commercial VR in the 2010s, their significance has been obfuscated by mainstream VR techno-hype. Davies explained the framing that she gives to her work in response to this continued technologically dominated discourse: "I have always preferred the phrase 'immersive virtual space,' emphasizing its character as a spatiotemporal *medium*, rather than the technology behind it."[22]

It was during the 1980s—prior to the creation of her landmark works—when Davies was already actively pursuing her drive toward working in 3D virtual space—that she became a founding director of Softimage, what would become a world-leading 3D software company. Founded in 1986, Softimage—the name given to the company by Davies—developed a creative software environment called Softimage 3D. Davies formally joined as a founding director in early 1988 and later became the company's first vice-president of virtual research. Davies said:

> Computer graphics software for 3D was technically very complex and could only be used by engineers. There were no intuitive interfaces. What Softimage did was develop an intuitive user interface that emulated the creative process so an art director, or an animator, could use such software directly. This removed the bottleneck between the technology and the creators. And, in doing so, Softimage changed the industry because then other 3D software companies like Wavefront and Alias were pressured by their own user groups to make their interfaces more intuitive. This is why Softimage became so successful. Then a few years later, Softimage moved on to PCs, away from the huge expense of Silicon Graphics machines.[23]

The shift to PCs and the impact that had on the wider industry was profound. "It made the technology so much more accessible," said Davies. "That is why the company was important at the time—for example, the software was used by Industrial Light and Magic for *Jurassic Park* [1993]; all the scenes with running raptors were animated using Soft-image. None of that could have happened without the Softimage software. . . . There is indeed a legacy. The company reconfigured the industry."[24] The software was eventually used in *Terminator 2: Judgment Day* (1991), *Titanic* (1997), and *The Fifth Element* (1997). Softimage received a Technological and Scientific Academy Award for innovation in its implementation of "inverse kinematics" for character animation, which were used in *Terminator 2*—a film that also won the Academy Award for Best Visual Effects. The next version of the software—Softimage XSI—was

Figure 2.15. *Osmose.* 1995. Char Davies. Roots, Rocks, and Particle Flow in the Under-Earth. Digital still taken in real-time through head-mounted display during live performance of immersive virtual environment.

used in the production of the Oscar-winning film *Happy Feet* (2006), *300* (2006), and *Charlotte's Web* (2006) and in the production of computer games, including *Metal Gear Solid 4: Guns of the Patriots* (Konami, 2008). Softimage successfully transcended the boundary between film and game production and was responsible for the accessible design of 3D creative systems that are in use today, driving forward innovation in visual effects (VFX) and paving the way for the most recent technological innovation in the screen industries—virtual production.

Even though Davies played an instrumental role in the early years of the company, she never received public acknowledgment or recognition, whereas her then partner (Daniel Langlois) was showered with awards. "I was never even thanked," she remembered. "Yes, I received stock options from the beginning, which is why I can afford to do what I'm doing now. But I was essentially written out of the history of the company."[25]

Davies started conceptualizing *Osmose* in 1993, assembling a team for the project in 1994. That same year, she began acquiring land on a small mountain in southern Quebec, whose forests inspired both *Osmose* and *Ephémère*. When early VR technology disappeared later in the 1990s, Davies continued creating immersive environments, but as large-scale compositions set within the land itself, using stone, earth, water, and trees. Through this work, she demonstrates her propensity toward the leadership of interdisciplinary teams. She stated: "I am working simultaneously in physical and so-called virtual space. I am presently directing three teams here—architectural, land, and software. But it is all interconnected, with the same goal."[26]

Since 2009, Davies has been taking digital technology into the forest while concurrently developing software for portraying it, not as a collection of objects but as a realm of subtle energies—building on the semi-transparent texturing that she developed in her earlier works.[27] According to Davies, she had no choice but to start developing custom software with her team, an exploratory process that has become as much a part of the artwork as the resulting imagery itself. "When commercially available software serves to reinforce the status quo, my only option has been to develop alternatives,"[28] she said. She went on to recount: "Going back 30 years, I believed that the medium of 'immersive virtual space' was not only unprecedented, but was capable of facilitating profound shifts in awareness, if its conventions were subverted. I have *always* sought ways to dismantle the so-called Western patriarchal dualistic instrumental worldview, whereby the nonhuman world is 'seen' as a collection of 'objects' for human use."[29] Reflecting on the path that she has forged through the lens of her gender identity, Davies said:

> My work has long sought to reaffirm our embodiment in the living earth-world, by subverting the biases inherent in the technology (associated with VR and so on) due to its origins in a militaristic patriarchal culture. . . . For me, it has always been about *returning attention* to our "being here," reaffirming our embodiment in the earth, which comes, I'm sure, from being female. Whether it's through shaping land and setting stones or creating this virtual work. That's what I've been doing for decades. And I should emphasize, such work has an ethical dimension; it is all about *care*.[30]

Davies has been at the vanguard of immersive virtual world creation from the outset, and her ideas, vision, and approach have been far-reaching in their impact and influence. Because she has been such a powerful force in shaping creative practice, artistic aesthetics, and industry process, she should take her rightful place in the history of the evolution of 3D immersive space creation. By advocating for a critical and reflexive approach in the technologies that she uses and develops, she has forged a path for artists, creatives, and content producers who have followed and those who will follow in the future.

When asked if VR could become a dominant artistic medium, Davies replied, "I think a more pertinent question would be, can artists overcome the inherent biases of the technology and the profit-imperative of the giant corporations gathering behind it, to create meaningful, relevant work?"[31] This question provides a fitting conclusion in our summary of the unique contribution that Davies has made and one befitting of the research that this book has sought to undertake.

Nonny de la Peña

Nonny de la Peña has been one of the central figures in the technological development and creative use of VR/AR for almost 20 years. Prior to this, de la Peña was a journalist, writing for *Newsweek* and the *New York Times*, and a documentary filmmaker. As founder and CEO of Emblematic Group (2011), her company has created projects across a variety of genres, but her work is primarily focused on the field that she has essentially defined and named, "immersive journalism." In 2021 she was hired as founding director of the Center for Emerging Media and Narrative at Arizona State University.

Her journey to the cutting edge of emergent technology, pathbreaking journalism, and academic innovation has been filled with challenges, and as she noted when accepting the 2022 Peabody Field Builder Legacy Award, there was bountiful "pushback" along the way from the worlds of gaming, journalism, and academia.[32] Her technical skills were in the main self-taught, even going back to her Harvard undergraduate days. "I was teaching all of my friends BASIC," she recalled, "but I was too nervous to really advance into the more intense programming courses. Everybody kept saying how hard they were, and [they were] full of guys,

Figure 2.16. *Gone Gitmo*, Second Life installation. 2007–12. Nonny de la Peña and Peggy Weil.

etc."[33] After graduation, she continued to teach herself coding and other computer skills and worked for several years as a journalist and documentary filmmaker. Her interest was then raised by a new platform. "I'd read Howard Rheingold's book about virtual reality [1991], and I just really wanted to get into virtual reality," she said. "I just didn't know how. Maybe I should have realized I should go back to school, but I just didn't really know what to do other than keep trying to teach myself things."[34]

The turn to immersive journalism for de la Peña began with a project in partnership with Peggy Weil, *Gone Gitmo* (2007–12), which was based on some of the material in de la Peña's documentary film, *Unconstitutional: The War on Our Civil Liberties* (2004). This project (which we discuss in chapter 7) was made in the virtual world Second Life and played a pivotal role in her reimagining a journalistic practice focused on embodied experiences. She received a master's in online communities at the Annenberg School at USC and shortly thereafter was up for a faculty position there. As she reflected, "I can remember very much the feeling when I was showing the *Gitmo* thing and saying, 'This is the future!' I remember one of the professors saying, 'Well, how many people are doing this in the world?' 'I guess just me, but I'm sure all the other people will soon!'"[35]

Although she did not get the post, she was offered a research fellowship at USC. During that time, de la Peña was invited to the Virtual Environment Lab in Barcelona, run by Mel Slater. Here, as she tried out a VR setup with a head-mounted display (HMD) and watched the story of a bar fight unfold on the platform, she quickly realized this was the direction she wanted to pursue. As she pulled off the VR goggles, she thought, "I cannot build for my audience to be outside the story. I've got to put them in the story."[36]

As a research fellow, de la Peña continued with coursework at USC, but still had difficulty finding others with a similar mindset for transforming journalistic storytelling. She recounted the events leading up to her working on the first VR documentary, *Hunger in Los Angeles* (2012):

> I joined a class that Sandy Tolan was teaching called "Hunger in the Golden State" where students were being taught to do web-reporting using audio, video, photography, and so on. I held up my hand and said, "Who here wants to do a piece in VR?" Not a single

student was interested. I was doing a talk down in UC Irvine, and I said that I was going to do this piece and needed some help. The professor told me to wait there, and she called her daughter who had just done a little documentary about food banks and who is graduating from high school. She got her high school students to come be my interns.

Michaela Kobsa-Mark moved into my garage office, and we started recording audio from food banks. One day she came back to my office, and she was bawling. She had just captured a moment where a guy waiting in a long line with diabetes, waiting for food and his blood sugar had dropped too low. He collapsed into a diabetic coma. That's when I decided to build with that.[37]

Despite facing enormous challenges in funding and equipment, *Hunger in Los Angeles* premiered at Sundance New Frontier program in 2012 (discussed in chapter 4). The responses from the New Frontier viewings were overwhelmingly enthusiastic for the groundbreaking work, but funding for other projects and personal finances presented serious ongoing difficulties for de la Peña and her family. Interestingly, de la Peña noted, Chris Milk—founder of the VR company Within, whose much-touted TED talk on VR as the "ultimate empathy machine" prompted robust debate—first experienced VR through her project *Hunger in Los Angeles*.[38] Undeterred by these struggles, de la Peña continued her work in VR while also pursuing a PhD at USC, and after an intense period of study and work, she began to find some breakthroughs. Her business, Emblematic Group, successfully took on commercial and entertainment-oriented work, and the sale of Palmer Luckey's Oculus headset to Facebook, the prototype for which had been advanced through the *Hunger in Los Angeles* project, increased the demand for VR content (figure 2.17).[39]

De la Peña then worked on numerous groundbreaking VR documentary pieces, including *Project Syria* (2014, commissioned by the World Economic Forum), *Across the Line* (2016, commissioned by Planned Parenthood), *Out of Exile: Daniel's Story* (2017) (figure 2.18), and *Greenland Melting* (2017, *Frontline, Nova*). All these works are noteworthy for their technical innovations incorporating photogrammetry and volumetric and holographic imagery as well as for their timely explorations of

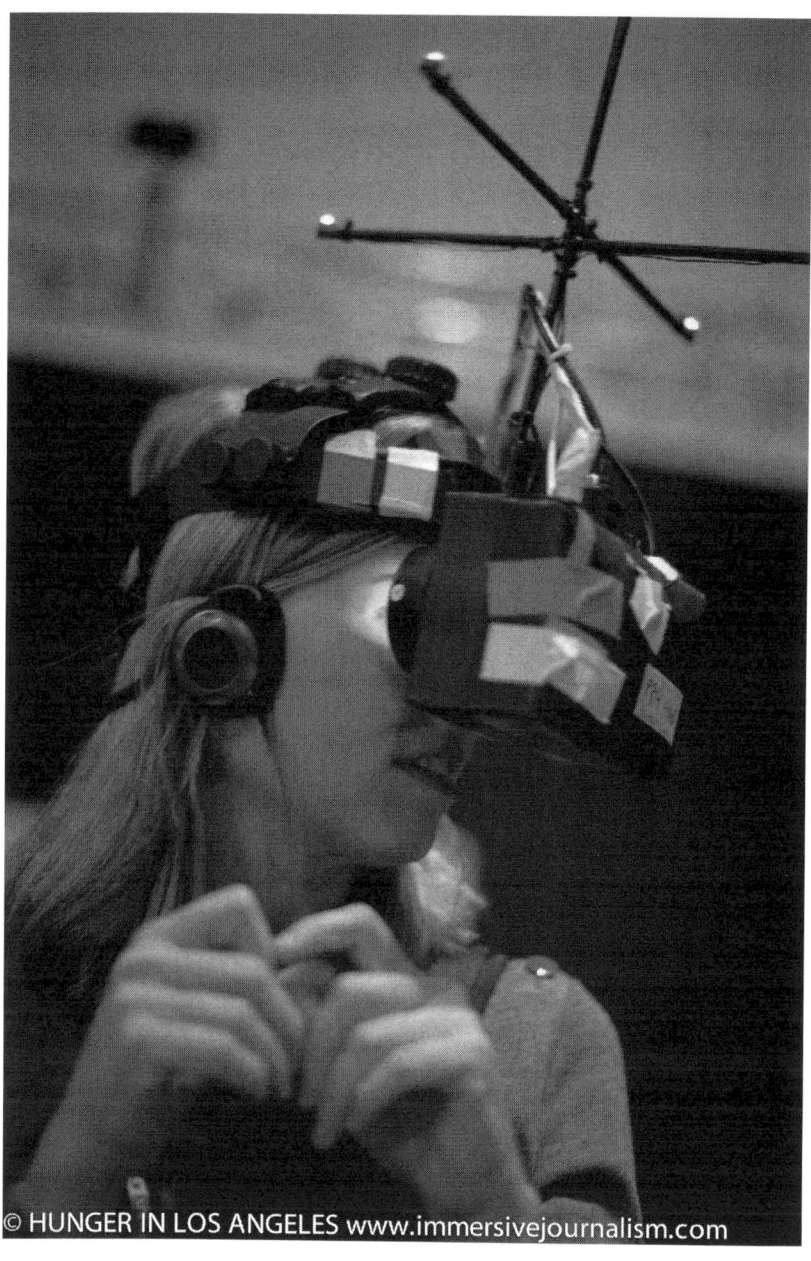

Figure 2.17. *Hunger in Los Angeles*, VR installation. Sundance, 2012. Nonny de la Peña. The image shows an audience member wearing the mobile VR headset that was an early prototype for the Oculus Rift.

Figure 2.18. *Out of Exile: Daniel's Story*, VR installation. 2017. Nonny de la Peña.

critical and, at times, contentious issues, including the Syrian refugee crisis, women's health care rights, LGBT youth homelessness, and climate change. Several projects also created additional 360-degree videos to expand the possibilities for audience access.

De la Peña noted the vicissitudes of her career path, but with her new role at Arizona State University and her ongoing work at Emblematic Group, she felt vindication in her accomplishments:

> Well, sometimes I laugh when I talk about that I have a stubborn streak a mile wide and a memory for pain that is so short. I tend to just forget all the trouble and the pain as fast as I can. Running a start-up is very difficult. I had to travel way more than I would've liked to, be away from my kids way more than I've liked to, but I think the body of work really speaks for itself. We've had an extraordinary run. I mean, there was a very tough period in 2018 for a lot of extended reality companies, and I was certainly one of them and we shrank considerably, but even through that I had a wonderful piece [*A Life in Pieces: The Diary and Letters of Stanley Hayami*, 2021] that premiered at Tribeca

last year, based on a child who was in the Japanese American concentration camp.[40]

At the time of writing, de la Peña was also in production for a VR piece on Lyme disease, which then premiered at Tribeca in 2022, as well as in development for an AR project in collaboration with the National Center for Civil and Human Rights in Atlanta on journalist and civil rights leader Jesse Max Barber. Barber, editor of the journal *Voice of the Negro*, was forced to relocate to Chicago along with the publication after the Atlanta Race Massacre of 1906.[41]

De la Peña's commitment to making these uncomfortable histories visible continues, as does her dedication to providing opportunities for women, BIPOC, and LGBTQ+ communities. One of the reasons she took on the new post was the opportunity to "scale the attempt to bring diversity and inclusion to these emerging technologies, particularly around narrative."[42] Through her Emblematic Group, she also has under development (in beta testing) a free web platform, Reach, for creating and sharing VR and AR projects. The tool, using simple drag-and-drop technology, will provide another venue for easy and open access to working in XR.[43] De la Peña's sizable contributions to a more accessible, inclusive, and equitable emergent media resonates through journalism, academia, and the VR/XR industry.

3
People

Contributions, Careers, and Communities

The preceding profiles provide an instructive introduction to the women and nonbinary practitioners working in the emergent media space. From these profiles, we find consistencies that are echoed throughout our interviews: each of the individuals profiled (including those who shared their experiences with us but are not featured in these pages), while unique in their groundbreaking contributions, have seen their work slighted, ignored, or uncredited, and each needed a varied and flexible skill set ranging across the technical, the social, and the interpersonal. Many of the innovations described (unconventional user interfaces, shifts in perspective, and focus on social rather than corporate outcomes) are often explicitly labeled by these participants as related to a gendered frame of reference—not in line with an essentialist logic but as an effort to provide a much-needed counter to established and oppressive centers of power. It is through these detailed accounts of the day-to-day work experiences from our diverse group of interviewees that we can begin to form an understanding of the tasks undertaken, the contributions made, the barriers faced, and sites of mentorship, community, and resistance. We begin with a focus on "people," not with technology or artifacts, because it is here that we find the personal stories that form an essential foundation to understanding the breadth of our current media ecology.

We approached the interviews curious to know if the issues of inequity and the "glass ceiling" within legacy media felt as intransigent in these transitional and emergent spaces. In turn, we were interested if this particular transitional moment brought changes within established media. Not unrelated to this, we wanted to know from those interviewed the kinds of tasks undertaken and role titles assigned and the relation between those areas; we especially wanted to know if work was fairly allocated, acknowledged, and compensated. As these conversations unfolded, we found a range of strategies toward a more equitable work-place, which included from personal tenacity, honest dialogues engaged, and the formation of alternative networks.

Based on the insights garnered through our interviews, we identi-fied the various roles our participants have taken on, as well as the kinds of backgrounds, training, and support they have experienced. Our focus is on broad divisions or classifications of labor drawing from established categories within media production and distribution, with the under-standing particularly that within these emergent fields, titles and roles can overlap. The categories used are not to affix or limit interviewees in any one area, and we found individuals' work experiences spanned across areas due to their interests and need for versatility, adaptability, and resilience.

We noted the difficulty among participants at times to shed cus-tomary labels and to advance into other areas or roles due to gendered assumptions about skill sets, temperament, and appropriate spaces. We look at the backgrounds, challenges, and strategies of participants as they have navigated an ever-evolving media landscape. Our research found a pattern of invisible labor, professional roadblocks, and old stereotypes alongside a determination to develop new funding streams, collaborative communities, and inclusive workplace cultures. We also found among interviewees divestment in the mythology of tech with enthusiasm to test, learn, teach, share across platforms and applications.

The participants are grouped into the following main roles, based on how they identified their role/title when describing the jobs/functions they performed: curators, programmers, and archivists; producers; cre-atives; community builders; entrepreneurs; funders; technologists; and futurists and thought leaders (see figure 1.4). By way of clarification, tech-nologists work on the applied side of emergent media, whereas futur-ists and thought leaders concentrate on the theoretical or conceptual questions of how, where, and why the media should be employed, with close attention especially to the ethics of these spaces. This is, of course, not a rigid distinction, and many interviewees cross over these areas—a robust mix of roles is evident among many of those interviewed—but this is the general definition we are working with to distinguish those latter two categories.

Curators, Programmers, and Archivists: Incubation and Preservation

We begin with the question of history, asking how the story is told, and by whom. Kamal Sinclair writes in "Challenging the Innovator Stereotype" from the series *Making a New Reality*, that "the story of innovation is told through the lens of those in power" and can generate a "cultural amnesia," erasing even recent contributions of those outside established circles.[1] Here we expand the lens of history to share the experiences of some of those not included in that visual field. Much of the critical foundation needed to create more inclusive and equitable spaces and opportunities for, and knowledge of, emerging media makers is found in the work undertaken by directors, curators, and programmers of festivals and nonprofit institutions.

Christiane Paul, a noted scholar and curator, is professor at the New School, where she is director/chief curator of galleries at the Parsons School of Design and has been curator of digital art at the Whitney Museum of American Art for more than two decades. Our 2022 interview with Christiane Paul revealed a core infrastructural difficulty facing any history of digital and emergent media. Although there has been a move toward the acceptance of digital work and a drive toward addressing issues of equity, Paul outlined a critical gap to be filled to ensure an informed selection and exhibition of the medium:

> There still aren't enough digital art curators. If you look at that landscape, it's partly due to the educational system, which is incorporating more and more digital. I've been invited to teach as an adjunct at programs all over, because ultimately they didn't have digital art classes at Bard and the curatorial program. . . . I think young curators have to be educated much better. That's really not been happening so much. But, of course, there have been female curators all over the world who really have changed the landscape. I would mention Sarah Cook and Beryl Graham in the UK, Sabine Himmelsbach at HEK [House of Electronic Art, Basel], and also fantastic younger generation curators—Tina Rivers Ryan is really on top of the field.[2]

Along with this new wave of curatorial talent noted by Paul, Kamal Sinclair, speaking in 2017 as the director of the Sundance New Frontier Lab, pointed to the festival's conscious efforts to write an inclusive history through a strategy of amplification:

> We noticed that Nonny de la Peña . . . was very much ahead of most of the people that are working today. There are people around that have been working in VR for 40 years, but she's at the beginning of this second wave in terms of content-makers and entrepreneurs. We noticed that she wasn't getting a lot of time and attention and that it was more the men that were getting the time and attention, from the press, from industry, investment. . . . In 2015 we said, "Let's do some amplification so the history books don't write her out of her role." We did a strategic, simple intervention of just making sure that we had talking points that included Nonny at every turn. . . . It wasn't just us, there were other places that Nonny was speaking, but we definitely employed an amplification strategy around her. Just at the very least not letting her historic role get lost in the mix. That was the year that Engadget called her "the godmother of VR."[3]

Engadget's accolade signaled a welcome recognition of the significance of de la Peña's work, while at the same time revealed a cliché upholding gendered norms where men are often labeled as pioneers, gurus, and innovators while women remain primarily assigned a caregiver identity. Engadget's label signaled women's ongoing dual role in emergent media as valuable but not centered.

Gendered assumptions on workplace roles speak to the critical need for venues committed to reimaging the media landscape. Highlighting de la Peña's work is but one example of the Sundance New Frontier Lab's countless contributions as one of the leading spaces supporting experimental, emerging, and inclusive media. Shari Frilot, who had come to Sundance as a film programmer from Los Angeles's Outfest in 1998 began working with the little-known Frontier section, a showcase fitting well with her experimental film background. Excited and energized by this challenge, Frilot brought in an array of experimental work that used or blended media, performance, and projection. While taking note of a shift in the media ecosystem in 2006–7 when New Frontier was inaugurated, Frilot commented: "This was around the rise of YouTube. . . . I saw a lot of the filmmakers from Sundance start to take on and engage with new media technologies in different ways and a lot of the artists were making films that were ready to be shown at Sundance. I had experience with the art world and also engaging with new media technology. So I convinced everybody, we need to go down this road and see what's here, because I think it's really important."[4] Since that time, New Frontier has been at the forefront of amplifying and supporting groundbreaking work in, as Frilot notes, one of the most diverse areas of the festival. For Frilot, innovation at New Frontier was not happenstance but distinctly personal:

> In the beginning, in the '90s, being a gay woman of color, made me an interesting but contained force in the field. It was one of the reasons why I was drawn to different approaches, because I had to find different ways to express myself. I was convinced that it was necessary to create a new world, to rip open a portal into the landscape of storytelling. . . . This is very much a part of the story, why I did this to begin with, is there were limitations in my ability to rise up, but also limitations for expression that I was interested in. . . . This points to my constant and deep belief that diversity is our strength. Because it does open up these new opportunities and expands our way to communicate and be with each other and to build our world.[5]

For our participants, in the curatorial and programming spaces, much of their attention was on experimentation and innovation but also specifically in relation to social responsibility and to democratic processes. Sarah Wolozin (2016), director and cofounder with William Uricchio of the MIT Open Documentary Lab, pointed to the larger goals of the space in our first interview: "The overall philosophy behind the lab when we started was that it represented a changing relationship between author, subject, and audience. With the availability of cell phones and the Internet for distribution and networking—the audience would now participate in the making of the story. That was a fundamental shift that interactive technologies allowed for."[6] In our follow-up interview, Wolozin (2022) talked about the evolution of the curatorial mission of the lab's invaluable interactive resource for documentary projects, Docu-base, and reinforced the necessity of casting a wider lens over media history and the challenges of capturing history in this uniquely and often ephemeral space:

> We were mindful of trying not to repeat that history of just putting in dominant, white male history. . . . If you do your job as a good documenter and preserver, you will be preserving the history of marginalized people because they're creating the work and being shown. . . . [I]t's very important as we document this work to make sure we learn from our mistakes in the past, and when we include women to make sure the story is told the way it actually happened. That's why the day-to-day documentation of Docubase is impor-tant, because if you look at the festivals, there is a lot of work by women and people of color and projects from other parts of the world, and you just have to make sure to include those.
>
> Our question is also Docubase itself, and how to keep that alive. That's why we're working with the MIT digital libraries. . . . [I]t really has become about preserving the work because it is disap-pearing so quickly already—the need always to think about the legacy of your work while you're doing it and not have that be an afterthought, especially when you're working with such unstable platforms. It's like it's happening in real time—the disappearance of your work.[7]

Our participants working in this critical development space bring together a unique set of diverse skills often due to the incredible breadth of background, as evidenced by Sinclair's work as artist, producer, cura-tor, and arts adviser; Frilot's strong network across experimental arts and film; and Wolozin's work as both documentary filmmaker, program director, and curator.

Liz Rosenthal's career has equally spanned across a diverse media terrain, from indie film production and distribution; to her work as founder and CEO of Power to the Pixel, a company fostering digital inno-vation across media practices; to her work as curator of Venice Immer-sive at the Venice Film Festival and the immersive content section of the

Venice Production Bridge Market. Rosenthal has been a vital force in identifying new artists and forms, crucial to the incubation and acceleration of project development. Because of her wide-ranging perspective, we interviewed her three times over the course of our research. In 2016 she described the challenges of working in a shifting media landscape, including the adoption of an ill-fitting title that hid the labor of analysis, strategy, organizational, and communication skills essential to the tasks at hand:

> I remember when Power to the Pixel was quite established, and people used to describe me as an "events producer." I was thinking strategically, analyzing where the industry's going. As well as running the company and these programs, you're having to catch innovation and predict where it's going and find strategic routes, you're helping large amounts of people to move forward . . . so you've got to be really careful that you're doing it well because you're the first. When you're challenged, you're the first person to get criticized so I always wanted to be logical and try to demystify a sector that is commonly full of inexplicable acronyms and hyperbole.[8]

Ingrid Kopp's impact on emerging media has also been significant as director and consultant on interactive nonfiction for Tribeca Film Festival, cofounder of Immerse.news, and codirector of Electric South, a nonprofit company based in Cape Town, South Africa, which develops virtual reality and other new forms of storytelling across Africa. Kopp has played important roles in this field through her work as curator, entrepreneur, and funder during her time running the TFI New Media Fund (in conjunction with the Ford Foundation). Her interest in issues of access, development, and diversity goes back to her early work in the UK at Channel 4 and has been a consistent thread in her career. From the beginnings of her career, Kopp (2016) has been attentive to the issues of inclusivity in technology and fostering a culture in which new voices emerge: "I got interested in this idea of the relationship between the technology being used and then who gets to tell the stories, and with these cheaper cameras, not being considered broadcast standard, I thought that was really interesting. I ran a lot of workshops at Channel 4 for new talent. That became quite a big issue for me—the idea of who gets to be on the Channel, who gets to tell these stories?"[9]

Wendy Levy's work as creative director of the Bay Area Video Coalition (now BAVC Media) and as executive director of the Alliance of Media Arts + Culture has been another formative influence on the field. Kamal Sinclair (2017) provided insight on how crucial these incubation/development skills are by citing Levy's key role in mentoring the design process for *Question Bridge*, a distinguished transmedia work on Black masculinity, produced by Sinclair: "We wrote to the Bay Area Video Coalition, which Wendy Levy was running at the time, and we applied. Just applying for that Producer's Institute alone helped to define our transmedia design, because she had asked all these questions that we hadn't considered before. Just in answering those questions we were slowly furthering the design of that project."[10]

It is clear from the insights provided by our participants that the curators, programmers, lab directors, and archivists play a key part in shaping the opportunities, recognition, and history of an emerging media field. As we identify other people and professions in this chapter, we acknowledge the essential role of this labor in expanding the vision of what is possible.

Producers: Women's Work

While our participants represent the spectrum of professions in a range of emerging media, we found marked consistencies in our interviews. First, the conventional divide in the media industry among management, creative, and technical leads and those areas designated as "soft skills" (including communication, connections, emotional and social labor) has held fast in these still-evolving spaces. Our participants revealed that women are particularly well represented in the producer role, although the title itself seemed to stretch beyond organizational and logistical tasks and often encompassed creative work as well. Although many of our participants noted in interviews (and confirmed in our "Women in VR" workshop[11]) that emerging media working environments faced the same problems of "silos" or "buckets" for personnel as in "traditional" media with stark divides between "creatives" and "suits," several of our participants said that they took on multiple roles. Samantha Storr, discussed her role as VP / executive producer at the VR company Here Be Dragons (2013–17) in terms of the pragmatics of the field: "I wear a few hats at Dragons, as do many people on my team. Working in a medium that's new, you have to be adaptable—we're paving the road for where VR can go. As vice president, I had to focus most of my first year on building an infrastructure that allowed us to carry this technology out of its infancy."[12]

Madeline Power, freelance film producer and former producer at 371 Productions and Custom Reality, worked on VR projects such as *Ashe '68* and *Across the Line*. She told us that her multitasking spanned everything from doing research, designing impact campaigns, to booking flights, hiring set designers, arranging conference and festival screenings and filming for 360-degree video projects.[13] While some of that wide-ranging crossover work was a necessary part of starting out or working with smaller companies, as noted above, other participants found that they worked from design to production to social media under the umbrella title of producer in order to fill in gaps to bring a project to completion or, more disquietingly, to minimize or deflect their contributions in other areas.

If we look at the Producers Guild of America's guidelines[14] for the credits aligned to the producer title, ranging from theatrical to new media, we find a consistency in the producer's role consisting of shaping the vision and providing the organizational infrastructure to ensure the completion of a project. In the case of new media, under which the emerging media of transmedia and multiplatform, VR, AR, and immersive media fall, there is an opaque flexibility in the credit designation, especially within the area of transmedia given its multiplatform structure and varied temporal dispersion. The language employed identifies the producer as the essential and constant thread across "planning, development, production, and/or maintenance of narrative continuity."[15] In other words, the producer must have the capacity for the bigger picture and a skill set that ranges across the creative and management dimensions. Caitlin Burns, former National Board Member of the PGA, former co-chair of the PGA Women's Impact Network, and longtime producer with established companies such as Starlight Runner and StoryTech Immersive Now, noted that emerging media projects (e.g., transmedia, immersive, VR) provided women with distinctive opportunities:

> I think that every big franchise production that I was working on, the executive in charge was actually female. There were plenty of men who were head of production, but the executives who were really pioneering this comprehensive understanding of these big intellectual property storyworlds were always female leaders. They were able to do the really careful diplomatic work that comes from overseeing many divisions of different specialties within an intellectual-property conglomerate, like a studio or a game publisher, and also understand the need to think about it in a different way.[16]

As Burns noted, the PGA is unique regarding gender parity in the organization, "almost 50–50" of its membership across an array of productions from theatrical to new media forms. She acknowledged the multiple challenges a producer faces:

> There are women who are also fantastic at it, who have been able to build their careers on really being trusted collaborators and trusted organizers that can deal with people from all walks of life, all personalities, all talents and all expertise in a way that's been fruitful. . . . They're doing it by being in that position, being able to see the overview, work with everyone, and being able to navigate the intricacies of those complex personal environments . . . these giant storyworlds—*Pirates of the Caribbean*, "Halo," "the happiness factor" for Coca-Cola—being able to take the ideas of the technique of coordinated narrative across multiple platforms and apply them to the traditional business models.[17]

Burns steered away from essentialist readings of women's participation in the space and pointed to cultural factors that might produce the opportunities beyond the usual gendered barriers:

> There seems to be a greater comfort, institutionally, with women taking on these supervisory complicated roles. It is also a place

where hard work can get you further, sometimes. Because it's entrepreneurial, you see a lot of people who are building their own projects. For a woman that can work hard and wants to experiment with something, there are fewer barriers than if you are a woman and you're trying to get into a clear career path where there are certain gatekeepers, like directing for example. . . .

I don't want to say that women are better at these things. I think, culturally, women are often in roles where they are coordinating, or they are understanding the bigger system, or keeping track of multiple parts in ways that men find less threatening, or the systems find less threatening.[18]

Many of our participants echoed their recognition of contributions by women in organizational, management, and "soft" social skills roles while also referencing the so-called glass ceiling. While the tasks of day-to-day scheduling, logistics, and interaction with personnel often fell to women workers, the passage in management from the middle to higher ranks for women was not seamless and at times tempered by gendered assumptions of abilities and temperament. As one participant, who wished to remain anonymous, noted in reference to their specific field:

I'd say 80-plus percent of the management field is female, from PA to all the way up. Of course, that's your stepping-stone to getting to producer and coming up through those ranks. . . . I would say there's still that problem where it's male-dominated for producer level. . . . [Y]ou still have to push harder to be respected in strategic and in analytical thinking. I couldn't possibly do my job well if I wasn't really good at it. But I can guarantee that side by side to a male doing it, I have to be stronger and smarter about getting my voice heard than a male would in this role. . . . The male voice is just heard stronger. . . . I think it's changing. . . . It's a slow cruise ship that's turning.[19]

From our interviews, it emerged that gender stereotypes that relate to temperament, a cultural reticence toward encouraging female self-confidence, and unconscious bias, incognizance, or willful ignorance all contribute to a relentless imbalance in opportunities. Research has shown that the "likability" issue is in play for almost any hiring and leadership context.[20] We found consistently in our interviews that pushing back against this "double bind" was an ongoing challenge. The constant need to advocate and even engage in self-promotion, is critical for visibility. As Jennifer Palais, creative strategist and digital producer, shared:

> With men—I need to really be in their faces when I'm looking for a new opportunity. With my female colleagues, I am front and center at all times and they are consistently sending me opportunities and leads without me having to constantly ask. I do the same for them. I see that men support each other pretty exclusively so I have been focusing on supporting as many women as I can. I think the real key to creating equality quickly is to continue to back each other.
>
> We should be represented equally on panels, in the workplace, in journals, in education etc. I think a lot of it comes down to having equal economic opportunities in the workplace. If there are less opportunities for women heading up projects (meaning top titles and the salaries that go along with those roles) then there will be less women on panels, less women in the leadership at major studios, etc., and less awareness of our contributions.[21]

Maureen Fan, CEO and cofounder of the VR animation company, Baobab Studios, who works on both the creative and business side of the industry, expressed the need for women to be their own best champion:

> My motto is "Always be asking." I found that if you don't ask, you don't get it. I learned this by observing when I was a manager. I observed that all my male employees would always be asking for promotions, raises, and the women wouldn't. I would ask the women, "Why aren't you?" They just don't feel comfortable. But I tell them, when promotion time comes around and I only have this tiny little bucket of money to give to people and I have to decide who gets it, who am I going to remember? . . . [Y]ou have to be asking for it because by not asking, you're automatically disadvantaging yourself.[22]

Along with advocacy, said Fan, comes an opportunity for education. She recounted a story of a boss and mentor who had hesitated to promote her out of a misplaced sense of "protectiveness" (due to a ruthlessly competitive environment) but who had listened to her reasoned and researched argument on gender bias in career advancement, which transformed his thinking. He subsequently gave her the promotion that she was seeking. "I feel like it's oftentimes more valuable to educate men than it is to educate women," Fan said, "because a lot of literature telling women how to be is telling us to be more like men. But I don't think that's fair. I think that there's great things about being a woman and they should meet us halfway."[23]

Jennifer Palais suggested, like Fan, that the disparity in hiring and promotion could be helped by the education of both men and women.

> I don't think men are even aware on a conscious level of what they are doing when they resist putting a woman in charge or "forget" to call one of us when they hear about an opportunity. . . . When women realize the disparity that is happening there is a lot of shock and disbelief. I was this way myself. It is almost impossible to believe you are being overlooked, underpaid, undervalued and ignored because of your gender. . . . But while there is more awareness than in the past, there has been a lot of backsliding and we are nowhere near a solution to discrimination against women in general or in the workplace. . . . I think it is important to make men (and women) aware of the issues in a mature, compassionate, and supportive way. To avoid pointing fingers, . . . to wake them up slowly so they don't get the bends. This is an issue that affects the quality of work for us all; it isn't even about individuals. It isn't about taking men down—it is about sharing and collaboration.[24]

Creatives: Invisible Labor

Despite the broad skill set frequently cited by our participants, the default view for many of the "gatekeepers" or even interested bystanders was that women's roles in projects were not on the creative or technical side. Jan Libby, writer, experience designer, and producer, who has worked on immersive and cross-platform projects for No Mimes Media, Fox Broadcasting, and Oxygen, as well as running her own company, Storees, noted:

> With my branding and TV stuff, even with CD [creative director] positions, they look to guys for CDs. If you look around the ad industry, it's mostly men. I mostly work with guys. Then we go to social media, that's where the ladies are put. I had one client who will remain nameless who after a very, very successful, big, big money project, came to me and said, "Oh, the agency really loved this"—P.S. I was the creative and the story person and everything else on it—"We'd love to bring you in full-time as a community manager."[25]

The inability to imagine women in charge of the tech or as creative lead was a frequent observation among our participants. Niema Jordan, a Bay Area producer and writer, noted however, that while there could be differences across genres and regions, stereotyping often interceded:

> I think I have very different experiences because documentary film is a lot more woman friendly than traditional Hollywood spaces. If you look at the statistics for women in film, it's horrible across the board, but it's better in documentary than it is in narrative film fiction. . . . There are more women producers than there are women directors—why is that? Because people feel like women are organized and can get things done, and they feel like men are leaders. Your director is a man, and your producer is a woman. I think you do see that space in the way things are gendered. . . . [Y]ou do see a lot of those divisions, you'll see a lot more DPs, or directors of photography, who are men. That also translates into directing because a lot of people think that in order to be the director of a film, you also have to be the person with the camera . . . I think that documentary film has fewer of the gender issues. . . . I guess it's a little bit more toned down.
>
> Also, living in the Bay Area, which is very social justice heavy, you're in spaces that are very supportive of women, of queer

folk. We try to embody diversity within the Bay Area as a part of our culture, and it comes out in our media in certain spaces, mainly in the independent media and I definitely see it in documentary film.[26]

We found a somewhat different response in the Southern California context, when speaking to Ashley York, who has worked in documentary, games, and transmedia in Los Angeles. The documentary genre, especially now within its Hollywood industry contexts, is not without its own blind spots:

> Even though women do participate more actively as authors or as directors, as producers, that shouldn't mislead anyone to think that the space is not as deeply troubled as other fields of media, where there are imbalances that are quite profound, deeply sad when you start thinking about the abysmal gender imbalance in tech and in the Hollywood system. That has an impact on transmedia, on documentary storytelling, on news . . . and I think that reflects our culture with media. . . .
>
> I did some research regarding race and media, and specifically around the Academy Awards and the Oscars. . . . [I]t becomes apparent quickly that this is not just about the Academy Awards. That's the last stop on the train. By the time a film gets to that level, so many things have happened, regarding who's going to participate, who's not, who's in creatively controlling roles.
>
> I can think about that from so many levels. . . . [T]his culture of internships being unpaid, that's all part of this system of inequality. The Ford Foundation have released a report about how people working for free perpetuates inequality. It's not helpful or useful for anyone. . . . That's something that I am deeply interested in, beyond just making projects that explore social issues in one way or another. I really would love to see this industry, from the Independents to Hollywood, games, in the universities, move in a space where we're talking about labor practices, openly, and all the time . . . people getting paid and people knowing what people get paid. . . . It's like these imbalances exist at every level.[27]

Changing a culture and building an inclusive workplace is challenged by continuing conscious and unconscious bias. York went on to recount a personal experience while working on a television documentary series. In this case a producer aware and commiserate with the ideals of inclusivity, nevertheless fell back on tired and hierarchical imagery:

> I was doing a short contract gig, mostly in a producing/research capacity, writing treatments, preparing things for the network. I hadn't applied to be a field director. I hadn't expressed any kind of interest in working in the field, but I was told that the executive producer said, "Well, I don't think she can command the field." . . . I would assume, this was just a way this executive producer works, and I honestly do think that it's a blind spot for him, I would understand if I had never directed crews, never delivered shows. This is a job that I've done, and if you look on paper, it's there—*Variety* magazine put me as a filmmaker to watch.[28]

We found through our interviews that work falling under the creative label, which includes writing, directing, show creating, or showrunning, continues to be a difficult area for women to access or, often, to get credit. Despite all the cross-boundary work performed by women, the assumption across media formats is that you belong in a particular silo, and that is not one typically labeled creative or project/company lead if you are female. Nancy Bennett, chief creative officer / studio head and one of the founders of Two Bit Circus has a long and diverse career in the entertainment industry in music video, commercials, film and television before her work in the VR/AR/MR space. Bennett (2017) discussed barriers for creatives:

> When I started working in the film business [in late 1980s, early 1990s], I was about 23. I was really lucky—I've been around guys who've been really supportive, but when it comes to male leadership—the good creative roles, I've never had the opportunities until I got older and really had to fight for them and found myself in that subjugated role of being the producer or the midwife in support of the male who was leading the charge, but oftentimes actually almost ghost writing everything that they were doing.

There were a lot of instances in my mid-20s where I was drawing storyboards and writing the treatments and the director guys would go in and do it all.

That's why, when I got the offer from Atlantic, a woman hired me, her name is Lori Weintraub. . . . She recognized something in me and I'm really grateful for it, but part of the negotiation was, "I'll do it for your tiny salary as long as I get to direct as much as possible," and that's how I got my opportunities. I directed for the home video division which are very low budget, where I was shooting, producing, editing, interviewing, doing the whole nine yards for very low sums of money on the project . . . and learned a ton. . . .

I couldn't get arrested to direct without the same scenario happening again for probably 10 years. I think that has a lot to do with the time. . . . Even in 2008–9, I was working on making a start-up company after I left MTV and I put a lot of my own money in it and developed a cool idea that a lot of people were really interested in doing, but I couldn't seem to close funding.[29]

The fundamental challenge of attracting and securing funding was experienced by many of our participants and will be discussed in much greater detail in chapter 6.

Creatives: Gendered Genres

Many participants noted that working in emergent media afforded them the opportunity to break out of the restrictive roles or siloed responsibilities typically demarcated in legacy media; additionally, they were drawn to the chance of experimentation these new forms might offer. Susana Ruiz, artist and scholar at University of Santa Cruz and creative lead on the pioneering serious game *Darfur Is Dying*,[30] had a different take on the question of an artistic medium, thinking through the perspective of "user agency" rather than solely the form and material as she develops a work. Ruiz's "medium agnostic" strategy departs from the norm of cinema and media training, which cultivates specialization. She discussed the attraction particularly of working in forms like transmedia, a "format" that engages multiple platforms, is at times quite loosely defined, and fits more closely with her identity as a "generalist."

Figure 3.1. *Darfur Is Dying*, online video game. 2006. Directed by Susana Ruiz. Produced by Ashley York, Susana Ruiz, and Huy Truong.

Ruiz wanted to avoid the usual pigeonholes found in media, from the academy to the arts: "The reason I went to iMAP [USC's Media Arts and Practice PhD program] is because I had this notion that theory and practice were interwoven, if not the same thing. . . . I am not fully a filmmaker. I am not fully a game designer. I am not fully a humanities scholar. I am this thing that's much more hybrid. . . . I would suspect that people you find doing transmedia are a little bit like me. They thrive on all of these things."[31]

Illya Szilak, the writer and digital artist whose projects *Reconstructing Mayakovsky*, *Queerskins*, and *Atomic Vacation* fall under the designation of transmedia that employs online multimedia narratives and VR installations, also does not fit neatly into a silo. Szilak, a practicing physician, has had an unconventional career outside the media industry or formal art training. After 9/11, she felt compelled to take up writing stories, particularly stories designed for the web, without knowing completely what that might entail. Szilak reached out to the artist Mark Amerika after seeing his hypertext work, *GRAMMATRON*. Amerika encouraged her to develop *Reconstructing Mayakovsky* and connected her to others working in this area. With her next work, *Queerskins: A Novel*, a web-based project designed by longtime collaborator, Cyril Tsiboulski, Szilak (2016) realized there was still not an established path for her to follow easily:

> I put it out there wherever I could. So it got recognized by the Webby Awards as net art, because there was no other category to put it in, and at that point I didn't even try an agent. . . . I'm really an outsider. I don't have any background in fine arts, I don't have any background in writing. Those creative arts have largely been institutionalized, so if you don't have degrees, it's actually difficult to break into . . . I just put things out here. I don't ask permission anymore. [In] 2011, I started writing pieces, blogging

Figure 3.2. *Queerskins: Ark*, the third of four chapters, VR experience. 2018. Illya Szilak and Cyril Tsiboulski in collaboration with Brandon Powers. In headset view, participants witness an intimate conversation between Alex (Christopher Vo, *left*) and Sebastian (Michael DeBartolo, *right*), captured in volumetric video, on a stunning photogrammetry rendering of El Matador beach just outside of Los Angeles.

for the *Huffington Post* on electronic literature, I did interviews with some major people, including Lev Manovich. Some of those have been excerpted into books, so it was a serious endeavor, and I spent a lot of time on them. I didn't get paid, of course, but that showed that literary community that I was smart, could write, and talk intelligently about these topics.[32]

The experiences of Ruiz and Szilak point to the difficulties creatives encounter when they take on more experimental narrative strategies and stories, crossing genres and forms: funding, visibility, and institutional support all become less accessible.

Community Builders

Efforts to seek out, create, and support community came up often in our interviews. In part, this was traced to the gaps in educational systems or isolation of working in this technology for some of our participants. For others, the online community was an important space of entry. Tonia B., an experience designer and cofounder/director of the media collective Browntourage, had a formative internship as well as a graduate degree from USC's Interactive Media and Games division but gained significant creative and coding background through essentially self-taught online experiences at an early age:

> I already knew HTML and CSS just from growing up with Neopets and then from these forums with girls in Japan, Korea, America, and Canada. We'd make our own art and share it with each other. Some people would have domains and you could apply to get your own art website hosted on a subdomain. . . . [I]t was like a sorority; you would be like a family with your host and your fellow "hostees." Everyone's art website would have a "me" section about themselves and a "you" section with things for the visitors: art that you're giving away—icons or stickers, and tutorials. I learned a lot from the tutorials on other people's sites.[33]

Browntourage follows a similar community building ethos, foregrounding socially conscious work of diverse voices across a range of creative forms and experimental styles.[34] Tonia B. originally used the term "Browntourage" randomly at a party to talk about a close group of friends, but this developed to a supportive arts network, magazine, and media collective, which organized collaborative events and online artworks. She noted the evolution:

> The concept caught on and we were at first using it as a hashtag on lifestyle type posts on social media, and we made a Tumblr where we would highlight other cool brown women using #Browntourage as a way to build up the concept. Eventually, it became more opinions, where we would review stuff or give our thoughts—which sparked it to turn into a full-on magazine. At that point, we began using it as a learning tool for us to get into videos, music, events, and mixed media collaborations.[35]

Mimi Ọnụọha is visual artist and researcher with a background in anthropology who holds a master's in professional studies from New York University's Interactive Telecommunications program. Her work looks at the intersection of technology, knowledge production, and systems of power. Ọnụọha noted one of her frequent collaborators, Romi Morrison, and her ongoing collaboration with Diana J. Nucera (aka Mother Cyborg), with whom Ọnụọha coformed the organization the People's Guide to Tech,[36] while sharing the genesis of the project:

> We met at an event that was talking about AI. Both of us had the same thought: "Wow—this event is talking about a lot of Black and Brown groups, and a lot of especially poor communities. . . . These are the people who are going to feel the brunt of the effects of these technologies. but they're not here, where's the interfacing?" Both of us had experience . . . making zines—DIY, community-driven materials that could educate but also allow people to organize on their own. . . . We made this zine, a guide called *A People's Guide to AI*. It was this beginner comprehensive approach. It was pretty rigorous while using these frameworks from popular education, so very accessible. It did really well. We ended up doing a ton of workshops around it, creating other materials from it. From there, we expanded into our organization—A People's Guide to

Tech—it essentially does what we did for AI but with a variety of different topics.[37]

An urgent need for inclusive spaces, accessible media/technology, and community-led work was expressed repeatedly in our interviews. *BlackTransArchive.com / We Are Here Because of Those That Are Not*, by Danielle Brathwaite-Shirley, an artist working in animation, games, sound, and performance, is another important model of collaborative work. Brathwaite-Shirley, self-taught in much of the technology around animation and gaming, described the process behind the game, which was commissioned in 2019 by the Science Gallery London. Brathwaite-Shirley had not built a game before but was determined to move forward with the archive:

> I knew that I wanted to work with a team of Black trans people and pay everyone where everyone is part of the team and made all the decisions. . . . I really believed [in] a top-down, bottom-up perspective. I want them to be there before we write any code, so that everything that we talk about can be made into the game. . . . [I]n the first meeting, we talked about making this game. People said, "I want it to be accessible. I want it as an archive, I think Black trans people aren't protected with an archive [i.e., archives not made by or monitored by the trans community], because there's a lot of problems with archives or misuse of images and having to go to news outlets and correct them on that." In listening, I thought, "Fine, you want it to be accessible, let's put it online." Then someone said, "Well, if it's online, anyone can access it, how do we know who's accessing it?" Then maybe you have to put your own identity just like we have to usually—and from that all the choices—the entire game came. I am not taking credit for that, that was the environment that was made, we managed to make all those decisions together, it was a hard conversation. But what came out of it was that everyone designed the character to represent themselves.[38]

Despite the very short turnaround time, Brathwaite-Shirley had to produce, collate, and organize the project, their very first effort in the game space was a success.

Everything ended up working really well. We had made a terms and conditions in the group. We had agreed not to re-create any trauma in the work and to let ourselves tell a story we want to tell rather than focus on explaining what we're doing. We wanted to focus on how Black trans people tell stories. I personally think it is one of my most successful works because it was just such a team effort. . . . It's super amazing to see that was my foray into this technology. I wasn't thinking of technology. I was thinking more of just games—interactivity and accessibility.[39]

Another important collaborative space, founded by Phoenix Perry on International Women's Day in 2013, is the Code Liberation Foundation, which runs events in New York and London in support of women, nonbinary, femme, and girl-identifying people in STEAM (science, technology, engineering, the arts, and mathematics) fields, using workshops, exhibitions, and creative research.[40] Perry, artist, activist, and game designer, whose background in tech is largely self-taught, has been an important

Figure 3.3. *BlackTransArchive.com / We Are Here Because of Those That Are Not*, installation. 2020–22. Danielle Brathwaite-Shirley.

force in bringing STEAM skills both to academic program development and university teaching (including Goldsmiths University of London and University of the Arts, London) and to public-facing works like Code Liberation. Perry discussed various efforts to open the tech space:

> I definitely think that I brought the first wave of women into that space, and I get thanked all the time by random women that I helped. . . . [I]t makes me feel like we did something really important. . . . I think that the women that I originally mentored in the Code Lib space have gone on to be amazing thought leaders. I think that we helped bring about a change. But we were just one piece of it, there was also Dame's Making Games and Pixelles. I think the three of us really did start a trend that then led to a lot of other organizations—now there's also Black Girls CODE.[41]

Code Liberation was crucial to the development of the work of Irene Fubara-Manuel, an artist working in animation, game design, and installation art, whose work explores surveillance and border policing, talked about the importance of Code Liberation to the development of their work. "It was my first step into coding," they said, "because every time that I tried to code on my own, it just felt overwhelming. They simplified the process for me, what made it easier to understand was being taught the fact that you could ask questions, the fact that we had our output that we're supposed to generate from it. People were fun, it was very joyful. It didn't feel hidden. That gave me a lot of confidence."[42]

Entrepreneurs

The ambitious and at times sprawling missions described above are not unlike the path taken by Taryn Southern, a digital innovator, whose career has spanned television, YouTube, music, and VR. Southern began acquiring media skills as a journalism student at the University of Miami. She then moved to Los Angeles, where she worked as a television host, actress, writer, and producer. She was working on YouTube content, mainly in comedic music videos, when her 2007 clip, "Hot for Hillary," a parody of Obama Girl's "I Got a Crush on Obama," went viral, producing a shift in her thinking about media work:

That was my first taste of seeing how creating something and having no connections, no real resources, the potential impact of that. Prior to that moment, my entire life as a performer, or as a journalist, or as a producer, or a director, or writer was contingent upon the gatekeeper saying, "Yes, I will publish your work," "Yes, I will give you your first job." This was the first time where I did something all on my own and I didn't have to ask anyone's permission. I could just upload it, and boom, it could be seen. That was a powerful lesson for me.[43]

Although Southern continued to work in traditional media as a writer, actress, producer and in internet video, by 2013, the disruption in the Hollywood landscape by online media was such that she decided to pursue a more independent route. She recalled asking herself:

Do I want to place my bet on the thing that is dying a slow death . . . or do I want to place my bets on the thing that gets me most excited and it's still in its very early growth stage? I ended up choosing the latter. I quit everything. I stopped auditioning, writing pilots. I basically quit the entire traditional media side of what I was pursuing and went full on into YouTube. I made a channel. I started uploading weekly videos and doing collaborations and all the things you're supposed to do to grow an audience.[44]

Southern worked on her YouTube channel, producing about 1,500 videos, until 2015 when she decided to move on to something new. She has since been working in AI musical compositions, VR, and documentary film. Like many of the women we spoke with, the diverse skills across media formats were largely self-taught:

I've just always been incredibly curious . . . I just always want to know how things are made. . . . Now, the internet is my greatest tool. I typically go and I just start researching. That's how it was with the AI music. When I started, it was just googling hundreds of stories and reading as much as I could, playing around. Even with my early YouTube videos, I didn't know how to produce a video.

When I was a teenager, I taught myself how to code websites. I did not categorize that as science or math. I was making stuff. But I think it gave me some confidence in my ability to build a technical skillset. . . . So now, while I still wouldn't consider myself someone who would be great at science or math, if someone throws a technical problem my way, I want to learn.

I think with VR and AR, there certainly is a barrier to entry around those who may feel that they don't have the technical skillsets to master creating content. But I feel like I've seen a much better representation of women in that space than what I've seen in traditional Hollywood.[45]

Working in a smaller media market and within the indie film and start-up contexts can also offer opportunities in emergent media, such as VR, and while we do see many women working in this space, as Southern noted, issues of "invisibility" can be present in media formats considered more "tech" driven.

Madeline Power, whose multitasking abilities were noted earlier, experienced a diverse work culture and supportive mentorship fostered by documentary media maker Brad Lichtenstein within the Milwaukee company 371 Productions. Nonetheless, Power encountered gender bias outside of 371's inclusive workspace:

I've had on occasion, guys who don't even work in VR, explain VR to me. . . . It happens in Milwaukee a lot. We're the only VR company. . . . If I go somewhere with male coworkers, we will hear, "Oh, you guys do VR?" And they'll default to the guys. The guys will say, "Just Maddy does it." They will default to the guys again, and they'll be like, "No, seriously, ask Maddy these questions. We don't know." . . . It's so hard as a woman. Then you're weighing up: Is this sexism, or am I just being too sensitive? That's another part of the problem, that women question themselves more and wonder if it's their fault, if I'm being too sensitive, or I'm overanalyzing this social interaction I'm having with someone.[46]

Nonny de la Peña, noted earlier for her pioneering work in documentary VR and as founder and CEO of the Emblematic Group, has faced innumerable challenges in her pathbreaking career, which has brought her to spaces generally reserved for men.

> A head of a major, very well-funded company said, "Oh, that Nonny de la Peña, she's tenacious." Is that a good thing or a bad thing? I often look to women leaders, and they often have a very soft, quiet way of how they talk. . . . I'm just not like that. I'm like this Latina loud, aggressive, busy, noisy. . . . Then I think, "Oh my god, I'm never going to make it in this place." . . . Then, when people say stupid stuff to me, like "Oh yeah, I'd share a hotel room with you," all kinds of stuff, I think, "How do I call somebody out on their stupid stuff and turn them into an ally instead of an enemy?"[47]

Kate Parsons is another creative who wears many hats as educator, entrepreneur, and festival director. She is cofounder of FLOAT LAND, a studio that works across a variety of audiovisual formats, including live cinema, VR, and AR, and she leads FEMMEBIT, a video art festival featuring LA-based female artists working in video and new media. Parsons spoke about gender bias in the emergent digital media space, even within her more art-focused context. Like many of our participants, Parsons's technical skills were largely self-taught. Her education in the late 1990s and early 2000s had a deep divide between the worlds of arts and tech, which was reinforced by gender. She completed two graduate degrees to fill in the gaps, and when she moved to Los Angeles, she sought out and found and created collaborative communities that shared knowledge and skills across diverse digital media. Even within these new spaces, old problems persisted. The VR space, however, Parsons noted, may present a cultural shift:

> There were some early 360[-degree] video workshops I went to, where students, people eager to learn, and were very open, and people seemed to be very comfortable. Over the span of a few months, you could feel it getting a lot more focused into this male gamer—I'm trying to think of how else to describe it that's not really terrible—but just very masculine and misogynistic in some ways. It's the microaggression of just having a bunch of men come in and completely disregard your existence. That's what it's like.

Seeing that happen made me really sad. There's still a lot of that stuff out there. But there's really good efforts being made to counteract that, because VR is still new, the rules are still being written, it's still the Wild West. There's a lot of Women in VR Groups . . . and other women that are legitimately, and very honestly working to bring other women into the fold, which is amazing. . . . My hope is that a lot of the efforts that are being made to educate the younger women in art and coding, in particular, that those efforts will pay off in the next few years, and maybe that gender bias won't exist quite so much.[48]

The impact of gender bias in spaces that teach media, whether formally or informally, was referenced by many interviewees and often was a keen motivator to seek out or design newer models for learning. Erin Reilly is director of innovation and entrepreneurship for Moody College of Communication at University of Texas at Austin. Before that, she was a founding member of the USC Annenberg Innovation Lab and research director for Project New Media Literacies at MIT. Her own entrepreneurial efforts include the founding of ReillyWorks and Zoey's Room, a nonprofit afterschool media literacy program for girls. Zoey's Room was originally part of Reilly's MFA thesis, an experience that shaped her more expansive approach to media. Of her graduate experience, she recalled:

When I was getting my MFA, my advisers were still encouraging me to be a producer instead of the creative director. . . . I remember shooting my first hundred feet of film, which I thought was great. He [my advisor] and everyone asked, "Why are you doing this? You're a producer. Why are you shooting film?"

I think that's why I did *Zoey's Room*, because they didn't know what I was doing. They left me alone to be creative because they didn't understand it. That moment pushed me to always explore areas that the general public don't understand. Because I felt like then I could get credit.[49]

Emerging media entrepreneurs face the challenges of handling multiple creative and business tasks as well as needing to shape the understanding culturally and artistically of these new forms. Our participants have played a crucial role in setting out and shaping a field. Catherine Allen, CEO of Limina Immersive and industry advocate for gender diversity, has been at the forefront of this work. She spoke of the unformulated nature of the industry in relation to the challenges of defining her own organization: "Are we a tech company, a tech start-up? Are we an events agency? Are we a consultancy who does events pop ups? Are we an arts theater? Are we an arts organization? There's so many things and we don't fit into any template. What role models do I have? What template do I fit into? Am I an arts leader . . . or somebody like the head of the National Theatre or South Bank Centre? Or am I a tech start-up CEO? They're all really different."[50]

Futurists and Thought Leaders

Given the experimental nature, innovative material, and entrepreneurial nature of the labor generated in emerging media fields, many of our participants aptly fit the designations of "futurists" and "thought leaders." Indeed, several of our participants are members of the Guild of Future Architects,[51] and some identify specifically as "futurists" (including Jessica Clark and Monika Bielskyte). Their responses and insights feature in more detail in chapter 8. For now, we highlight here some of those who have taken on the role of explicitly pushing the public discourse on these new forms. Many women have actively mentored and launched community groups, as Parsons noted above. Jenn Duong and Julie Young cofounded two groups, Women in VR/AR and SH//FT (Shaping Holistic Inclusion in Future Technology), which focus on supporting diverse voices in XR spaces. SH//FT began in 2015 with the goals of equity and inclusion in tech and partnered with companies on immersive storytelling projects for young artists from underrepresented groups. Women in VR/AR, the ever-growing and resource-rich Facebook group, was founded in 2016 and, at the time of writing, had more than 11,000 members. The group was an effort to address the tech industry's less-than-welcoming culture to women in the sector. Julie Young's crucial essay, "The Invitation Effect," signaled the negative impact of women's and other minorities' absence from emergent media on diverse groups' participation, asking to what extent underrepresented groups avoid participation in industries, like the tech world, where they rarely see individuals like themselves.[52] Women in VR/AR was established to bring together those already in the field as well as appeal to those outside to join in. Duong and Young decided on an 80% women to 20% men ratio in the group to create, as Young wrote, "a place for women to feel an OVERWHELMING sense of welcome. We need to make women pretty much feel like they are being handed a diamond-encrusted golden invitation to join the VR/AR industry."[53] While some might imagine a goal of gender balance in such a group, Young saw their carefully considered "imbalance" of membership numbers as both an empowerment space for those often typically outside the tech sector and a consciousness raising arena for those already within.[54]

Jenn Duong, who wants to work both on the creative side as a director in traditional and immersive media and on the development side to address issues of inclusion and equity, talked about the larger vision of Women and VR and SH//FT:

> We really wanted it to be this open-source reference for the community, and for women and underrepresented groups, immediately for there to be an overwhelming presence of people that resembled them. Whether they were women, or women of color, of people of LGBTQ, we wanted to reverse the feeling that we get when we go to conferences and it's predominately male. We felt like we could do that through this online community. It got to the point where we wanted to take it to the next step. We wanted to host an event, or if we wanted to partner with someone like Oculus to give away scholarship tickets. We should have a legal entity to do this.
>
> One of the goals of Women in VR was never to just focus on women. It was to focus on equality, diversity, and inclusion overall. Women, men, people of color, the gay community, the trans community, it couldn't just be called Women in VR. So we came up with SH//FT.
>
> . . . We strongly felt that no one should ever own the Women in VR community. . . . [I]t's very much one of those things that we feel like this belongs to the people. Everyone should be able to throw a Women in VR mixer or gathering. We shouldn't be the gatekeepers to that, it should be a community thing.[55]

We will further discuss the contributions that many of our participants have made to the establishment of community-building initiatives in chapter 5.

Technologists

Many of our participants discussed the need for more women working on the technology side of emerging media. Most of our conversations and most of the research has demonstrated this is largely a culture rather than a pipeline issue. Amelia Winger-Bearskin, an artist and technologist and chair of Artificial Intelligence and the Arts at the Digital Worlds Institute/University of Florida, addressed this very point:

> Being a developer in general, in any kind of start-up or tech focused company, it's still so incredibly male dominated. You wouldn't think that we live in 2022, if you go into most developer rooms of most companies, and it's shocking, if anyone at all is a woman. The culture is very strange because of that. I think they lose a lot of male talent as well, who don't like a monoculture. It's a very narrow culture. A lot of men are very dissatisfied with the way it is. It's incredibly competitive and locker-room-like. I think a lot of men hate it—they'll leave and start as a developer, and then move into customer service or something else because [they], especially men who have families, don't feel comfortable. It's still a very toxic culture. A lot of women go into it and leave within a year or two. We don't have a pipeline problem—people thought there was a pipeline problem (that is, get more women in STEM). So women go and they get bachelor's and master's and PhDs in STEM fields, and they go and work at a tech company for one or two years. And then they just leave, they go to a radically different field, they don't even usually go to a different place in tech. They just bail entirely because they have such negative experiences. It's really not a pipeline issue or a capacity issue or a training issue. It's really just how incredibly toxic the cultures are. There's just a very small margin of acceptable difference that you're allowed to be.[56]

One technology lead and producer from the UK, who wished to remain anonymous, noted how stubborn blind spots could be:

> I was one of four heads of technology in my previous job—two of us were female and there were two males, and it was not that uncommon for people to be really surprised when they found out I actually had an engineering degree. They just make a subconscious assumption that can't be my background, I must be something else. And I find that mind boggling because my actual title is "head of technology." I don't know a single person with that title who doesn't have a technical background. . . . [I]t's easy to get underestimated and you have to show your credentials in a way that I don't think everybody has to do. If I have to share it, if I have to play my card, I can say I have this degree and I also have a certain pedigree in terms of the companies I worked for, being well-known companies. I shouldn't have to show that for people to take me seriously.[57]

Winger-Bearskin, whose diverse career spans the arts, academia, and technology, also spent time as a "developer evangelist." The goal of the developer evangelist, as noted by Jennifer Helene Maher in *Software Evangelism and the Rhetoric of Morality*, is seen within tech companies as a significant one. It is ambitiously imagined not merely as a marketing tool for a piece of technology but rather as a performance directed to developers that relays the larger vision, spirit, or "belief system" of a company.[58] Winger-Bearskin discussed her experience with this unique role and its productive personal by-product:

> I went to Silicon Valley in California, and I worked for a start-up called Contempo. That was really the first time I ever worked for a Silicon Valley start-up, which was really fun, and I got to join them when they were a very small 70-person organization. Now they're a unicorn and about to IPO [initial public offering]. I was there for about two and a half years, which is incredible. I've really learned an enormous amount about the industry and also just perfected my technology skills even further, I worked as a developer evangelist—you're someone who performs the act of

coding on stage every day constantly, traveling all over the world, and you just code live for people as an entertainment form, which was an amazing opportunity. I think I got over any type of impostor syndrome I ever might have had, someone telling me that I don't know how to do something, I just learned how to do it in front of thousands of people![59]

Winger-Bearskin, has also been a prominent voice for reimagining technology through an ethical rather than instrumentalist lens, one that is responsive to Indigenous values and environmental concerns. Wampum Codes—Winger-Bearskin's name for an ethical framework with which to engage with technology—is also the title of her ongoing podcast:

[*Wampum.Codes* is] where I interview Indigenous technologists [about] how they're co-creating with technology in their communities to make positive change. Wampum Codes is also an ethical framework for software development, inspired by Indigenous values of co-creation, for which I do as a workshop with a lot of different companies in Silicon Valley. I work primarily with coders, who want to make ethical decisions; they want to have ethics and values within their company culture. But oftentimes, you have the people who are ethicist[s] and philosophers, and maybe social critics on one side, and they write very amazing books. A coder is tasked with taking seven different 300-page books and distilling it into code. That's very difficult, and it's a huge burden to assume that those people can do that by themselves. I'm primarily focused on coders having all these great ideas, but when the rubber meets the road, how are we actually coding when the systems that we are coding are not neutral, and it's more than just input in and then output out with AI? It's the process of how these algorithms are looking . . . it's not just what data you are using.[60]

Funders

Martina Welkhoff, cofounder of the WXR Fund, an investment company that looks to support women founders of companies working in spatial computing (VR, AR) and AI, has worked in several start-ups reimagining the use of technology in communication from mobile games to VR, and for the last several years she has been focused on issues of gender and equity in the extended reality (XR) space. Welkhoff also founded ConveneVR, which focused on using VR for live events. "The original vision I had for Convene," she said, "was to start experimenting with special events and the types of experiences we could build in VR that could be shared and be spontaneous. The big differentiator was I didn't want to work with any kind of recorded medium . . . [and] I'm very interested in experiences that you can relive and share."[61] In 2017 Welkhoff, working with the artist Drue Kataoka, used ConveneVR to host a live event showing her VR sculpture, *Yes, Now Is the Time*, which allowed invited participants across the United States to walk around the work and learn of famous firsts for women in history. This innovative live event was, according to Denise Restauri, writing for *Forbes*, a "'first of its kind' convergence of virtual reality art and social VR for social change."[62] Welkhoff explained:

> We brought women inside of the art from all over the country and streamed the conversation in VR about the political moment and how VR could be a tool for social advocacy, and how we could use VR to elevate women's voices. That was just an amazing project right out of the gate and got me very excited about the potential for how we could translate what happens in VR into change in the real world and how we can connect the two, which at the time, and I would say even now, tend to be thought of very disparately.
>
> I think increasingly that line will blur. We wanted to try to get ahead of that and see how we could influence people's thinking and particularly women's thinking in ways that they could use the technology in an empowering and human way that could be sustained in the real world.[63]

Welkhoff's work as founder with WXR and ConveneVR and as board president for Seattle Women in Tech, has focused, like many of our participants, on developing a network of women in the emerging tech sector.

> I've devoted a lot of energy to building up communities of women in technology because of my own need for that now. Two or three

years into Zealyst [a mobile gaming app], I started to really recognize that I have very few women in my professional circles and that was a detriment and really weighing on me emotionally. In the more recent years, more of my peers and mentors are women. However, I'd say the majority are still men. Another shift I'd say that's happened in my network in the last few years is the men I associated most closely, very strongly identify as allies and actually seek me out to get advice on how they can be better allies and how they can better support. I find that really encouraging. From a numbers perspective, most of my assistants are men, but there are more and more women I am finding all the time and through things like WXR. What Julie [Young] is doing with the Facebook community, it's easier to find those likeminded women than ever. I think that a huge part of the solution is just the visibility and how do we seek each other out, and the tools to sustain those relationships.[64]

Having a strong network for communication and funding is vitally important in emerging media spaces. Unlike an earlier era of digital culture, when relatively cheap tools fueled a wave of creative work in video, social media, and online work, which included a ripple of participatory and cross-platform media, media making today in the immersive and interactive spaces can be prohibitively expensive for the maker and the audience. Sadah Espii Proctor (2017), creative/entrepreneur and founder of Espii Studios, is a VR director and sound/media designer for theater and immersive experiences. She directed *Girl Icon*, a 360-degree video documentary, which was created as part of Oculus's VR for Good Creators Lab and worked in a mentorship role in the 2020 "Cannes XR Challenge" with Garage Stories. She discussed the issue of access and its direct link to funding for makers and audiences, especially for communities of color:

The challenge that I have had with VR is accessibility. . . . Hardware Hack Lab, ThoughtWorks had sponsored an art and tech hackathon called Art-A-Hack. That was my first time venturing into VR—because there are not really many solid answers on how to do things, there is a lot of room for experimentation. For my group, we created the Afrofuturistic click, the Afrofuturistic Carnival. I worked on sound design and narrative design. . . . Even with borrowing equipment, accessibility is still a problem. I have a Mac, so I have been limited to just mobile VR. I've watched so many developers in articles cry about how mobile VR is not really real VR and that it's extremely limiting. So, I wrote an article on Medium in response. . . . and people responded pretty well. But I have come to my own understanding that mobile VR as of today is more accessible to your everyday audience than PC VR. The reality is that a lot of people do not have access to that because not only the headsets are expensive but also the computers to run them cost a lot of money.[65]

Espii draws attention to significant and complex issues related to access and funding, which will be addressed in more detail in chapters 4 and 6.

Liz Rosenthal (2019), whose work crosses over from curatorship to funding, discussed her role of development and incubation with artists in conjunction with CreativeXR, which provides more holistic support alongside funding for projects:

I think doing content accelerator programs, incubator programs are brilliant—we finance 20 teams with creative prototypes, and we give them strategic workshops and mentoring, provide finance to create a prototype, and we help them with their business plan and pitch. Then there's the showcase market at the end where we invite potential financiers and distributors. I believe that these wrap-around programs are really good support instead of just giving money to people and saying "go and work it out."[66]

But many roadblocks to funding are still stubbornly in place. Kamal Sinclair commented at the opening of this chapter on Sundance's efforts to amplify the innovative work of Nonny de la Peña—part of a series of interventions by the organization, as exemplified by Sinclair's expansive inquiry on media equity, *Making a New Reality*, noted earlier. We interviewed Sinclair in 2017 and 2022. While still in her research process for the series in 2017, she generously shared her thoughts at that time on some of the dilemmas in funding for diversity, particularly in our context of a discussion of gender:

> It's about making sure that we're all aware of amplifying what is truly already there in terms of diversity and women. I also think that there are more explicit strategies that need to be put into place that lower the barriers to entry and increase access. I think the investment space is really a place that needs support. I spoke with a group of wealthy women philanthropists, and we talked about this issue, and a few of them came up to me and said, "You know, when it comes to my philanthropy I invest in women and girls all day long. When it comes to my portfolio, I invest in men." . . . I definitely think it has something to do with mitigating implicit bias and with really investing in women at the same level that we invest in men.[67]

Promising Futures

There were feelings of optimism among several of our participants, especially in the earlier 2016–17 interviews, that the VR space more generally provided opportunity, as Kate Parsons noted above. Whether due to the more experimental space that VR represents, the quite conscious efforts toward networking and funding for diversity—as evidenced by Facebook's Women in VR, Sundance New Frontiers, and WXR—or the reckoning of accountability that the #MeToo movement brought to the media industry, there is a sense that something is changing. Samantha Storr, who at the time of our 2017 interview was at Here Be Dragons, then vice president of content at Within, and then, at the time of this writing, vice president of content at Supernatural, expressed an optimistic view:

> I collaborated with Chris Milk for 12-plus years, so we got into it together when we made Beck's "Hello Again," which is considered to be the first VR music video. . . . Tech industries have their boys' clubs, definitely. Occasionally I'll come across an old-world mentality in the workplace. But I welcome those interactions as an

opportunity to fight the good fight. I know what I'm doing, where I'm going, and how to get there. And I'm surrounded by intelligent men and women who support one another. One of the best parts of working in emerging media is the new ways of thinking that emerge around it—there's potential to alter perceptions here and combat discrimination. The pace of positive change is inspiring. Our head of camera, head of production, EP [executive producer] of development, head of post—all women. For me, I'm really interested in their unique success stories.[68]

Kamal Sinclair (2017) noted that change would require multiple strategies and returned to the importance of amplification and history, the point where we began this chapter:

I think it'll be a mix of strategies. I do think it's important to consider, not only for women and people of color, LGBT communities, but for everybody. I think we all benefit from having a more diverse perspective on what reality is. I think that telling the truth of the stories of who is an innovator and who's participating and platforming work from different places, I think that enriches us all and helps us all to mitigate our bias, because nobody is without that bias, none of us. Not even against our own identity groups or against our own selves.[69]

Shari Frilot had mixed feelings on where things stand regarding gender equity but cautioned against a belief that women were absent or not central to emerging media:

I'm torn, because there's a distinct disparity of investment to companies that are owned by women. . . . But at the same time, this familiar narrative that men own the space is a narrative and doesn't connect all the time with the realities that I'm seeing. I see a lot of women in the space, a lot of women doing really interesting things from all over the world. Take with a grain of salt that men own the space. Certainly, it's Chris Milk that gets to sell his company for $400 million. It's Palmer Luckey, the intern, that gets all of the $2 billion, selling the Oculus Rift. There are definitely things like that. But it doesn't mean that this field is developing without women. Women are key to expanding the exhibition, the artistic, the creative technology, the community. On a certain level, it is important to acknowledge the disparity of investment, but also to acknowledge that the fact that these women are here, working and building this work. . . . [T]here are a lot of women in the space, and that's what we should be talking about.[70]

Conclusion

As Frilot notes, the stories we tell about the space can either contribute to our own erasure or be empowering and inspirational. This chapter demonstrates an effort to accept Kamal Sinclair's challenge to broaden our lens and explore the diverse contributions and roles that women / gender nonbinary / genderqueer individuals have made to the emerging field. We have highlighted the many roles that our participants have undertaken, some of which have been hidden, uncredited, and undervalued, but that have nonetheless been crucial to the success of numerous projects and initiatives. The roles we have foregrounded—curators, programmers, and archivists; producers; creatives; community builders; entrepreneurs; technologists; futurists and thought leaders; and funders—have proven essential in establishing practices, principles, values, and approaches within the emerging media spaces that they have been situated.

What we have learned from our conversations with participants is that these histories are about more than individual recognition; they raise larger questions about the world we want to live in. When women and historically underrepresented groups are blocked from advancement or even entire areas of employment because of long-standing gendered assumptions and biases about job "suitability," there are serious economic consequences. The loss of these undervalued or invisible contributions magnifies as we consider the runoff cycle this produces in terms of educational opportunities, restricted self-goals and self-worth, and silos not simply of jobs but of people. Losing the ability to communicate across divides of gender, race, class; shutting down or silencing uncomfortable conversations about inequities, and, most tragically, fostering isolation rather than community result in culturally profound damage.

As inspiring as individual stories of resilience might be, they lessen everyone's ability to thrive if we must reinvent opportunity anew for each place and person.

We saw in this chapter our participants take on these challenges with a range of strategies: speaking up in the workplace, educating coworkers across lines of difference, and building their own spaces for work and creativity. We saw several initiatives where participants organized new communities to address inequities, demythologize technologies with empowering training/education, and begin the difficult but essential tasks of reimagining nontoxic spaces and communities. The efforts by participants recounted in this chapter, which we will encounter again in chapters 4 through 7, is in the last analysis about producing vibrant and healthy cultures.

We may well be at a tipping point in the recognition and centering of women's contributions to emergent media, thanks to a convergence of forces such as the #MeToo movement, the long-term activities of women-organized spaces for training and empowerment, formal and informal DEI (diversity, equity, and inclusion) in educational spaces and workplaces, and especially our first group of curators, programmers, and archivists who have been absolutely critical in the shaping and promoting of essential new histories in media.

4
Platform

Transitional Media Moments

In this chapter, we take the term "platform" as our point of departure and apply it in its broadest terminological sense—a site on which content is delivered. As we heard in chapter 3, our participants have engaged with, and are experts in, a spectrum of media platforms across transmedia and multiplatform, VR, interactive, and immersive media. These platforms include the conventional (cinema/television/radio/print), to the digital (web/online/mobile) and range across time-based narratives to spatialized experiences.

We begin this chapter with a consideration of what it means to work across platforms and to use multiple platforms—a phenomenon commonly referred to as transmedia. Here we expand on the use of the term as shorthand for transitional media—which characterizes the spaces of innovation that we are seeking to understand in this book. We then turn our attention to VR platforms—initially covering a period of activity from 2012–22—but through our interviews we uncover earlier participation with these technologies, which extends back to the 1980s. Our research participants have been able to share a wide range of perspectives, from working on highly commercialized platforms right through to community-based participatory platforms that create or provide venues for voices and experiences previously marginalized and disenfranchised.

We start with an in-depth discussion of transmedia and multiplatform work, exploring its definition and application within different industry contexts. We then examine how platforms may not be the primary driving force that is fueling experimentation—rather, our participants place the focus on innovating new ways to tell stories, produce media, and create artworks. We explore the potentiality of transmedia as a set of work practices, principles, and values. We move next into a discussion about the transition into the second wave of commercial VR in

2012 and the key women who amplified the potential of this technology as well as the creatives who were leading innovation. We look at virtual world creation as a precursor to "stereo" VR and consider the impact and influence of our participants' documentary practice on the platform's evolution. We examine the increasing proprietary and limiting nature of VR, revealing the barriers of and the gendering of technologies that our participants experienced. Like transmedia, VR, for women and non-binary media makers, shows waves of opportunity for experimentation and innovation but is hindered ultimately by an emphasis on monetary gains that focus on narrow market casting, for example, marketing for transmedia, games and enterprise for VR, and the metaverse. We conclude by charting a shift toward social VR as a platform that emerged during the COVID-19 pandemic. Many of our participants led the way in its evolution and raised critical awareness of its development.

Transmedia and Multiplatform

"Transmedia," primarily an academic term adopted to account for a particular set of industry practices, was first used by Marsha Kinder in 1991 and later adopted in 2006 by Henry Jenkins.[1] Jenkins famously conjoined "storytelling" as a suffix to the term to account for a particular strategy adopted by the entertainment industries to tell a coherent story or present an expanded coherent and persistent storyworld across multiple platforms. Jenkins's work spawned a vibrant subfield of transmedia studies within media and communications scholarship, which still persists. For our purposes, we are using transmedia to account for two interrelated phenomena—first, as a way to consider the use of multiple platforms and technologies adopted within one particular project or creative endeavor through transmedia practice and, second, as a way to account for the characteristics inherent in transitional media moments that we will shortly go on to explain through our cyclical model of experimentation to platformization to commercialization (see figure 4.1). Transmedia practice involves both fictional and documentary storytelling but also includes marketing and charity campaigns. It is important to note that although transmedia is a helpful term for the purposes of academic classification and analysis, it is not one that was embraced by many of our participants and it has not been widely or consistently adopted in either artistic or industry contexts. Instead, many of our participants described their work as being multiplatform, "cross-platform," and cross-media.

Innovations in this field of creative space can be tracked back to the early aughts, with a peak in activity occurring in around 2010. Caitlin Burns, a producer and editor from New York, introduced in chapter 3 and who has spent more than a decade creating multiplatform content strategies for well-known intellectual property, described the origins of the industrial/franchise mode of transmedia: "They're creating consistent storyworlds where you can start in a game and move to a film, go to a book series. . . . My personal definition of transmedia production fits in with the PGA [Producers Guild of America] credit, which is someone who is developing a narrative across three or more platforms for intellectual property."[2]

However, despite this formal recognition by the PGA, a screen industry recognized body, the transmedia producer credit held less relevance in other sectors of the industry. Jennifer Magee-Cook, a senior producer from Sony in Los Angeles stated: "When they tried to title me [in *Descendants: Wicked World*, 2015–17], they had me as transmedia producer for a while. . . . It's a confusing word because it's too broad, and it's too general. I'm not even sure I could define it because to me—I work on movies, and I work with multiple platforms—does that make me a transmedia producer? Or am I a movie producer who knows how to utilize additional partners within the system to help me?"[3]

Furthermore, although the credit may have signaled the professionalization of the sector in its recognition of a transmedia producer, it did not convince others of the existence of a transmedia "industry." Kim Plowright, an independent producer from London, with extensive expertise in designing and delivering cross-platform projects for Channel 4 and the BBC, talked about the commercial limitations of transmedia as a nonprofit-making form, therefore rendering it less significant to the wider commercial screen industries: "There really isn't a business model for it. . . . They're trying to make the industry a thing by defining it. I think the problem is that unlike the film industry and unlike the games industry, nobody's actually buying transmedia experiences—they are marketing at best."[4]

Robin Benty, from Fox Broadcasting, Los Angeles, and the executive producer of the *Sleepy Hollow* VR experience,[5] also attested to the industry using the term inconsistently: "I never considered myself a transmedia person until I submitted something for an Emmy and that was the only category where we could submit in. It's weird because it's such a taboo word in the digital space because no one understands what it is."[6]

Liz Rosenthal (2016), founder of Power to the Pixel, curator of Venice Immersive, and executive producer of Creative XR, reflected on why the term may not hold a consistent credence among industry professionals: "Nearly every year there's a new hype word which comes in and out of fashion. 'Transmedia' is an academic term as opposed to a practical term. . . . I really believe that the whole media and creator space is multiplatformed . . . the way that we engage with media today, and ideas and communication is totally multiplatform and is constantly evolving."[7]

Hazel Grian, a UK-based independent artist, writer and director of VR and multimedia works (including the renowned web series *KateModern*), explained: "Transmedia is more of a commercialized version of the grassroots stuff—the alternate reality game or anything which is experience-designed which uses non-traditional platforms to tell stories. I would say that transmedia to me is not a separate thing. It's just a term."[8]

This agnosticism around the nomenclature resonated in many of our participants' responses. Illya Szilak (2016), writer and artist, from New York, of *Queerskins* series recalled: "I didn't set out deciding that I wanted to work in transmedia. It was really just, 'How do I tell the story in a way that I need to tell the story to make it work?'"[9]

Platform agnosticism came up in numerous interviews, including with Carrie Cutforth, a creative producer and writer working across interactive, digital, web series, film, VR, AR, transmedia, and alternate reality games (ARGs). Carrie cofounded several community-building organizations, including Transmedia 101 and the Independent Web Series Creators of Canada. "My path is so divergent in terms of the various mixed realities and VR—creatively, I'm very platform agnostic" she recounted.[10] Juliana Loh, a VR worldbuilder for social spaces, an XR prototype designer and an interactive VR artist using Google Tilt Brush similarly stated: "I think it's really important to be platform agnostic initially. Do not put all your eggs in particular baskets. There are so many platforms out there and ways in which you can create . . . but sometimes software becomes obsolete."[11]

Originating from an ARG production perspective, Mary Feuer, a creative from Los Angeles and one of the writers on the critically acclaimed and hugely popular web series *lonelygirl15* (2006–8), also foregrounded and prioritized the story over the medium:

> I honestly knew nothing about this stuff until I met Jan Libby [another writer] on *lonelygirl15*. I remember her talking about placing a classified ad in the newspaper as part of an alternate reality game. I remember thinking, "Wow," because when you hear the word "transmedia," it sounds very high tech, and it sounds like you're going to be doing all these technical things . . . but it was really about what's the best way to tell a story that's going to give people the excitement of finding the story.[12]

Like Feuer, many of our participants were keen to emphasize the fact that platforms themselves did not matter, the emphasis is instead placed on the creative affordances and opportunities, as opposed to fetishizing the platform as a new technology. In many cases, a critical approach was taken to evaluating the potential of the platform with participants asking how it would be useful to enhance the content and approach of the project. Award-winning documentary filmmaker and journalist Carrie Lozano from San Francisco explained both the creative and pragmatic factors of her decision-making process when deciding what form or platform a project should take: "What should this story be? What does it merit? Is it an article, is it radio, is it online, is it a film, is it a short film, is it TV? I really start with this story. I don't think everything should be a 70-minute documentary film that costs $400,000 to make."[13]

Jasmine Idun Isdrake, a game designer and creative director of Playcentric in Sweden, noted a shift away from fetishizing emerging technology in her own communities of practice: "People are getting back to focusing on actual design and actual storytelling. . . . I think we are more mindful now about not just bringing the newest tech, but actually designing something with quality and a human centered perspective."[14]

Ingrid Kopp (2016), introduced in chapter 3, a director and curator of the Tribeca Film Festival who is based in South Africa, echoed this viewpoint: "I never felt particularly invested in transmedia. I just wanted to see what documentary could look like when it wasn't a feature length film. I'm not particularly invested in transmedia as an industry. I also never really saw the scale in terms of our audiences."[15]

May Abdalla, executive director and cofounder of the award-winning UK-based Anagram, similarly centralized documentary within her practice: "I'd always been interested in documentary and the quality of documentary; in the feeling of having to go into the imaginative space of inhabiting somebody's life. What else are we doing other than living our lives wondering about other lives that we could be living? It's the material of being alive."[16]

Sarah Wolozin (2016), director of the Open Documentary Lab at MIT, took these individual's views a step further in her belief that documentary is a driving force behind the uptake of new technologies and innovating approaches to emerging media practice: "If you look back at the emergence of every new technology from film to radio, to photography, it's documentary that people do first. It's documentarians, whether they're professional or amateur, who are the ones experimenting with the new technology and sometimes creating the new technologies for storytelling."[17]

An overwhelming sense continued to emerge from our interviews that the platforms themselves did not matter, but rather it was their capabilities and affordances in advancing storytelling forms and techniques and, crucially, their capacity to enable and introduce a more diverse range of creators. Lina Srivastava, a strategist, advocate, and producer, collaborating with organizations such as FilmAid, UNESCO, and UNICEF, explained the importance of ensuring that multiple voices are heard: "It has to be about multiple authorship. There has to be multiple voices. You can't make actual social change with one voice."[18]

Maya Zuckerman, a writer and consultant and cofounder of TransmediaSF, a network of Bay Area media and start-up creatives, also explained the importance of "giving space to these new voices. Looking at transmedia as this umbrella ecosystem for any kind of platform and understanding that VR is just another platform. AR is just another platform. How do we learn their language and bring that into this bigger cohesive idea of narrative worldbuilding and storytelling?"[19]

Many of our participants spoke with excitement and enthusiasm about working at the vanguard of technological change, Jenni Powell, a director on *lonelygirl15* reflected on their constant evaluation of their multiplatform approach: "Snapchat was something that *lonelygirl15* didn't have access to 10 years ago, but we're using it now. It really takes a mind that stays technologically advanced, because you have to be ready to incorporate the newest thing. I know for me, that's actually exciting. I love the idea of new technologies coming out and me being able to use them as storytelling devices."[20]

Key to our observations is the tendency and proclivity of our participants to experiment with the affordances of new and emergent media platforms. You only have to look at the CV of Christy Dena—a prolific writer-designer-director of multi–art form and interactive projects—which, read chronologically, represents a timeline of technological developments and innovations where she has been at the forefront of innovation spanning CD-ROMs from 1996 to VR and immersive media in 2021.[21]

Liz Miller, documentary maker and community media artist from Montreal, took an expansive and extended view of the affordances of working across platforms:

> I'm also wanting to move beyond the digital realm and think about the platforms that we take for granted. Platforms for dialogue, for conversation, for political and democratic processes . . . they could be online, they could be on the ground, and that's one of the dangers when we speak about cross-platform . . . this idea that the deep conversation and reflection can necessarily take place there. When you get past thinking of only the digital platforms, or online platforms, you can think about how platforms on the ground can complement platforms online, and what they do differently.[22]

These open and emphatic expressions of wanting to expand and complexify the canvases of experimentation were something that characterized many of our participant's responses.

Our participants also reflected on transmedia as a place of gender diversity. For example, Mary Feuer observed: "It seems like there is something unique about transmedia and about exploring the outlying methods of storytelling that seems to either attract women or have more opportunity for women."[23] Christy Dena reflected on the notable presence of women working in the space of ARGs, compared to the computer gaming workforce, which has historically suffered from a notably dire lack of gender diversity, despite the fact that the first graphic adventure computer game was designed by a woman (Roberta Williams): "A lot of people used to say [in] the early days, the reason there was a lot of women in ARGs is because it was so story focused . . . and predominately cooperative in their design rather than competitive. Whereas a majority of video games, especially in traditional video games, are competitive. They're about the emotions and the achievements of power. Whereas alternate reality games are about social mechanics and cooperation."[24]

Sandra Rodriguez, a creative director and producer of VR, XR, and AI experiences and a sociologist of new media technology based at MIT, also pointed to women's participation in newer forms of creative technological experimentation as a moment of opportunity: "I see a lot of women in my situation with a diversity of backgrounds that are targeting or exploring things that haven't been so boxed in yet."[25]

Monika Bielskyte, a futures researcher, futurist, and futures designer, as well as a founding member of Protopia Futures stated: "In 2014 I was giving a talk, saying that the future is *not* about virtual and augmented reality. The future is ultimately about these layers of transparency of digital overlay that you choose in your life. It's about moving through these different modes of transparency."[26] A similar idea was also expressed by Kim Plowright, who conceptualized the creative palette of technologies: "You can draw a Venn diagram of all of these different areas like UX [user experience] and design and coding, and it's just those technologies and formats applied to storytelling."[27]

The emergence of social platforms as an open space for more women to participate and to be included was foregrounded by a number of our participants, including Jennifer Palais, who at the time of our interview was head of integrated branded content strategy and production at Greenlight Media. Palais commented: "Anyone can join the conversation. . . . Things were getting flattened more. That means everybody who has been marginalized can find their way in and find their people that they relate to and then also tell their story in whatever way they want."[28]

Other participants reflected on the richness that collaboration across platforms brought to the creative process, as Christy Dena (2016) explained:

Embedded within the actual form is a mindset that leans towards diversity, towards understanding and respecting difference, and finding one of the common elements that actually connect us together. We do that through story; we do that with documentation; we do that with the ideas; we do that with the design; we do that with the teams, and so that is another factor and the reason why we have such a mix. . . . [T]here's a definite connection between the spirit of what transmedia is about and that's the inclusiveness as an entertainment form that then parleys into working practices.[29]

What comes through quite strongly in our participant's responses is an overriding set of principles and practices that characterize how the platforms are used and accessed by our participants. This becomes all the more pronounced as transmedia and interactive media transmuted into a new discourse of immersive and virtual spaces. "To my mind," explained Caitlin Burns, "the concept of transmedia has always been more of a technique than it's been a market category now and of its own. It's really about a way of thinking about creative development, and the business around a creative production."[30]

Kamal Sinclair (2017), director of the New Frontier Lab Programs at the Sundance Institute describes how transmedia provided a discursive lens through which to understand the manifold creative activity and experimentations: "Transmedia was a way of framing that new expansive canvas at a particular time when we needed a language to understand what the heck was happening, but I think now it's much more normalized as how people communicate, and therefore how story is transferred."[31]

Looking back at our participants' experiences and insights on transmedia, we see artists and practitioners—often outside of, or marginalized from, industry power centers—seeking out and creating opportunities in areas of digital creativity prior to their codification and exclusive instrumentalist and monetary valuation. Driven by new forms of storytelling and experimentation with medium and expression, rather than technology in itself, the participants in our research also found openings to reshape the workplace, through collaborative practices and the development of storytelling formats. Transmedia, despite its sometimes inconsistent or dismissive use as a term of reference, does have a real value then by marking a significant moment of transition in media making. It serves also as an important precursor to the resurgence of VR in the early 2010s.

Platforms in Transition: Virtual Reality

During our research, we tracked a shift between 2016 and 2019 when more of our participants started talking less about cross-platform, transmedia, and interactivity and much more about VR and immersion, with many of them making a transition into those spaces as the second wave of commercial VR took hold. Ingrid Kopp (2016) explained the palpable sense of absence in transmedia creative output as people shifted from one medium to another: "I really noticed that there's a lot less web documentaries and those kinds of projects because the people who would have done this now are just doing them in VR instead."[32] We learned of the origins of this shift from some key visionaries whom we introduced in chapter 3 and who brought new work and new ideas into the spaces of discussion. Shari Frilot, chief curator, New Frontier, and senior film programmer at Sundance, talked about the genesis of the New Frontier festival:

> I was very interested in bringing art into the New Frontier that was legible to a film festival audience—innovations in new technology that I knew would spark the imaginations of filmmakers and industry who are really wanting to do something new. . . . If I did this at Sundance, not only would it live in the discussion and shift the discussion to ideas and creativity, but by bringing these worlds together would spawn something new and it did generate a lot of new things.[33]

Kamal Sinclair (2017) elaborated on the forms and formats that have been embraced and included within the festival: "It has spanned everything from participatory storytelling to biometric response storytelling to interactive film to gaming to VR, augmented reality . . . early generative art and early AI art."[34]

Frilot recalled the inauguration of "walk-around VR" in 2012, by Nonny de la Peña, and expressed the importance of enabling both the platform for this work and a space for experimentation: "Nonny and Palmer Luckey created the prototype for the Oculus Rift for New Frontier to be able to show *Hunger in Los Angeles*. It's that kind of thing that is incredibly gratifying when you know that this experiment [New Frontier] actually worked."[35]

As Sinclair explained, "The first prototype of the Rift was created by Palmer to bring Nonny's piece to Park City, because they couldn't bring the USC equipment off that campus, and so he [Luckey] said, 'I think I can figure out a way to do it on a mobile phone.'"[36] The headset, which showed de la Peña's 12-minute piece, was built at USC by Mark Bolas, Palmer Luckey, Thai Phan, and Evan Suma, and in our interview de la Peña expanded on the context of the evolution of this landmark innovation: "With this Unity working group, it was a really small group of us hanging out together. I started pulling people in to help me make this piece. I spent $700 of my own money, I begged and borrowed favors. This was the fall of 2011, and the lab says, 'You cannot take our goggles because they're the last ones I have and they're $50,000 a pair.' It became this great push, to get Palmer to get the goggles together."[37] Here, de la Peña described the first iteration of what would go on to become the Oculus Rift.[38] She explained what happened next: "Project Syria goes to the World Economic Forum in January of 2014 and that Spring; Palmer sells the goggles through Facebook for $2.5 million. Then everything changes. The interest grows, the technology gets better."[39]

These accounts bring us back to the arguments illustrated by our cycles of innovation model that we laid out in chapter 1 (see figure 1.1), which showed moments of women's experimentation with different creative technological mediums before they become commercialized or professionalized. The introduction of portable VR and the subsequent commercial success of the Oculus Rift present to us a similar case to those that preceded it in our model—film, animation, coding, electronic music production, and VR in the 1990s. In the case of portable VR in the early 2010s—we can bring to bear deeper understandings of the characteristics of a transitional media moment through the rich accounts provided by our participants. In figure 4.1 we present the introduction of portable

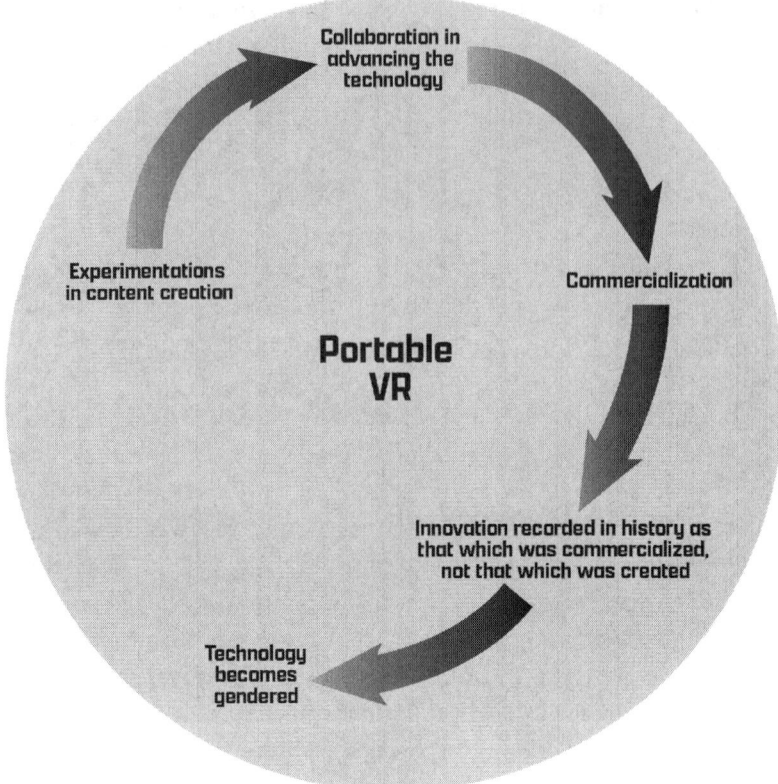

Figure 4.1. Cyclical model of experimentation to platformization to commercialization using the example of earlier experimentation of portable VR in 2012 and the subsequent commercialization of the Oculus Rift in 2014. Graphic design by Bullet Creative.

VR as a cyclical model of experimentation to platformization to commercialization, where we outline the key processes of a transitional media moment. These are innovation, collaboration, commercialization and historicization which result in a gendered rendering of the technology shaped by those who commercialize and make proprietary as opposed to those at the vanguard of creative innovation and experimentation.

Although the subsequent commercial success of the Oculus Rift eclipses de la Peña's important contributions within mainstream understandings of those responsible for innovation in VR, de la Peña's work has nonetheless stimulated a vibrant field of research into what she coined "immersive journalism"[40] and a fruitful strand of creative experimentation and inquiry. It is that which should be elevated and amplified in historical accounts of the evolution of VR genres, aesthetics, and creative innovation. Sinclair went on to explain the growth and expansion that the New Frontier festival subsequently experienced as a result of the inception of portable VR: "We went from having about 6,000 people coming to the New Frontier space within a 10-day period—which is pretty average for a venue at Sundance—to 13,000. It was all these gaming companies and studios and venture capitalists, as well as the grassroots media maker activists and the DIYers."[41]

The year 2012 clearly marked a key moment in VR's evolution in its mainstream and commercial adoption, which, as our participants accounts reveal, was initiated by key women creatives and curators. However, our highlighting of the significance of these contributions should not serve to overwrite the significant leaps which had already been made in VR creative innovation during an earlier wave of VR experimentation in the 1990s prior to investment and commercial interest being withdrawn. Some of our participants provided rich insights into that earlier moment.

Early VR Experimentations

Some of our participants revealed how they had been working at the vanguard of VR production and creation well in advance of the 2012 moment described above—these included Tamiko Thiel and Char Davies, who had both created groundbreaking 3D immersive, virtual world works three decades prior (see chapter 2 for more on their contributions). Thiel, an independent artist now working in Berlin, originally collaborated with Steven Spielberg, chair of the Starbright Foundation, to create the virtual Starbright World for children in 1994. She explained how Spielberg

> had heard of this VR technology that could now run on PCs and came up with this idea to create a 3D online virtual world where kids could run around as avatars, and he would go there as ET. So even if they couldn't leave the hospital, they would be able to

meet online in that way. . . . But because in those days the stereo VR helmets were lousy and gave everyone nausea within about 10 minutes, they said, "Please, no helmets"—the kids are already connected to machines, they are nauseous from all these medications. Let's just run it on a screen. . . . This is the same technology that turned into 3D computer game technology. It's exactly the same as what is called VR. The only difference is that people use the term "VR" with the Oculus and stereo VR. That's why it took so long for those helmets to come up, because you had to have very fast processors that could send you both eye images at a high enough rate, so you didn't get sick. So, between 1994 and 2015, when people talked about VR, they were also talking about these [on-screen] virtual worlds . . . it was the same code.[42]

The mid-1990s also saw the first wave of *commercial* stereoscopic VR hardware, and it was within this period that the artist Char Davies created *the* first works in virtual immersive space that were designed for viewing in a stereo headset [*Osmose* (1995) and *Ephémère* (1998)]. This wave was short lived, and the technology quickly died out, as Davies explained:

By the mid-'90s, those HMDs [head-mounted displays] disappeared. The companies making such helmets went bankrupt. So I bought out the last HMDs, called D-visors, from Division, which we started cannibalizing; when one would break, we'd have spare parts. I should add that, commercially, certain HMDs still existed, but the emphasis in the market had shifted, to higher graphic resolution with a narrow field of view (i.e., 60 degrees), suitable for scientific visualization. Whereas the HMDs I had been using had relatively low resolution and a field of view that was 110+ degrees. But basically, when the technology disappeared, my medium disappeared too.[43]

Davies discussed how she directly responded to the existing technologies with her earlier (1990s) VR artworks: "When I began conceptualizing *Osmose* back in 1993, I was extremely aware of the patriarchal values embedded in the technology. And very deliberately went about making a work to prove there could be an alternative. I do believe *Osmose* succeeded in that way. And *Ephémère* (which was essentially *Osmose*, part 2) took this even further."[44] More detail on these projects is found in chapter 2; for our purposes here we acknowledge their key place in the developmental history of the creative application of VR. Such important and groundbreaking works by women are obscured in the history of VR. Char Davies is somewhat of an exception in having received considerable critical and academic recognition for her works.

Other illustrative instances of the "first" experimentations are raised by our participants here. They include Toni Dove, who explained, "I did a project [*Archeology of a Mother Tongue*] with Michael Mackenzie and it was probably the first narrative VR piece, and I think we were the only people doing narrative."[45] Earlier virtual world projects created by women also include *Gone Gitmo* by de la Peña and Peggy Weil, which was originally produced in Second Life in 2007 (discussed further in chapter 7). Another "first" was described by Katerina Cizek (2022), a documentary film director whose works extend across many media platforms including the Emmy-winning *HIGHRISE—One Millionth Tower*:

> We used WebGL (3D space in a web browser) to create the first WebGL documentary. We were one of the first depth-kit projects using the depth kit system in universe. . . . We were doing 360 [-degree] long before VR was really back in the picture. . . . So definitely a sort of the *proto*-prototype for the full VR experience, even though we didn't do stuff in the in the headset, especially around *HIGHRISE*, which was so much about space. . . . I'm much more interested in 3D space, accessible through devices that are much more ubiquitous.[46]

These underpinning values and motivations to ensure open access expressed in Cizek's account were also highlighted by several of our participants. For example, Lily Baldwin, an artist, filmmaker, and performer who works with hybrid forms, spanning film, documentary, VR, mixed reality, and performance, spoke about her project *Through You*, which premiered in 2017: "It was an all-live action dance narrative. I was

Figure 4.2. *Through You*. 2017. Lily Baldwin and Saschka Unseld.

obsessed with making it flat—we need to democratize this, not everyone has a headset."[47]

We heard in our interviews an ongoing concern for the lack of diverse voices in the VR space. Artsy Marie, an independent social VR architect, who has been creating VR environments since 2020, raises a stark access and inclusivity issue:

> The closest comparison I can think of is redlining. . . . [T]he intentional separation of opportunities is happening in the space where we're not privy to all of the opportunities that come to these different platforms until it's too late or we've transformed the platform and our ideas get taken by corporates and we don't see any compensation for it. I've struggled a lot with Microsoft not paying me any attention, even though I've been the most transformative artist on the platform. I haven't been invited to anything that my copiers have been invited to.[48]

This troubling experience of "redlining" revealed in Artsy Marie's account is something that we will return in the next section of this chapter, but it is striking to note how her insights resonate with our own earlier observations—the systemic exclusion of creative contributions that occur through the processes of massive expansion and commercialization.

Our participants described the ways in which they have been work-ing to open up access to platforms in order to unlock their creative potential. Valencia James, performer, maker, and researcher working at the intersection of dance, theater, technology, and activism and the creator of *Suga': A Live Virtual Dance Performance*, which premiered in the SIGGRAPH Art Gallery in 2021 and later screened in the 2022 New Frontier Sundance Film Festival, described how James and the project's collaborative team "wanted to address the accessibility for performing artists to actually create their own virtual performances at home. We had issues of affordability of the technology that's usually used for this kind of volumetric streaming. . . . So we're thinking about how we can simplify it and make it the most affordable equipment possible."[49]

Accounts from other participants illustrate a renewed interest in the VR platform by women producers and creatives post-2012. Debra McGrory (2016), cofounder of a New York–based start-up that builds cross-platform 3D visualization software, explained why there was such a widespread transition into the platform's use: "It's just a really organic next step, but it's a very disruptive one and it's wide open and it's a new frontier. Coming from transmedia and transmedia production, this is the next thing. Everyone needs to be playing in this sandbox right now."[50] She went on to account for the creative and collaborative potential of VR: "The things feeding into VR and the making of it are coming from very different sectors, from art and theatre, film and games, and perfor-mance art. I think it really demands collaboration and it opens up huge opportunities for invention and innovation from interaction design and production in new ways."[51]

Many of our participants spoke of how they have been at the vanguard of experimentations with new technology. According to a North American–based tech start-up founder, who wished to remain anonymous: "The opportunities for women to just build something entirely innovative and very complicated in terms of production and user-interface design, things that we really are testing and asking ques-tions about every day. . . . [I]t's exciting to start to see the kind of work that has been produced, even in a short timeline and increments, and with very little budget, for the most part."[52]

Nancy Bennett (2017), a creative artist working at the nexus of groundbreaking technologies, cinematic storytelling, and creative design

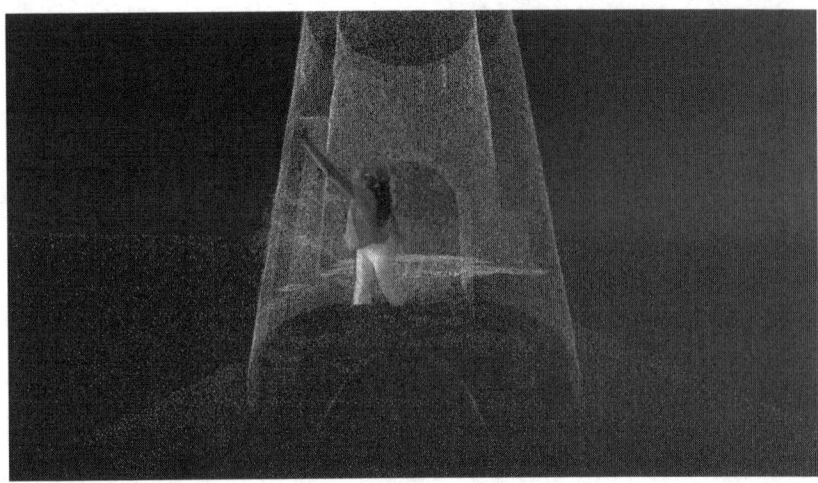

Figure 4.3. *Suga': A Live Virtual Dance Performance*, 25 minutes. 2021. Valencia James. Performance still. Photo credit: Simon Boas. Courtesy Valencia James.

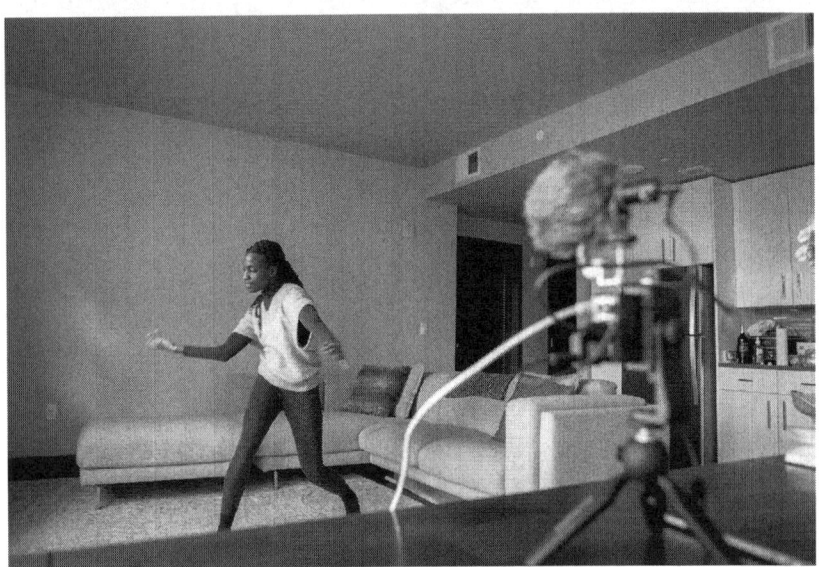

Figure 4.4. Behind the scenes of *Suga': A Live Virtual Dance Performance* (2021). Valencia James (*left*) performs in her living room and her 3D image is seen in the virtual world using a custom-made portable low-cost kit (*right*). Photo credit: Whitney Legge. Courtesy Eyebeam.

and cofounder of Two Bit Circus, described her own journey into VR innovation:

> I got the opportunity to see the Oculus Developer Kit number 1, which Two Bit Circus and Team were working with as early developers. I thought to myself, "This is the time to shoot for this," and I got a phone call: "I hear you guys are working with DK1 and we want to make this. Can you do it?" And I said, "Yes." Thus began five, six years of making VR content. It made perfect sense to me. . . . I've been fortunate enough to be at the right place at the right time to be innovating with the next formats.[53]

These accounts and many others demonstrate a proclivity and propensity to working with technologies that are not yet defined, that are in their nascent and beta stages, where there is instability and unpredictability, and, crucially, that are situated within a moment of transition. As a founder and director of a UK-based VR production company, who wished to remain anonymous, explained: "I'm making a piece of content at the moment, which is on the Magic Leap headset, and we've literally just written contracts with the developers where they're anxious . . . signing off something that might crash the next day. We're working with code and a platform that's still in development."[54] Robin Benty, a digital strategist with 20 years of entertainment experience, also expressed the transient and temporary nature of technologies:

> It's women and not men who say there's no future in VR. . . . I'm talking with women who are senior executives at major digital companies. I've said to [many] of them, you know it's funny, all the women say that, but if you talk to men, it's the second coming. They're all leaving their jobs, going to those VR companies. In LA alone, there's probably 50 VR companies that have gotten so much funding. Every day in trades and in *Variety*, there's a new VR company that's gotten investments from Silicon Valley and is aligning themselves with a studio. There's a VR shop on every corner in LA.[55]

Liz Rosenthal (2019) spoke about the challenges ingrained in working with new technologies and the impact that mainstream media discourse has on those working within it: "[I]t is constantly evolving with hype cycles and troughs of disillusionment, where there are news headlines every other week that can influence investors, . . . you're always fighting these fast-moving perceptions, so money comes in and out of the sector with these peaks and troughs the whole time."[56]

This constant threat of imminent and inevitable obsolescence is keenly illustrated in a practical example from Zillah Watson, who at the time of our interview was working as a commissioning editor for BBC VR. "We were trying to create a groundbreaking piece for Google Daydream . . . and it was disappointing to find how quickly Google pulled away from Daydream," she said. "And you just think, 'Hey, I didn't get any sleep for weeks creating this thing . . . and now you tell me that was just an experiment, it didn't work, so we've moved on to AR.'"[57]

Katy Morrison, cofounder and producer of VRTOV—a studio exploring the emerging language of narrative VR talked through the practical challenges of sustaining accessibility and availability and the unintended aesthetic outcomes that this can lead to: "It is a problem because we have these projects which have come out that require a certain set of hardware to run on and it will be this version of the run time and this version of this specification for a computer. One good example is *Assent*, which was the project that was originally made for the Oculus DK1, and it's been ported now to the DK2 and the CV1. So we've updated it so we can still send it off to festivals, because they all have the latest versions of everything."[58]

The idea that VR is technology in constant development and a transitional technology was framed by a number of our participants, including Heidi Boisvert, a designer and technologist, from futurePerfect Lab in New York: "VR is a transitional technology, where we might be proto-typing the future."[59] Similarly, Vicki Lau, a VFX artist and producer from Singapore, stated: "AR and VR are just the baby steps; they have some utility in certain industries—for example, VR in education, enterprise, and architecture. They could use VR just for that limited scope, but when we're talking about entertainment, it has always been heading in the direction of XR, mixed reality and extended reality. The final end goal was never VR."[60]

Exclusionary Interfaces and Accessibility

In our exploration of the creative and collaborative potentialities of platforms that are malleable, free flowing, expressive, and traversable, we revealed a space that enabled and supported a more diverse representation of gender. In contrast, when examining the uptake and evolution of VR platforms, we uncovered how proprietary platforms can be limiting and inhibitory in instances that Safiya Umoja Noble has referred to as "technological redlining," where "digital decisions reinforce oppressive social relationships"[61]—an example of which Artsy Marie recounted through her own lived experience detailed above. A further instance can be drawn from Zillah Watson's account, which alludes to this possibility in relation to the proprietary and closed nature of the VR headsets:

> There is not the same sense as there was with early computing technologies, where there was more openness about the technology being available and people having opportunities to try and exploit and understand it for different things. I think you can feel it is a much more closed world now, than the opportunities we had in those previous times. . . . You're not just buying a headset and then you choose which provider you go to, to download an interesting range of things that suit you. That's all being predetermined with the headset.[62]

Caitlin Burns further explained the difficulties and barriers that the hardware creates: "When you look at the big head mounted displays—the Oculus, the HTC Vive, and the PlayStation Morpheus, you're looking at really intense hardware. You're asking people to do a lot of work and spend money. Today, there are some interesting pieces out, but they aren't necessarily inspiring the mass market to overcome all of those hurdles to engage with it."[63] Toni Dove raised still another issue of accessibility that relates to public spaces: "I don't really want to work on a corporate platform. I don't want to work on a platform at this point in which the language is determined or predetermined."[64]

Debra McGrory (2016) talked about the gate-keeping limitations inherent within the technologies: "We really started to see the inherent biases built into those platforms around the business models, the app store model and the closed-systems and gatekeepers. I went through that process where it was difficult to release my film on those platforms because of those gatekeeper practices."[65]

An XR and health care specialist and founder of a UK-based XR design studio spoke of limitations of a different nature, those imposed by the creators' own subjectivities, though still aligned with Noble's "technological redlining": "In experiences where you're embodied, you'll often be embodied in a white person. I think you just need to look to the VR porn industry—I think that's quite telling. . . . [I]t's really fascinating that you're just embodied in white men's bodies the whole time. It's not very diverse. It's still very much male dominated and it's still very much focused on development by white people."[66]

One of the VR hosts from the Limina VR cinema (2019) (which was open from April 2019 until early 2020 in Bristol, UK), working with hardware among a diverse range of audience members (which totaled over 10,000 people), shared their observations that "headsets themselves are often too big, especially for petite women. The headsets are designed [for] an average human. . . . People who don't have Western face shapes and have quite low brow ridges or nose bridges, that kind of thing, sometimes they don't quite fit. To Oculus's credit, they have different shapes for lower brow, nose bridges, and stuff. So there is an attempt at being better."[67] This insight underscores how our relationship with technology is neither seamless nor uniform, and several artists sought to address issues of access and well-being directly in their work. Carmen Aguilar y Wedge discussed how she is trying to meet some of these challenges within the context of her own work with Ece Tankal, with whom she cofounded Hyphen-Labs:

> The technology isn't made for certain groups of people, and also how quickly my eyes were just degenerating from having another screen right in front of them and it felt like it was antithetical to the kind of healthy practices that we're trying to incorporate into our lives. What I'm really excited about right now is instead of fetishizing the technology itself, looking for ways to incorporate technology into immersive experiences that we are creating: through performance, through sculpture, through architecture, and having technology be something that augments

the experience but isn't the only reason why people are going to the space.[68]

Similarly, Lauren Lee McCarthy, an artist working across various media, spoke of her own open-source response to overcoming challenges of platform access: "An open-source tool for making code on the web—what would it feel like if the tool itself was built on these values of access and inclusion? That basically anyone that wants to participate should be welcomed in and encouraged, that you shouldn't need to prove your experience or your worth in the space, and then really trying to think about representation and diversity and how do you do the outreach. So from the get-go, you're building a different kind of space."[69]

Phoenix Perry, founder of Code Liberation Front, whose significant contributions to community building were detailed in chapter 3, raised a further issue about the accessibility of VR and how she addressed this through her own interaction design in response to "how hard it is to use the interface is in any position other than exactly how they think you should be positioned. For example, a lot of people who use sign language are struggling to use VR because you can't sign in VR, and they can't hear people talking. There's not much transcription. . . . I made InteractML to try and bring through gestural interfaces into VR and AR!"[70]

There have also been gendered issues with the technology with research revealing that women have been more susceptible to motion sickness than men.[71] Sara Lisa Vogl, a VR user experience designer from Berlin, described numerous barriers that women faced in accessing immersive spaces: "There's a higher entry barrier if you're a female. The other thing is that women are very sensitive when it comes to intimate interactions. It's not a given in all of the online social spaces that you actually have boundaries. What I'm frequently seeing is that a lot of my peers are actually rather scared and intimidated and don't feel empowered by the possibilities."[72] Nettrice Gaskins, a digital artist, academic, and cultural critic, reflected on such fears: "People are afraid of technology. . . . [M]any generations of having been oppressed by technologies have created a distrust of what technology does and what it can do and their role and how they use technology."[73]

Turning to issues of consent, Becca Caddy, a UK-based technology journalist illustrated in her own account of why such fears are well founded: "I actually went to an immersive future experience last week, there was no consent asked before, from four different people putting equipment on me. . . . [I]t was a really jarring example of why we need to talk about it. This is why there needs to be some kind of standard practice in how we describe touch and consent in VR and how we ask for it."[74]

Verity McIntosh, a VR practitioner and UK-based academic, also reflected on these innate and implicit barriers that have been encoded into the technology:

> Even from that first experiment when we brought *WormSlayer* into the studio, it was apparent that a lot of people experiencing the work were feeling quite unwell, and we had a go with Mitch Altman from the States who was very heavily involved in the 1990s movement around VR; he had some really useful reflections on what generated nausea and also that that was disproportionately felt amongst women, so that piqued interest around what inequality of experience might be in this field.[75]

Sarah Wolozin (2016) reflected on the wider issues relating to the inaccessible nature of these technologies:

> All this money and hype around VR means that a lot of spaces that normally were really experimenting with the web, which is much more fundamentally accessible and interactive and community and network building. . . . There's that fine tension and balance between working on technologies that are not accessible . . . versus technologies that are immediately accessible and more low-tech that allow more participation for more people—whether it's your audience or the people you're co-creating with. It means that immediately the lower technology projects are more democratic and accessible.[76]

Issues of accessibility emerged across several vectors, from the hardware and the platform to the virtual spaces, through which an inverse evolution appeared to emerge—as platforms advanced, they become increasingly exclusionary. We will return to these discussions in chapter 7; for now, we turn to consider the most recent technological transitional moment that a number of our participants discussed.

Social VR

Just as creative and experimental interest in VR began to dwindle, a renewed surge in its use in the form of "social VR" was precipitated by the COVID-19 pandemic and social distancing measures. Social VR is a form of web-based social interaction within 3D virtual worlds where individuals, represented by an avatar, can engage in real-time exchanges and shared activities. These worlds can be accessed either via a standard computer screen interface or by wearing a VR headset. Many of our participants explained how they quickly innovated in the transitional space of social VR, which was wrought by the need for social engagement and interaction that was not permitted through face-to-face encounters. For example, Shari Frilot described how they evolved their New Frontier online platform and expanded audience engagement using WebVR when the physical version of the Sundance Film Festival was canceled: "We figured out how to do a WebXR spaceship. We realized that we could platform a very ambitious XR lineup as well as create something that held all the social activity of the festival as well as show some films in the cinema house (in Park City, it was impossible to meet the demand to see the show). In 2020 we were able to quadruple the amount of people that could come and see the show, see the worlds in different ways."[77] Frilot's account reveals the positive corollary of being forced to move exhibition online—thus enabling access to what had previously been exclusive cultural experiences to a much wider audience.

Michela Ledwidge, creative and technical director, specializing in real-time and virtual production, and CEO and founder of MOD Films in Sydney, Australia, described the benefits of MOD's early adoption of social VR and virtual games production and their own agility in moving into the spaces:

> The IEEE Conference in 2020 pivoted to being a VR-only event, and we got involved in putting that on. Straight after the conference, we decided to go hard into Mozilla hubs, which is an

open-source platform that existed well before Facebook started talking about this. . . . We've just turned virtual world creation and operations into a core pillar of our studio and quite regularly now we'll have occasion for our internal team or a client to just use web-based VR, and because we have all these systems rolling literally every day, we can spin this stuff up really quickly. We don't use video conferencing as a standard tool at MOD. . . . [I]f we need to do anything beyond audio, we're more likely to jump into Mozilla hubs. We are natives in this space now and we are constantly juggling web-based XR with game engine VR.[78]

Liz Rosenthal (2022) talked about the significant growth of social VR use and its accessible potential. There was "an incredible explosion of creativity in VRChat, which for VR is what YouTube is to video. The platform has a huge community of worldbuilders and users and, with its Unity-based SDK [software development kit], enables creators to design any type of spatial multiplayer environment or 'world' and upload it to the platform. There is also an extraordinary range of user-created avatars to pick from allowing for infinite modes of self-expression and identity."[79] Rosenthal went on to explain the diverse range of social VR spaces or "worlds" that are available on the platform and that range "from super creative fantasy hangout spaces, to a beautiful, architecturally designed space, to an art piece, to an adventure quest game that could last several hours, to a music video, to a multimedia club world that's iterating on a weekly basis, to spaces where people teach sign language and hold dance, meditation, or exercise classes."[80]

Sara Lisa Vogl expressed a similar observation in terms of the explosion of social VR use: "It has never been a better time to be there than right now because all of a sudden people are there. There are people online and I can reach them, and people can see what I'm creating."[81]

The positivity by which these technologies and the sharp uptake by which they were embraced is described by their affordances and creative potential. Valencia James foregrounded the opportunities that these spaces afford to artistic practice:

I think volumetric performance can offer artists something that's very powerful—the autonomy in designing your own virtual spaces, performance world and the way of interaction. We found in Mozilla hubs—the social VR platform—we're really aligned with their vision for Internet health and accessibility. I found it to be an incredibly powerful tool for artists, especially those of marginalized communities where in these traditional gaming spaces it's been so historically saturated by white male presence. And . . . as a Black fan, I found that incredibly radical to just take up space in the form that I am in a virtual world. But what I love is that it's a new opportunity for artists who haven't been heard or haven't been represented in this space to tell powerful stories.[82]

Similarly, Artsy Marie recounted a positive experience related to her work as an artist using social VR spaces:

I had an online retail store called "Pretty Darn Artsy," and that's what led me to coming into VR during the pandemic. I came in on the Oculus Go and different social VR spaces like Altspace. . . . [H]undreds of people were visiting my gallery on a daily basis and I was blown away that could even be possible. . . . That's why I stayed because I immediately knew the power of this technology in removing the barriers and the gatekeepers and being able to build things that I don't have access to in regular life.[83]

Artsy Marie here underscores the value of these spaces to those who have been historically underrepresented. But as with most accounts, there is a dual dimension to the experience of emergent technologies, where inequities are transposed from real into virtual spaces. Although enthusiastic about the opening of access and opportunity to engage and experiment, Artsy Marie also described how this "openness" can allow access to be unwelcome with highly negative elements: "We had a situation where there were some hackers that came in, they took over our megaphone and were saying the N word repeatedly very loudly. This happened concurrently, and it startled people. We had to have town halls about it. They eventually got the scammer off the platform, but it took a lot out of us as a team to host events and get hijacked, and it's very scary."[84]

Sarah Lisa Vogl described the gender balance of social VR spaces and how she handles any difficult situations that may arise: "They just act like kids that are not able to keep their stuff together. It's just like they start trolling and wanting to make fun of you; they don't know what else to do. It's very often like kindergarten and I only have a few other females as soon as I'm on a new platform. . . . If anything is too much for me, I just take my headset off."[85]

Many of our participants raised the urgent need to address safety and trust within these platforms. Martina Welkhoff, serial entrepreneur and cofounder of the WXR Fund, described the benefit and importance of showing VR experiences in public venues: "It's a lot more difficult to dehumanize someone that you're sharing that experience with because it feels so real. It's harder to abstract and 'other' someone's identity and, in turn, to act on any of those cruel or base impulses that we often see online because you actually recognize that you're standing next to another human being."[86]

Safety and well-being are clearly fundamental issues. Heidi Boisvert expressed concern over this and the imminent and widespread uptake of VR technology across all aspects of our daily life: "Most of these VR projects drop you into a space where there's no pre- and aftercare model, which could potentially lead to retraumatization with people. I think in terms of the ethics of VR, I'm very concerned, and also [in terms of] the neurobiological issues—how is this technology not only affecting us now, but epigenetically, over the long term as it becomes more mainstream."[87]

We will examine in greater detail the ways in which our participants have responded to issues of safety, health, and well-being in chapter 7. But for now, we can conclude with our observation that use of social VR as an emergent media form, for creating different kinds of spaces that are safe, open, and inclusive was profound, in spite of the challenges faced.

Conclusion

As for the future of VR and immersive technology platforms, our participants expressed mixed feelings and offered a range of perspectives. Some felt that the rhetoric around the technology had become all-consuming: "The words 'immersive' and 'virtual' have become meaningless," remarked Char Davies, referring to the saturation of these terms used in contemporary entertainment media and broader promotional discourse within the burgeoning experience economy.[88] Heidi Boisvert talked about the dangers of the pervasive infiltration of VR into our everyday lives: "People are talking about it becoming the next operating system—which means that we'll be in VR in our offices, in our homes and all these things. It's like the black mirror."[89] Others took a more pragmatic stance in relation to the realities of the uptake of these technologies. Addressing whether the VR sector had achieved the status of an industry, Zillah Watson stated: "It's people scrambling around trying to do stuff rather than a formal industry. Many of the VR start-ups that started a few years ago are now going bust.... Others are having to diversify and do other things. It's not an industry yet."[90] Martina Welkhoff provided useful insights into the business factors at play and how they influence the future direction of these technologies:

> It's definitely cooled over the last year after a lot of hyperinflated expectations at the beginning of 2016. I think unfortunately it wasn't really set up for success because of the money that rushed in and the expectations of exponential growth in the first 18 months, which really wasn't realistic at all.... AR is the new shiny thing that investors are really excited about, and I've seen more and more companies that are either folding in an AR component into what they're already doing in VR or vice versa.[91]

These latter accounts point to the more negative aspects of the accelerated uptake of VR technologies and their impact on our participants, as discussed earlier in this chapter. These include the loss of technologies and the withdrawal of their support—meaning works are no longer accessible or, at best, very difficult to access. This was revealed most acutely in the accounts we included from the first wave of VR in the 1990s and in the commercialization of the Oculus Rift in the 2010s. Our accounts suggested that existing histories of VR technologies have favored and fetishized the head-mounted hardware of stereo VR over the rich practices of virtual world creation, which make use of identical source code and design in their production. This has led to the erasure of numerous women artists from the story of VR. This absence is compounded by terminological confusion and inconsistency, particularly around transmedia, which has led to further omissions in history—when works and activities elude definition and easy categorization, they can become easily obfuscated and lost in later accounts. By uncovering those lesser-known accounts in this chapter, we have shed light on the significance of women's participation and contributions. We revealed many insights into how our participants have been at the vanguard of platform experimentation and innovation—making new discoveries and creating works that have been central to the evolution and development of VR and immersive technologies. What many of our accounts also revealed is that once these platforms become more widely used, co-opted, commercialized, and made proprietary, the creative contributions are sidelined. Furthermore, the platforms can become more exclusionary and fail to accommodate a diverse range of participants with varying types of accessibility needs. The history of innovation is too often told through a history of technology, which claims innovation through naming high-profile product releases and acquisitions. Products and items of technology are too often foregrounded at the expense of the creative and artistic experimentations that have been instrumental to their development and successful commercialization. This invariably leads to a lack of acknowledgment of the contributions of artists and innovators.

Taken together, the accounts featured in this chapter strongly argue for the need for a more cautious and reflexive development cycle, and they also reveal how the fundamental principles, values and working practices that our participants have developed can be carried forward into the next technological context. It is exceptionally clear that the affordances of new emerging platforms and digital tools, which are open, undeveloped, and enable sandbox experimentation, in the transitional moment of their becoming, are what attracts many of our participants to these spaces, to innovate and advance storytelling, media making, and artistic creation.

5

Place

Legacies, Resilience, and Resistances

The thing that I'm best at is places. You can take me to a place once, and 10 years later I'll get you back there again. I think that's why VR works so well for me—in that I understand spatially right away how to design a story. That's how I live, that's how I think, that's how I feel.

—Nonny de la Peña[1]

Our participants have worked across a wide spectrum of places and contexts: from large commercial tech entities (including Disney Imagineering, Oculus, Sony, Epic Games), to cultural organizations and festivals (Sundance, Venice, Tribeca), to independent production companies and across a range of different roles. We have taken "place" to refer to a wide range of locations, from the place of work and production to the places of consumption, engagement, and promotion, acknowledging that there has been a conflation between platform and place as the line between the physical and digital has blurred, particularly during the COVID-19 pandemic, which significantly disrupted conventional notions of place.

This chapter examines the very constitution of "place and space" and its impact on opportunities and challenges for our participants. By drawing together key insights and observations taken from the interviews, we set up a series of "dualities," which all comprise a negative dimension—in which our participants have faced an exclusionary domain—and a secondary positive dimension—in which their responses result in the establishment of an inclusionary context or initiative. We first look at what have been described as male-dominated work cultures, establishing why our participants either sought out alternative working cultures or set up their own work environments. We then consider the traditional industry forums of conferences and the challenges and exclusions that our participants have experienced within these venues. We then look at the alternative forums that our participants have either sought out or established. Finally, we look at how our participants have responded to institutionally led diversity initiatives and how gender-inclusive support venues have been established and sustained in response.

Early Places of Creative Innovation

We begin by looking at our participants experiences in early creative computing environments. Peggy Weil, an artist, designer, and academic whose award-winning work spans such genres as digital urban signboards, VR, apps, and games, was an original member of the MIT Media Lab. She described working in what was initially called the MIT Architecture Machine Group (Arch Mac) between 1980 and 1982:[2]

> Even though it was extremely male in terms of numbers, I did not experience what I would say were really adverse issues related to being a female—partly because I was brought into the group with no expectations that I was an engineer. . . . They found that having an artist with creative experience in the lab helped with these models because the business of the lab was essentially to create demonstrations and to model future uses, and so creative thinking was honored and qualified. I did feel valued there because I wasn't competing, because I offered something that was valued.[3]

Rebecca Allen, whose detailed profile is featured in chapter 2, joined the Arch Mac lab in 1978 as a graduate student and research assistant, also commented on the gendered nature of the space as being indicative of the wider context: "It was very clear that the computer world was a very male engineering environment. At that time, it certainly was and unfortunately there still needs much improvement. . . . I felt fortunate as a woman and as an artist to be allowed into that technical environment at that time, MIT was about 10% women when I joined. You definitely felt like you were not quite where you belong. But I was determined that we had to change all of this."[4]

Weil went on to explain the work of the lab and how it informed her future projects:

> They got funding from military and industrial to create demonstrations of how some of these things inform future worldbuilding. So there would be a hypothetical issue for the future and how might that be solved. One of them was the sense of transmission of presence. That is something that I was given which figured prominently in my work later, certainly the work with Nonny [de la Peña], and *Gone Gitmo* had to do with transmission of presence in these virtual places.[5]

Gone Gitmo will be discussed in more detail in chapter 7; however, one particular project of significance that Weil talked about was one undertaken during her time at the lab:

> I picked up a book on lip reading and it had an illustration of 16 lip positions, and that was the "aha" moment for this piece called *LIPSYNC*. . . . Each [mouth] was assigned phonemes from the vocal tracks, which you could coordinate with typing. So you could type in "Hello. I'm from Architecture Machine Group," and the big lips would say "Hello. I'm from Architecture Machine Group," so that, you know, deepfakes—it's my fault . . . [W]e pasted the lips crudely on a still picture because the idea was to send as little bandwidth as possible, and you could almost make it look like somebody was talking. We showed it to a naval officer who said, on the basis of this, nobody will ever be able to make the order to "push the button" based on a digital transmission alone. That was in 1978 and that was chilling.[6]

Given how groundbreaking this innovation was, and its status as an early example of AI-generated art, we inquired as to whether Weil had been recognized for this work, or if the historical significance of the work had ever been highlighted, particularly in recent years within the context of emergent deepfake phenomenon. She responded:

> We were aware that we were breaking ground. . . . I did not feel marginalized for being a female in any of this—so that's clear. A

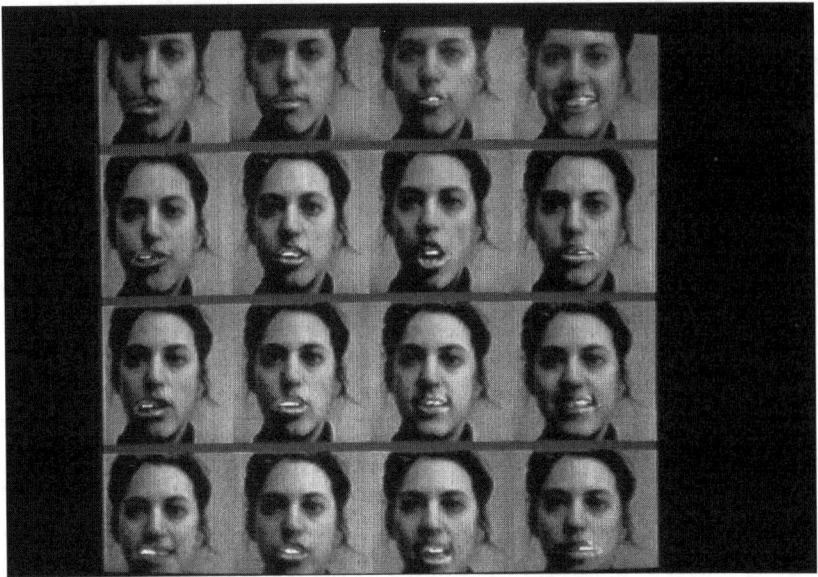

Figure 5.1. *LIPSYNC.* 1980. Peggy Weil.

book was written about the Media Lab by Stewart Brand in which
there's an account of this. I am nowhere mentioned. . . . I don't
believe it was deliberate. I was here raising babies and making
some of the first interactive games, and I wasn't in that world, and
I wasn't acknowledged either. Whoever talked to Stewart Brand
about it didn't say, "This was Peggy Weil."[7]

We here again see a recurrence of the marginalization of an exceptionally significant and groundbreaking experimentation, as exemplified
by our cycles of innovation model (see figure 1.1). In this case, Weil's
innovation is overwritten by the dominant media institutional narrative.
However inadvertent, this points to the recurring and systemic issue that
historians, documentarians, and authors need to consistently attend.
There is an ongoing need to amplify and clearly identify those responsible for innovation at times of technological transition to avoid such
glaring historical omissions in the future. Similarly, Allen also described
a project of significant note that lacked appropriate attribution. This was

Figure 5.2. *LIPSYNC*, frame buffer animation with Votrax and typed input. 1980. Peggy Weil.

one that she led at the Computer Graphics Lab, New York Institute of Technology, which she joined in 1980:

> The very first female 3D model was built by Ed Catmull, who was the director of the lab in the 1970s. When I was there in 1980, we were developing one of the first 3D animation programs, and I wanted to take the human female form and animate it, to bring her to life in the computer. . . . My first result was a short piece called *Swimmer*, then a piece called *Women Ascending a Staircase*. From the research side, it was about trying to get a 3D model to move like a human, and that was considered a really hard technical problem at that point. I created the first example of a female figure moving in 1981. There was a piece that's sometimes credited as the first human motion animation called "the sexy robot." It's a commercial for selling canned food.[8]

The commercial that Allen was referring to was made in 1984 and first broadcast during an American Super Bowl game on January 20, 1985, three years after her own experimentations (see figure 2.1). We asked if she received any recognition for her work, either at the time or retroactively, and she replied, "It wasn't until I more recently looked at the history and dates that I could confirm that this was a first. I know people have certainly written about my very early work in this area, but not that this was the first because I didn't quite realize that either and didn't want to draw attention to myself in that way. . . . So yeah, it didn't get credited as such."[9]

Weil's and Allen's experiences provide two illustrative cases of the innovation-to-commercialization model we presented in figure 4.1; only when there is a commercially exploitable logic of the technology is it amplified and promoted. In the case of Allen, her "sexy robot" claims the space in computer animation history as the first computer-generated imagery (CGI) of a female figure.[10] In the case of Weil, considerations of deepfake technology have only recently been documented and historicized, the origins of which are situated only in very recent developments (ca. 2017). The images of a lip-synced video of Barack Obama, widely attributed to the research group at the University of Washington, brought the concept of the "deepfake" into mainstream public consciousness. In both cases, it is the "institutional" narrative that is documented and promoted. (We have already revealed several other instances in the participant profiles featured in chapter 2).

Further accounts from participants with longer and sustained career trajectories reflected on the gendered dimensions of tech industry spaces. Allen described an early experience of a games industry working environment at Virgin Interactive, where she worked in the early 1990s: "There were very few women working there and I must say it was pretty sexist as a workplace. The video game world was just that way at that time. It was kind of shocking. I hadn't been in that type of environment. I expect they were probably better than other game companies, so I don't want to say they were unique in any kind of way."[11]

Mandy Rose, speaking as a professor of documentary and digital cultures had previously worked as a TV and film sound recordist and documentary director, including for 20 years at the BBC, reflected on her own industry experience across a number of different traditional media contexts in the United Kingdom:

> I've spent a lifetime working in spaces which are slightly uncomfortable in terms of gender relationships and technology. When I was 22, as a trainee sound recordist, I went into a department where I was the only woman alongside 50 men, and there was some pretty straight-up hostility towards me in that job (notably from the younger men). Then, at the BBC where I worked for a long time, I was relatively early into what was then called the "new media" space. I set up the first interactive / new media department at BBC Wales. I'm used to working in contexts where the relationship to technology is quite gendered, which can be difficult to navigate. Over the years I think I probably built up a thick skin and sense of what my strengths were—and that these were more about the editorial application of technology than the tech itself, as well as the understanding that underpins my research—that it's the social purpose and impact of technology that's really at stake.[12]

Char Davies recounted her experiences as a founding board member of Softimage in the late 1980s: "In 1987 I was not allowed to attend the first meeting for potential investors because it was held in a private men's club where women were not permitted, even though the first contact for such investment had come through me."[13] And on another occasion: "In 1992, instead of being handed a bottle of scotch by the investment bankers at the celebratory IPO (NASDAQ) dinner, I was presented with a pair of black suede short-shorts, even though I had worked alongside them on all the offering documents. (I always wore pants, so I assume this was their way of saying they wanted to see my legs.)"[14] In perhaps an even more concerning account, Davies revealed: "During the decade I was at the company, there was behavior among senior executives that now, in the #MeToo era, would be considered completely unacceptable. I'm referring to sexual affairs between executives and their assistants. A cliché, I know. As the only female senior executive, when I objected to what I sensed was happening, I was lied to and gaslighted for many years and told I needed therapy. I could say more but will refrain."[15]

Despite Davies's reluctance to elaborate further, her reflections of these highly troubling experiences are, as they were in her chapter 2 profile, very open and frank. Speaking from positions of experience, career stability, and, in some cases, levels of critical acclaim, the candid accounts in this section reveal the exclusionary and challenging experiences of earlier "legacy" industry environments. We were keen to explore with other participants whether there has been a continuation of these types of experience and behaviors, while also being mindful that younger participants were less likely to want to go on the record given the contemporaneous nature of their current context related to their role and to existing companies and organizations.

Contemporary "Traditional" Working Cultures

We now move forward with a consideration of our participants experiences in traditional mainstream-media working cultures. Jennifer Magee-Cook, a senior producer from Sony in Los Angeles, explained how women are not equally represented within the workspace in which she is based:

> The people I have been in conversations with who have done start-ups—it's all male based. I think that's because it's initially technology driven, which tends to be a more male-based field. . . . I have a very animation-centric point of view, so I can't talk from anything but the animation world. I can say that there are just a handful of women that are in that industry. . . . I do feel that management levels are usually filled by females and technology by males. There's a lot of creative women, but rising to the top are always the males. It's still quite a glass ceiling for women being able to get up to the top and noticed in creative fields.[16]

Our participants described differing levels of impact on their ability to perform in the ongoing face of gender-based challenges. Kaya Jabar, a preproduction supervisor at Framestore, a virtual cinematographer, and on-set supervisor, offered a perspective on working within male-dominated spaces, including the nascent virtual production sector. Virtual production is a suite of tools and practices that uses real-time game engine (RTGE) technologies in film and television production. Jabar compared virtual production to the traditional spaces of film and video production:

> It's a new industry so it wasn't as mired in the old boys' club as . . . if you had joined a postproduction company straight away where you do have women in management, but then all of the creative supervisors would be men, so there aren't many women role models. . . . [O]ne of our DPs [director of photography] was a woman, but in terms of communication you're facing off [with] a bunch of lads, because on [film] crews it's a little bit worse. It's more military in its execution. The expectation of how you speak, how to behave, can be more aggressive on a male crew.[17]

Uneasy atmospheres can be made further uncomfortable through the disconcerting persistence of familiar microaggressions, as explained by a managing director of a UK-based creative SME (small and midsize enterprise) who wished to remain anonymous: "I think that the BBC back in the day was full of male bosses with very keen women wanting to work their way up, and I think that was abused to a certain extent. I've experienced casual sexism a lot. I've definitely experienced being the only woman in the boardroom a lot. I would say that there's definitely been times where I'm not listened to, and a man will repeat what I've said, and they're listened to. That is familiar to me."[18]

In addition to these everyday low-level microaggressions, participants described how their cumulative buildup could lead to even more wearing affective. Amelia Winger-Bearskin, an artist, technologist, and academic who has founded many organizations, including DBRS Innovation Lab, which specialized in the creative uses of AI, recalled her own experience of working in an industry context:

> I did find some women that were like me. You have a very narrowly defined way in which you're allowed to succeed, or what background you're allowed to have; you always have to be proving who you are at all times. I think men are OK doing that because they don't get challenged as much. But if you're a woman, you get challenged 1,000 times a day and it just gets exhausting, and

whenever you walk into a room, people always assume you're the secretary—it's very hard to say, "I am the one that created this." You have to be very aggressive about it. Not everyone feels comfortable doing that.[19]

Some participants described far more predatory environments and situations. Vicki Lau, a VFX artist who has already written extensively about her own experiences within the VFX industry, explained a particularly problematic situation in a film-based working context:

There was this dude that was deliberately hiring women crew members. I don't think it was for the right reason. . . . [H]e's this 60-year-old director from New York and all the crew members he hired were young, very attractive, and he said he was doing it because "I believe in women, I support women, and I love giving women opportunity," but from what I saw when I was on set that particular day—I was a visual effects supervisor for that one film— . . . [H]e was checking out his crew members and getting kind of handsy with one of them.[20]

Lau's candid account is representative of many shared by our participants, some of whom did not want to go on the record for fear of reprisal. While it was clearly difficult for some of our participants to reveal problematic experiences of either witnessing or being subjected to harassment, others spoke of the more quotidian observations—including the endemic issue of the lack of a visible diverse gender representation in creative media working cultures. Liz Rosenthal (2016) situated the root of the challenges within media-industry working cultures at the senior leadership level:

There's a real problem with the fact that women are so underrepresented in the majority of businesses, whether it's a film industry or finance industry. The big problem is when you look at the top level of companies, at the boards and the people who are making decisions, they are mostly men. It's very rare that you'll see women on executive boards, and I'm a real believer that's where decision making has got to change. We've got to have more diversity.[21]

Vassiliki Khonsari, who in 2006 cofounded iNK Stories in New York, where she is also a producer, director, and writer, spoke about her own experience working on a Triple-A game as a narrative designer. She described a meeting being held on the Zoom platform and the inequities that this accentuated:

> It was this Zoom checkerboard of 20-plus men and I was the only woman. You come to realize, unfortunately, that this barrier that you have in person is amplified digitally in a Zoom space where you can't hold your place as much on a digital platform, particularly in the game space, which is so male. It became that much more difficult to give feedback, to hold my place, and I was super exhausted for other reasons. We were working long hours [and taking care of our] children. So I started taking these shortcuts, which was just to give some of my notes to male counterparts, because trying to speak from a female perspective, you know, when you're the only woman in the room . . . We can talk all we want about these high-level ideals that we all hold, and not to say that these men in that space were misogynists, or in any way cognizant of this, but it was just the way these conditioned patterns played out.[22]

Here, the digital space of Zoom visually and affectively amplified the inherent gendered imbalance and biases of the established games industry.

Transitional Media Spaces and Cross over Cultures

We have already made a clear distinction between the entrenched spaces of mainstream media production and the transitional spaces of emergent media, which can often be characterized by openness and opportunity. As Liz Rosenthal (2016) suggested, "When you're working on an undefined space where there's not a templated business model—it's easier for women to be part of that space."[23] Ingrid Kopp (2016) reminded us of one such example where this is the case: "I was always working with incredibly high-profile women in documentaries. A lot of the commissioning editors at Channel 4 and the heads of departments were women. There were some amazing women working in documentaries and a lot of women producing and directing as well."[24]

Robin Benty, working for more than 20 years in the entertainment industry, also provided an example of a context in which gender diversity was more evenly represented: "In all the companies that I've talked to, their social teams are mostly women. I think that women are inherently better at social media because they're talkative and they're expressive and they're emotive. . . . I had a lot of women working at FOX in social media."[25] Sarah Ticho, founder of Hatsumi in the United Kingdom, a research and design studio that works at the intersection of arts, health, and immersive technology, also pointed to an area of gender diversity: "I've found in this work I've been doing around immersive tech and health care, there is a really awesome bunch of women that have gravitated to the same space. I think partially it's because it's a caring role and it involves community."[26]

Many of our participants described the ways they have attempted to alter and develop their own immediate and more institutionalized working cultures to improve the experiences of their colleagues and employees. Zillah Watson, commissioning editor for BBC VR and head of BBC's VR hub, described the working culture that she had established:

> I've created a very different team and way of working in the BBC. We work in a very different way around a table. I have sought out good women, so we're probably not a typical team, because I've created something deliberately because I found it hard to work part-time four days a week when I had young children. I've deliberately subverted that and we've got various groups working part-time because they're doing other jobs. I really have tried to create a new way of working.[27]

However, on the flip side of these positive interventions, some of our participants raised issues that were being inherited from the mainstream media spaces. Dee Harvey, a writer-director specializing in immersive media and founder of Controvert, explained: "The same dynamics come to bear in this industry as they do in any other. It's not a brand-new industry in that it's an industry that's growing out of gaming and filming, so both of those worlds have their own cultures that are sexist in different ways."[28]

Ingrid Kopp (2022) expressed a more positive dimension of convergent media environments: "Quite excited about how, at least in XR spaces, it feels like there's been spaces opened up because it's new and it's not inheriting all these legacies. But again, I don't know if it's just me because I'm in these more creative nonfiction spaces where there are more women in documentaries than in big Hollywood features."[29] Martina Welkhoff, who cofounded a venture fund focused on women-led companies, also referred to the "legacy issues" of mainstream media forms and described how she has sought to counterbalance them through the creation of a targeted funding opportunity: "One of the ways in which we framed WXR early on is we have to have the opportunity to build something from the ground up and to really establish a new foundation of inclusiveness without a lot of the legacy issues other industries have, which of course exist. It's not a perfect blank slate by any means, but I do think that there's a lot more opportunity to form what is going to be common."[30] And Lily Baldwin, an artist, filmmaker, and performer, highlighted the benefits that come from working within an emergent media space: "In the 360[-degree], digital, nonlinear, non-flatty space—there's not a lot of rules, which I love. Things are not codified in the same way as they are in the linear, flat, contained rectangular box film. I love that space and everyone I've met; there's not the same kind of hierarchy."[31]

An anonymous managing director of a UK-based creative SME talked about the positive working environment that they have established:

I try and behave like a role model in my company. But my experience at [company name] is that it is wonderfully collaborative and respectful. I think we're just missing the ability to bring on more diverse members of the team. I would say that actually this is a very open, nonproblematic environment. Everybody is very accountable. There's no "macho" working late into the evening. We're very good on flexible working for parents. I feel like we have an environment here which is very positive. . . . My previous company was quite old-style boardroom so quite 1990s—there were

11 people on the senior leadership team, and I was the only woman. I got used to it. I'm reasonably confident in my own opinions, but I do think men talked over me and things like that.[32]

Belén Santa-Olalla, a senior creative consultant at Conducttr, London, where she developed transmedia storytelling projects, spoke about the explosion of transmedia content and the positive and inclusive working environment that this had established, but she was simultaneously cautious about what might happen next: "I think that right now there's lots of creative force from individuals, regardless of their gender, creating things. My fear is if this becomes more like a fixed, strong industry, we'll start to have more gender issues."[33]

Nonny de la Peña also underscored the notable visibility of women but highlighted how their presence is focused on particular roles and platforms. For example, she notes the distinction between 360-degree video and VR opportunities due to programming skills needed in the latter and a need for more women trained in this area: "If you go into the 360-degree video world, you'll get a lot more women. It's really not a very far field from filmmaking, in which women have made great inroads. They're still not the power brokers, but when you get into Unity and the real programming stuff—as it is, my studio is very male dominated."[34]

May Abdalla, executive director and cofounder of Anagram in the United Kingdom considered why women may gravitate to working with VR as a medium:

There was something about the etiquette of space and people feeling welcome and comfortable. I'm not saying men are not capable of doing this [, but women tend to be attentive to] the invisible rules of what is going to be present in the creation of space and the creation of home or the creation of an environment. I'm not saying all women are good at that, but I think there is something there. I've had a very gendered upbringing—growing up . . . there were women's spaces and men spaces.[35]

Tamara Shogaolu is the founder and creative director of Ado Ato Pictures. As director and new media artist, she is focused on sharing intersectional stories across mediums, platforms, and virtual and physical spaces in order to promote cross-cultural understanding and to challenge preconceptions. Shogaolu explained how she has questioned the representation at leadership level in some of the new spaces of innovation that she has encountered:

> I asked: "Are there any people of color–owned companies or vendors that you guys are working with?" She said: "Yes, there's one." I asked: "Are any of them owned by women of color?" She said: "No." I just thought it was so interesting that these projects that they're pitching and promoting as being so diverse now that immersive is becoming profitable . . . now it's becoming more of a boys' club than it was before . . . when a lot of women have been in this field for a long time—some of these companies have been around for two or three years—and now they have a whole roster of guys working on projects that are about diversity. But none are led by women or by women of color. . . . That's the change in terms of gender that I've seen—there's a lot more men involved now and they're the ones who are getting the big contracts.[36]

Despite our initial claim that transitional media spaces and crossover cultures have in some cases been more open, inclusive, and gender diverse, we hear in the account above of that the barriers to equality at partnership and leadership levels are still very much in place, especially with regard to racial equity and with women of color, particularly, missing from key roles of decision making and power. Many places within the emergent media landscape have resisted change or have slipped back to the patterns within legacy media environments that were spoken about at the beginning of the chapter, which has spurred others to either move away or to establish new work environments and cultures.

Creating New Workspaces

Our participants often engaged in the reimagining of place in response to issues of equity while also gravitating toward the understanding that emergent media offered unique design opportunities across myriad venues. Our interviews were predominantly with those in the creative arts and entertainment sectors—where the gender-based issues that we have been highlighting throughout this chapter appear to be germane. We also spoke with women innovating in the use of these technologies for care in the establishment of their own businesses. These included Isabel Van De Keere founder of Immersive Rehab, a digital health start-up that offers personalized and engaging neurorehabilitation programs using VR. Van De Keere (2019) explained one such effective utility of VR in the health care sector: "VR really was a tool where we could allow people to actually engage with objects, where in the physical world, a lot of them are just not able to do it because of lack of strength, fine motor skills. We create interactive studio therapy programs within fully immersive VR with a specific focus on their rehabilitation. We focus on patients that had a stroke, spinal cord injury, MS, Parkinson's, and, specifically, upper limb and balance training."[37]

Neilda Pacquing is a user experience designer and prototyper and AR and VR consultant who has led the development of training software applications, including EmpowHER VR, a VR application providing self-defense training for women. Pacquing explained another application of immersive technologies in a specialized training and educational context:

> We have the epidemic of active shootings in the US. The way that it's taught right now is through online courses or reading materials, or in-person classes and drills. The way that some of these in-person drills take place—it's traumatizing for some people. . . . I understand that we have to prepare people as much as possible, but at the same time it should be carefully done. . . . We used gamification methods where you could see how fast you react in those activities. These are things that you could use in VR and compare to in-person classes—you're allowed to make mistakes in VR, you're not going to be physically hurt—so it's a great training tool for [rarely occurring events]. . . . [W]e realize that VR is going to be the best way to learn how to deal with dangerous situations.[38]

In the two examples described above, the individuals expressed a priority on the advancement and application of immersive technologies in these different scenarios. Others spoke of being motivated to set up new spaces of production, particularly to address gender inequities. For example, Carmen Aguilar y Wedge talked about the driving factors that led to the cofounding of Hyphen-Labs with Ece Tankal: "We wanted to have a platform where we could invite more women to work with us. We wanted to see more women in interaction design because it has a very commercial part to the discipline. A lot of that is driven by advertising and by men, and so we were also looking at some of the budgets and the hierarchies of how people were being paid, and it wasn't equitable."[39]

Our participants also conveyed a propensity toward establishing hybridized working environments. Debra McGrory (2016) explained her own motivation in this regard: "When virtual reality became a thing with Facebook purchasing Oculus for $2,000,000,000, I was already calling myself a curator of digital and physical space. . . . We founded Datavized out of this idea of seeing the potential intersection between big data and virtual reality. Really, what that meant was a data-driven VR studio, a data-driven lab where . . . that's data in the kind of broadest sense."[40]

Heidi Boisvert, who cofounded XTH and collaborated with David Byrne on Theater of the Mind, an immersive theater piece, spoke of the establishment of her own multiplatform business: "I have a creative boutique called futurePerfect Lab that makes pop culture with a purpose, so I make video games, transmedia storytelling, mobile apps, anything that's really pop but intersects with emerging technology and social change. It could be anything from immigration to racial profiling to climate or women's rights, but the idea is to make playful content that works across different touchpoints."[41]

Joanna Garner, a senior story creative director for Meow Wolf—a renowned arts and entertainment company in Santa Fe, New Mexico—described the complex working relations between multiple discipline-specific departments: "We have both a digital storytelling division and an XR department. They're often taking the narrative, the worldbuilding that we've done and then using that foundation to create a framework for those experiences. We work very closely with the digital storytelling team, which creates gameplay strategy and the technology in which those stray experiences can be experienced in the exhibition and then tied closely into our XR team."[42]

These enthusiastic and vibrant accounts are testament to the fact that our participants are excelling in environments that are hybridized, multiskilled, interdisciplinary, and, crucially, often women led and speak to their own principles and values. Despite the challenges, hostilities, and exclusions faced within traditional media environments described above, our participants have developed a range of strategies to circumvent the barriers that they have faced. By establishing their own spaces, which are built on different value systems, and the implementation of their own principles and practices; by applying the technologies to new areas; and by establishing their own companies from the ground up, our participants have made the space in which innovation and creativity can flourish. Furthermore, our participants once again demonstrate their abilities to bring together and work across multiple platforms (as we evidenced in chapter 4) and their proclivity to inhabit multiple roles (as revealed in chapter 3). Here, our participants have shown how they can create effective and productive spaces that successfully draw together different fields, skill sets, approaches, and technologies.

Conferences

Industry-based conferences are important sites for consideration, since these are the spaces where workplaces are represented to wider professional communities and publics and where issues of exclusion and lack of accessibility can simultaneously be hidden yet amplified, diminished yet distorted. Because many of our participants are recognized as important thought leaders in emergent media and immersive technologies, they speak at many of these forums and bring with them highly valuable insights drawn from their own lived experience. Monika Bielskyte, a futures researcher, futurist, and futures designer, has spoken at many such venues. Despite her own significant exposure in these places, she has noted a historical lack of the platforming of women:

> Nonny de la Peña was platformed a bit, but I find that the only women that were platformed were women that worked for large companies, so they were women that worked for Oculus—there's some very smart women. But the women that would be given a big platform were the women that ultimately worked for men's products, for men's companies. Then all the other women, especially women that had a critical regard, were either violently shut down or treated as curiosities, and I think I was somewhere in between.

They found that I was futuristic by my aesthetics. Somehow I was allowed to vaguely exist within that space, but at no point neither myself nor anybody who I saw were enabled to engage in critical discourse—and I'm talking about women and feminine nonbinary queer people, people of color—whoever wasn't singing to the tune of VR—and [this marginalization] was actually pointing at what could be the issues with that industry. We were again either ignored or being given very niche spaces and then everything that we were criticizing ultimately came to be.[43]

This troubling account of a lack of engagement in the space was echoed by other participants. Kaya Jabar addressed the inaccurate representation of the gender makeup of industry through the strategic inclusion of women at conferences:

What I do find difficult about it is, if you are actually doing the work, you never have the time [to speak at conferences]. So it's always someone from management who then presents the work for you, which can skew the optics of what that team is. . . . I think there are events that are better at trying to balance panels and going out of their way to do it. If anything, they might skew it too far the other way—you can feel like the token woman on the panel. They're much more complicated to navigate than my actual job![44]

Amelia Winger-Bearskin talked about her role as a "developer evangelist," an industry/software coder featured at conferences to promote products/companies (discussed in chapter 3), and how her presence could also potentially skew the perception of women's involvement in these spaces:

I think this last four years there have been more women than there have ever been in this role. It was primarily men. I think it's still pretty unusual to be a woman, but I've definitely been to our annual conferences in San Francisco, and the first time I went it was half women and half men, which was amazing. So it has now become a very equal field, and I think it's because it's very public. It's a very easy way of seeing if a company has a female representation and you get criticized in the community for not having it, whereas no one really knows the gender breakdown of the people behind the scenes that are building your product—and surprise, surprise, they're all men, but because it's a public role, there [are] more women in it. I would get messaged every day for a job—people really want to hire women in that because you're a spokesperson or a mascot.[45]

Other participants found themselves on the receiving end of conference organizers seeking to artificially amplify women's participation. Liz Rosenthal (2019) explained a recurring experience of being invited to speak based on her gender as opposed to her extensive track record: "They don't say, 'Oh, we'd love to have you talk because you're really good at this or for your expertise.' . . . It would be really nice if my speaking invitations were all in the vein of 'Oh, Liz, we'd love to have you talk about this' without saying 'Oh, we need a female speaker.'"[46]

This frustration was echoed by Nonny de la Peña: "I'm now the head founder of a company, and I now have to be the voice. People can never get Palmer [Luckey], they're always calling me—'Oh good, we can get Nonny, she'll be the woman on the panel.'"[47] Taryn Southern, a digital personality, writer, producer, director, and songwriter with more than 500 million views across her internet videos, voiced similar experiences: "I typically get asked to be on the 'Women of . . .' panel. At first, I was like great. I'm so happy to be representing women. Now I'm like no, you put me on the actual panel, and all of those other women that were sitting on those panels, put them on the other panels. Let's get equal representation on these other panels and not just the 'Women of . . .' panel."[48] And Tamara Shogaolu concurred:

My work isn't about promoting diversity. It's about socially grounded issues and we live in a diverse world, so why wouldn't that be reflected in the work? I got really tired of being pigeonholed and going on these panels and being asked questions like "Why do you think diversity is important?" I just think it's crazy that you would ask somebody who is underrepresented or systematically marginalized why their existence in a space would be important.[49]

Stephanie Dinkins is a transdisciplinary artist creating platforms for dialogue about AI as it intersects with race, gender, aging, and future histories. She described the balance she is constantly attempting to strike when agreeing to speaker engagements:

> I've done an awful lot of panel participations or Zoom panels. It depends—sometimes I can be the woman and the Black person, sometimes it's a little mixed, or sometimes it's all Black and brown, but those are much rarer. . . . I think I do them but know that you're this thing that they're inviting in—you're probably their diversity and equity thing for the month. And what does that mean? I always wonder about what that contact does, who it's serving and why. But I also hold out that hope that there's the little prickle that starts somewhere. I'm sitting here thinking, "Am I fooling myself or not?" But it's fraught.[50]

Among our participants there was widespread recognition that this was an ongoing and recurrent problem, but some noted that there was evidence of positive interventions. Martina Welkhoff observed:

> I see more women at VR events than I do at general tech events. Obviously, it's anecdotal, but I really have noticed that trend continuously and I also think there's more pressure on organizers to showcase women on panels and to have a more gender-balanced speaker roster overall. I think that's really helped. I don't mean to paint an overly rosy picture, but in my decade in tech, the tech industry now, there's a distinct difference in the VR events I'm going to versus the mobile gaming stuff.[51]

As well as receiving repeated "women panel member" invitations, our participants also reported experiencing discrimination at the conferences themselves. Tamara Shogaolu recounted one particular situation: "When I was at Tribeca presenting my project, I had one of our interns [with me]. He's a tall, white, cis male, and everyone kept going up to him, introducing themselves. The project was about a lesbian couple from Egypt. I would be standing next to him and [the] press would introduce themselves anytime there was a man [present]. They would go to the [men] and assume that they were the ones who made it—that happens all the time."[52]

Catherine Allen, a regular speaker at tech conferences, explained a strategy that she has evolved to counteract these types of recurring negative experience:

> I've got into this habit of only arriving just before I'm about to speak. It's partly because I find it really uncomfortable being talked down to when conference attendees I talk to apply their biases when speaking to a young woman and [make] assumptions. I don't want to have to claim my place—I'd much rather just speak and then people know who I am, so that we can just have a proper conversation without the discomfort. . . . I shouldn't have to do that—but it's been a coping mechanism for those male-dominated tech conferences.[53]

Verity McIntosh, a VR practitioner and academic, shared similar experiences at VR tech conferences she attends:

> I have had more instances of microaggressions and harassment and discrimination working in VR than I ever did in the more general creative tech sector, and I don't know what to make of that really. . . . I have certainly had more direct experiences of people making assumptions about my credibility or authority in a situation, looking for the man to talk to, because presumably I'm the salesperson or the booth supervisor. Particularly conferences and expos, where there's any kind of booth. . . . I think particularly when we were setting up Bristol VR Lab, when it was important to take the VR Lab out into the wider world . . . I was effectively there as the representative of that space, and I could attend to any questions they might have. They either just told me that wasn't the case and they wanted to speak to someone proper, or started to quiz me on what my development credibility's were, what I am proficient in, or what thing I have made millions on recently, which may just be a particularly aggressive mode of inquiry, but my guess is

that I would not have received quite the same sort of interrogation if I was the person that they expected in that context.[54]

Sarah Ticho recorded the limited presence of women at these events. "I took this 360-degree image because there were just no women there," she said. "There were literally two. It was the first time I'd really spoken about it, and I was tweeting about it all day. I made this comment to this guy saying, 'There should be more women here.' And he said, 'Why? Is it because you're a lesbian?'"[55]

Tech journalist Becca Caddy explained the affective impact of the microaggressions that she experienced: "It's at conferences and big events and people just making little comments about me not being a journalist, or why am I there. The little comments mount up to create a general feeling that I don't have a place at those events."[56]

These patterns of ill will are familiar, repeated, and often documented, particularly as they relate to the games sector and were indeed the starting point from which our original research project began (see preface). In addition to these experiences, our participants reported experiencing unrepresentative and problematic imagery at conferences. Ingrid Kopp (2016) provided an example of this: "It's not that easy, there's a huge push in this space to make sure that women are represented. There're images like the one of Mark Zuckerberg walking down the corridor with all the white men in suits in their VR goggles. I think everyone held up that image as this is just not the world we want to live in. If this is what VR looks like, we don't want to be part of that."[57]

These images and our own experiences[58] go beyond the conference environments that we are describing here. Sarah Jones (2019), a senior academic leader, educator, and VR practitioner who has previously worked for ITV as a correspondent and news anchor, explained: "With our VR Girls UK, immediately there was request for porn because that was the perception that if there were girls in VR, then it must be around porn. Which clearly was just creative technologists trying to form a community."[59] Jones also shared a troubling account of her experience "at one of those big horrible VR expos where there's nothing exciting or innovative being shown, it's just a commercial": "I was talking at one of those events and there was a car VR experience. I was trying it out and

I was wearing big heels and a pretty dress. You could tell the photographers were wanting that image of 'here's a female wearing a headset, and look, she's by a car and she's got heels on'—that kind of narrative. You could tell that was the image they wanted—I'm never going to play along with that."[60]

These stereotypical representations feed through into other areas of marketing and promotion and media narratives that gender these technologies.[61] As Neilda Pacquing described:

> When I was creating EmpowHER VR, a self-defense training app, I was looking for assets from a 3D model marketplace. I searched "women" and the search results were mostly women in adult content. When I searched for "men," it showed men in professional attire who look a lot more empowered. I actually did a side-by-side screen comparison between the two and shared it. The 3D marketplace reached out to me and told me they didn't realize that this is what was showing up. They changed their algorithm. They set up a contest so that more people [could] submit women who are not adult content, so they could diversify their marketplace.[62]

To try to counter this bias, our participants shared experiences where they have actively attempted to shift the balance and to diversify conference participation and representation on panels. As one anonymous participant working in the immersive space explained:

> At a conference people get known and then they get asked again and again, and that means it's very easy to end up in an echo chamber where you're not hearing from new people. So even people who come through who are new, maybe there are some diverse voices coming through. . . . I try and get people to nominate other people they work with who might not have spoken on one before. At least part of the panel is made up of new people that people won't have heard from before.[63]

Shari Frilot spoke about improving the gender diversity of the Sundance Film Festival board: "The last two editions have been 50% women across the board. . . . [W]e gave ourselves a challenge and found it easy to meet. And then we put on the most successful festival with record-breaking acquisitions. . . . It was a fantastic festival for two years in a row."[64] Lynette Wallworth, an Australian artist whose immersive video installations and film works reflect on the connections between people and the natural world, attested to the significance of the Sundance New Frontier and the influence it has had on her own career:

> The only reason I got to work in VR in the way I did was because I was supported by Sundance New Frontier, who made a deliberate decision, and a wonderful decision, to look at a powerful emerging technology and say: "What if we facilitate those people who might, because of the cost of this, because of access, because of the technology, might be able to manage this technology beautifully, but might come to it late, because of access issues." . . . Sundance made a preemptive jump. They said, "Okay, let's facilitate residencies for people who we think could use this technology but might have an access issue to it."[65]

These latter insights, which reveal the profound power and productivity of gender inclusive principles and spaces, lead us into our next consideration of the establishment of alternative conference spaces.

Alternative Spaces Led by Women

Although some of our participants noted a dominance of men in tech-based VR conferences in the discussions above, others remarked on a striking visible presence of women within more creative, immersive industry events. Several participants described setting up their own conference-style venues. For example, Nicoletta Iacobacci, who has been involved in convening TED talks since 2007, explained how she influenced the TED agenda through the establishment of TEDx Transmedia: "Since I was one of the first TEDxers, they gave me the opportunity to do it, because usually TEDx has to be a location. When I wrote the application for the license, I actually wrote something that is not a location but in a sense is a universe. Then the speakers are going to be the platform on how to enter into the subject. It was a little bit constructed in order to have the license, but they gave it to me."[66]

TEDx Transmedia went on to be a highly successful forum and a much-referenced source for the citation of the key professionals and thought leaders in transmedia. It included Alison Norrington—a leading figure in the transmedia world who also convened and chaired the major industry event "Storyworld"—a conference and expo—which ran for three editions (2010, 2011, 2018). "For me," said Norrington, "it was a global gathering of the mindset around transmedia, storytelling and story worldbuilding. I believe there's friendships made there in 2011 that still exist now, 11 years later. So it was a brilliant bringing together of people. I love doing that. I did it again in 2012. We moved it from San Francisco to LA. . . . [L]oads of careers were launched on the back of that."[67] Other participants attested to this claim and spoke very highly of their experience in this forum, including Carrie Cutforth, a creative producer and writer working across digital, WebVR, AR, transmedia, and ARGs: "You could feel the electricity that people had found each other," she recalled. "We didn't have the words that we do now—the neurodivergence, being neuroatypical and so forth. If you're trying to work in transmedia, you have a very neurodivergent brain, many tabs open, and it was like we finally discovered ones like us . . . and I found that the friendships forged through transmedia were the more sustaining ones."[68] The inclusive spirit and positive impact of "Storyworld" was also referenced by Juliana Loh, who has since gone on to be a highly successful virtual world creator: "What was really important was meeting a community of like-minded people. . . . We were able to connect to a community, not just a small community, but a world stage. . . . Being able to be seen as somebody legitimate on your own, writing stories as a member of the public, and being able to create fan-based works . . . helped us to bridge our fandom and our unique stories into core narratives."[69]

Although the "Storyworld" forum was not specifically aimed at tackling gender issues in the transmedia space, it was spearheaded and shaped by a woman. We already heard in chapter 3 of the major role women have played in shaping the agenda within these sectors and how they have profiled and amplified important work—but it is a role that has been underplayed and undervalued. We can see from the legacy that these forums and events have left in their wake—how critical and influential they have been in shaping the sector and the careers that have been launched and supported as a result.

Diversity Initiatives

Many of our participants referred to the emergence of organization- or institution-led diversity initiatives in recent years. Nancy Xu, a virtual production producer at Epic Games London Innovation Lab, described how the B3 "TalentLab" in the United Kingdom, a mentoring and development program, is

> specifically for storytellers that are from marginalized or under-represented communities—to get them into a room and let them collaborate, give them briefs, give them equipment, give them kit and software, and see what they come up with. I've been going to the pitch events when they finish their cycle and it's exciting. They're doing great things with the briefs or the problems they've been given. These kinds of initiatives are giving them opportunities to tell their own story, giving them a portfolio piece so that they can go out there and get that next big gig. I think that's a great way to inject the industry with that diversity.[70]

But not all initiatives are as sustaining and successful. Ingrid Kopp (2016), for example, expressed skepticism about the motivations of some of the more corporate-based initiatives and their potential to effect meaningful and enduring change, saying, "I do think that some of those, especially if you look at some of the stuff they're doing in Silicon Valley, it's so 'by-the-numbers' and unhelpful. It has to be baked into the organization all the way through. . . . Whenever I hear about those diversity initiatives, I'm always really skeptical because I think that it's an easy way out and actually it's about changing the organization all the way through."[71] And Samantha Gorman (2017), who cofounded the indie game and art studio Tender Claws, which creates novel approaches to interactive narrative through emerging media, similarly questioned the efficacy of these corporate actions:

> I was part of a diversity initiative at Warner Bros. and I was also part of "Oculus Launch Pad," which was a diversity initiative. I think there is a recognition on some level for multivocal, diverse creators to tell their stories, but I don't think there is a home [for] what you do with those new narratives yet. It can feel like a PR

move rather than something that can be easily actualized at this point. I think the people in charge of those programs are really well intentioned and well meaning, but within the systems they're working with, it just seems like a no-go . . . to get the studio to see that diversity. . . . No matter the intention, I think that you still have to put it in quantifiable terms—like money.[72]

While the existence of these initiatives was seen as important by many of our participants, there was a commonly held perception that they were "top down" and institutionally led and, in many cases, ineffectual. Instead, many of our participants foregrounded the grassroots communities and organizations, many of which were women led and women focused. Over the six-year period of our study, numerous community initiatives have been mentioned and highlighted by our participants, some of whom have been actively establishing and leading them.

Women-Only Communities

Our participants were unanimous in expressing the value of networking spaces. Neilda Pacquing explained why: "The working conditions—when you're building a product, it's almost solo—and if you have any questions, you reach out to your community. I feel very fortunate that I do have a very supportive community out there of AR/VR professionals who actually are thought leaders in the space. I feel very safe in that regard, but I know not everybody has that resource."[73]

Liz Rosenthal (2019) described one particular in-person event called "Mad Women VR": "It's a networking breakfast for leading women in the immersive creative sector that takes place at major festivals, for example SXSW [South by Southwest], Sundance, Tribeca, and Venice over the last 5 years. It was founded by Jacqui Bosnjak, a[n] NYC-based founder of the music and sound design studio Q Department. It's an important space where I've been able to build lasting connections, business relationships, and support."[74]

An anonymous participant (2019) commented on the value of these in-person events: "One thing I'll say about the women's breakfasts, things like that—I find it a lot easier to chat and network in an environment like that than a more general mixer. I find it somehow lowers the pressure.

If people are not natural networkers, which not everybody should feel that they have to be, then they can be a bit more open. They can feel a bit less high pressure."[75]

In addition to in-person events, there have been numerous online groups established within social media spaces, in particular on Facebook. They include Women in VR/AR (see chapter 3), ARVR Academy, ARVR Women and Allies, AR VR Women, and XR Studio by Mozilla—a program for women who are working on projects in VR, AR, XR, AI, and machine learning. Sarah Lisa Vogl is a VR user experience designer, creative entrepreneur, and futurist who explores and constructs new virtual and augmented realities as well as organizing VR events, hackathons, and investor days. Vogl also leads Women in Immersive Tech Europe. She expressed the importance of these spaces: "I think it is still such a fresh space that we can all come together to create. . . . I'm very much a believer in community and groups because that's how you navigate real life."[76]

Sarah Wolozin (2016), director of the Open Documentary Lab at MIT, also underlined the importance of these opportunities: "I talked to a woman at Jaunt [VR company]. She's the only woman there, and she feels very isolated. That's why they created Women in VR. The fact that you have this great Women in VR group, just says that they need to talk to each other, because they are the minorities."[77] Kim Plowright, a creative producer, digital product manager, consultant, and educator, talked about the emergence of a smaller online and more informal network:

> I'm part of a very strong women only support network. . . . It's basically a bunch of women who are all digital producers and creatives who work at the point of where the arts, digital, and production overlap. It's a loose acquaintance network. Literally, it came out of getting together one evening and us all saying: "We should have Slack," and then slowly other people have been pulled into it, and it's become really valuable.[78]

Neilda Pacquing described the shared motivations of the groups of which she is a member: "We all have very similar missions; we want to push this industry forward. We all want to create amazing experiences that are breaking barriers and making changes. Some of the entrepreneurs that I know are tackling implicit bias, some are tackling sexual harassment, some are tackling gender roles, and helping people see both sides of a situation. Because we all realize that this is such a powerful tool."[79]

Siobhan O'Flynn has consulted on digital, interactive, participatory, transmedia, AR and VR storytelling via her company NarrativeNow for almost 20 years. O'Flynn described the origins of another grass-roots online support community—Transmedia 101, which was inspired by the approach of another leading woman figure in transmedia, Jill Golick:

> We wanted to do a meetup so that we could organize a series of speakers as well as sharing of resources, with some kind of skills-based discussions as well. I think of Jill Golick who's been one of the lead individuals in the Canadian space, and producing Ruby Skye PI, which was a web series—an update of the Nancy Drew scenario for contemporary teens. Jill did a talk with us and did quite a number of conferences and media industry days. She was on her Facebook and social media platforms daily, interacting with the fans, cross-sharing, and really modeled a way to seed a fan community and to nurture and grow it. . . . Transmedia 101 was really about wanting to develop a community as well as the opportunity for knowledge sharing from people who were working in the space and who were achieving success.[80]

Transmedia 101 was cofounded by O'Flynn with Carrie Cutforth and Anthea Foyer in 2011. Although it began as a meetup group, it went on to become a more significant organization that engendered numerous collaborations between both transmedia professionals and creatives, with others from allied industries.

Sarah Ticho explained her involvement in a Facebook mentoring program for women in VR: "I think that it'd be interesting to see more investment opportunities specifically for women in VR as I think so far that most community support is just doing meetups, which is great. But I think most people are in agreement that we don't want to spend our lives just going to meet ups."[81]

While all our participants appreciated the importance of these places to exist, others also flagged issues with the time and emotional labor and effort required to sustain both contact and leadership of these communities. Catherine Allen talked through the challenges of the time and effort required to lead on these essential initiatives. In relation to the VWVR project, she explained: "There's always this tension with these kinds of projects, which is that something I care about deeply, but I also have to get on with my job as being a woman who happens to work in VR. . . . If I just dedicated everything I did to women and VR as a cause, then I'm taking myself out of the game as being a . . . a woman who works in VR."[82]

Allen's comments point to a key issue that emerged in the previous two chapters—the time-intensive and emotionally intense labor that supporting and mentoring requires. This can very often be invisible and not something that receives the same levels of credibility and recognition as other areas of creative innovation.

Conclusion

Through our in-depth consideration of place in this chapter, we have revealed the following insights: Places of creative technical production have historically been perceived as male-dominated spaces where our participants have found themselves working as the only, or among very few, women. The discoveries of women within these earlier spaces have latterly become obscured, often overwritten by a more dominant and pervasive "institutional" narrative. Within male-dominated work cultures, our participants experiences ranged from everyday microaggressions and exclusions to more extreme forms of harassment. Despite these barriers and challenges that our participants recounted, they have continued to propose, evolve, and develop numerous strategies to circumvent these including the establishment of their own places including their own working cultures, their own businesses, support groups, and more gender diverse places and events.

From these latter discussions that relate to the establishment of new spaces for women and created by women, we can start to segue into the fourth theme of this book: "process," which we will consider in more detail in the following chapter.

6
Process

Cash Flow, Workflow, Free Flow

This chapter is concerned with process—how projects and productions are financed, made, worked on, and managed. We cover different industry workflows and people processes from funding to sharing best practices. By drawing together key insights and observations from our participants, we consider the following aspects of process in detail: funding and financing; workflows and workloads across a range of emergent media sector contexts spanning independent, artistic, and commercial environments; and emergent working practices that respond to the challenges faced by our participants in order to circumvent, avoid, and overcome the obstacles that they encounter. These include collaboration, mentorship and allyship, self-teaching, archiving, and sharing best practices. We first look at the starting point of any creative or artistic project—access to funding—and consider how this shaped our participants' experiences and demonstrated their capacity to overcome them. We then turn to newly emerging areas of funding access, including the blockchain as an alternative mechanism for accessing funding that some of our participants have been exploring.

Funding and Financing

Funding, the starting point of any project, process, or product, shapes and defines how individuals can advance their work. During the course of our interviews, we heard firsthand accounts of how innate funding challenges stemmed from gender identity and learned why women in documentary fields were particularly adversely affected. Documentary became a genre of cross-platform innovation, using multimedia tools as aids in distribution, funding, and exhibition and, as our participants described it, a field with, generally speaking, more gender balance, fewer stereotypical roles, and lower budgets. "It's maybe a cynical thing," explained Ingrid Kopp (2016), "but a lot of people have pointed out that they think it's because there isn't so much money in documentaries. The documentaries are the underpaid segments of the film industry, so no wonder there's more women there—I think there's probably some truth in that."[1]

Sarah Wolozin (2016), director of the Open Documentary Lab at MIT, noted the role of emerging technologies in reshaping documentary as a form untethered from platforms and blurring the roles of authors and audiences, opening up possibilities in the field, but again with the financial caveat:

> It's like the internet and everything else. . . . [I]n order for women to be involved, it's not where the money is. VR becomes a money-making thing inevitably. [Then] sadly it gets taken over by men. . . . [A]s long as it's not mainstream, then the women are good. Documentary is not well paid, right? . . . [B]ut . . . social change and educational motivation is a lot of it [reasons for making a project], so you will find more women, versus making money or glory. In film it's a problem, it's a problem everywhere. I don't really see VR as being any different.[2]

Wolozin's insight underscores the cyclical model of experimentation to platformization to commercialization that we introduced in chapter 4.

May Abdalla, executive director and cofounder of Anagram, provided an illustrative example of her own organization's creative rather than commercial motivations:

> We were making *Goliath*, which is a VR piece about psychosis and being a gamer; we were making *A Face to Open Doors*, which is an installation at the Imperial War Museum about user technology at borders; and we're making this AR experience about plant intelligence and the end of the world. We had the businesspeople come in and say, "Why don't you make stuff that's a bit more formulaic so that you can be developing software and pitching for VC [venture capitalist] funding?"[3]

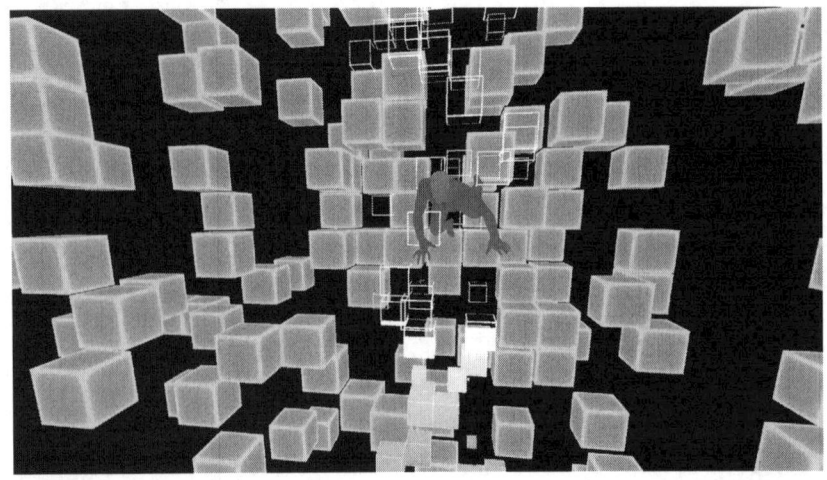

Figure 6.1. *Goliath: Playing with Reality*, animated VR experience, 25 minutes. 2021. Anagram.

Figure 6.2. *A Face to Open Doors*, interactive installation. 2020. Anagram.

Similarly, Catherine Allen talked about her own company, Limina, and their establishment of a VR theater, driven by the need to support artists and industry in getting their works out to audiences. Speaking in 2019, when the pop-up VR theater was in operation, she explained: "We're achieving our social goals. That makes me so happy and proud, but this doesn't scale. The staff ratio to the amount of audience members is more scalable than most other forms of VR and all these bespoke installations where the cost per audience member is so high, but at the same time, you have 3 members of staff to 12 audience members. That's not a business ratio. It's more like a restaurant or a spa currently, but not like a tech start-up."[4]

Mimi Onuoha, an artist and researcher working in multimedia using print, code, installation, and video to call attention to the ways in which those in the margins are differently abstracted, represented, and missed by sociotechnical systems, talked about the challenges of accessing financing: "I do think the hardest part of being an artist is staying an artist. The reason for that is just you're constantly navigating these webs of relevance and funding and support. It can be very challenging to figure out how to hold them all, and it demands wearing a lot of different hats. It's hard to find a model that can support just making work—in the US at least."[5] Jan Libby agreed. The award-winning writer and producer of immersive experiences for brands and media companies commented: "There really is not funding for just independent fictional work in this space. It's because it's hard to figure out how to monetize it."[6]

Many of our participants talked about the exclusions that women faced in attempting to secure venture capital funding. Nancy Bennett (2017), creative artist and cofounder of Two Bit Circus recalled "having a conversation with Dave Goldberg, who is now deceased unfortunately, who was a fantastic man (president of Survey Monkey, former executive at Yahoo!). . . . I went through my idea with him, and he said, 'This is fantastic, I love it. But, you're never going to get funded. . . . [V]enture capitalists invest in what they know, and they know men.'"[7]

The chances of securing funding appeared to decrease as women's identities intersected with other identities, including gender, ethnicity, and social status. As Michela Ledwidge, CEO and founder of MOD Films in Sydney, Australia, succinctly put it: "As a trans woman running and co-owning a small studio, I'm not wasting anymore time trying to get funding on a level plane because I don't think there's a market for hearing my voice and I don't think that's got as much to do with my storytelling ability—people want to give funding to people who look like themselves."[8]

An anonymous participant cited her ethnicity, among other reasons, for her own lack of motivation in pursuing funding:

> I was talking to someone about the evolution of my company and he's a CEO of a media company. We were talking about how I was thinking about growing it. . . . He asked if I was interested in looking for investment, I replied, "I really don't think so because I'm in social justice, I'm in media, things that are very low funded and often expected to be done for free, I'm a woman and I'm a woman of color." He said, "Yep, you're the perfect storm of unfundability, uninvestibility." . . . I'm not even going to try because I know it's going to be a waste of time to a certain extent. The amount of time it'll take me to try and get investment for my company . . . I'm just going to go with client work.[9]

Amelia Winger-Bearskin talked about her limited access to certain types of funding due to her particular socioeconomic status:

> I've done a lot of different rounds and raised in different ways with a lot of different funders and I don't know if it has to do with being a woman or just having to do with someone that doesn't have generational wealth, honestly, because most of the time [they just assume with] the money that they give you . . . that you don't need any money to live. I am a single mother, so that was just never my reality that if they gave me a 100K and asked, "What are you going to do with this 100K?," "I'll pay rent," and they'll reply, "No, you have to take that 100K and use every single dollar towards your company." . . . [I]f you're somebody who needs to pull a paycheck, then the VC route isn't going to work for you.[10]

In all three cases detailed above, the participants reveal that they have given up even trying to secure VC funding, which, to their detriment, has impacted the types of projects that they can then undertake;

instead of kick-starting their own ventures and creating their own original works, they opt for "client work" and service projects. These three accounts lay bare the innately challenging issue of accessing funding, whereby opportunities are foreclosed based on gender identity. In the few instances where participants did apply for this type of funding, other unexpected challenges arose. Neilda Pacquing, founder and CEO of MindGlow, a company using VR to maximize workplace safety and prepare employees for emergencies, provided insight into her own experience of pitching for funding:

> I've had an experience where we have a product, given a pitch, and then one investor [who] didn't realize I was talking to other investors in his firm, told me, "You have a really great product. Unfortunately, it's not something that we're looking to invest in, but on a personal side, do you want to get some drinks?" That caught me off guard because it showed that he's unaware of what else is happening around his firm and also felt like he had this power to ask me out when I am a female entrepreneur looking for funding and looking to push my product and my vision forward. I know that I'm not alone with this because I have heard other stories from other women.[11]

In other cases, our participants revealed the challenges of securing alternative sources of funding due to the perception of the gendered nature of the content they were producing. Dee Harvey, founder of Controvert, a company using immersive and interactive technology explained: "We're now talking to a VR distributor who wants to potentially commission the next thing that we do—we're not really looking at government funding, although we've applied for a lot of them. We get short-listed a lot, but I think because the subject matter that we're working in is so very specific to females, I think we struggle a bit with that. We get great feedback, but we often don't quite make the cut to get the money."[12]

Even when funding has been secured, our participants described the further challenges they faced wrought by a bias that manifested as a lack of trust and respect for their expertise. Char Davies recounted her experience of engaging in a successfully public-funded project in 2006:

l was invited by the Canada Council to be a lead investigator on a project[13] for which engineering teams from two Montreal universities were funded by NSERC [Natural Sciences and Engineering Research Council of Canada] to develop an HMD to my specifications with the specific goal of developing the wide-field-of-view HMD that l needed in order to continue my work in immersive virtual space. After accepting the first round of government funding, the lead engineers decided they were not interested in this objective (saying it was only based on my "intuition") and began cutting me out of the process so they could instead develop a spherical projection system. After l notified the Canada Council / NSERC, the engineers were denied the second round of funding, and the project was terminated. l later received an email from the head engineer who wrote that it had been a humbling experience.[14]

A clear line of consensus emerged among our participants when discussing, in contemporary contexts, the alignment between the investment/profitability of the immersive sector and the hardware, not the content being produced. One anonymous consultant in the VR/metaverse field (2019) underscored this: "The platforms need to make money. . . . [W]e've gone back to this situation where although all sorts of other forms of interesting narrative content have been explored, such as news and journalistic content, the monetization challenge around that content in VR means there's a danger that it could go no further. And the only content that Oculus really want to support is more readily monetizable content."[15]

From the accounts above, we can see that many of our participants are driven by social change and artistic endeavor rather than financial gain, although sometimes this is simply because they have no other choice. Familial financial responsibilities and the taking on of caring roles, where gender bias can play a significant role, can pose insurmountable barriers. Even so, we already see a push to finding alternative ways to achieving creative goals and company missions.

Alternative Pathways to Funding

Sandra Rodriguez, a creative director/producer of VR, XR, and AI experiences, highlighted the corollary impact of these seemingly insurmountable barriers detailed above—the development of abilities to overcome these to find new ways to access resources:

> Because of necessity and because of discrimination, women are pioneers. It's hard to get told no all the time. . . . [W]e're put in a position where it's easier for us to feel that we are going to be told no from the get-go. You start thinking about alternatives to get your point across or get your story across . . . but the more it gets marketized, the more the nos come first. I think maybe that's your key to where the discrimination happens because even when people are pretty sure that a woman and a male creator can both have the same projects, I think it's a lot easier still to say no to women than it is to men.[16]

Some of our participants talked about attending accelerators (mentor-based training programs aimed at start-ups) as a route to access alternative sources of funding. "I went through an accelerator," an anonymous creative director and founder told us. "I found it really useful as a way of learning how to articulate yourself in that world. But I realized that I didn't want to be a company that went for investment. I think I'm at a stage where it's more grant funding and it's around collaborations with universities and professionals—[and] that's not necessarily how start-ups operate."[17] Isabel Van De Keere, founder and CEO of Immersive Rehab, successfully pursued the same route:

> I had a small investment from an accelerator program in the beginning. That's basically how I was able to start the company, develop the first demo, . . . [and I've] funded it myself since then. In our field especially, within VR and health care, it's a very regulated space. . . . [I]t's such a new field, investors are playing the waiting game: "Let's see how it plays out and whether we think it will be valuable or not in the future, using VR in health care." That's what I mostly hear from investors.[18]

Accelerator programs are one type of contemporary industry innovation mechanism; another is the "hackathon"—an event in which a large
number of people collectively engage in a collaborative-making activity, such as computer programming or product design, within a short
period of time. Hackathons are usually competitive and involve funding
awards that result in investment. An anonymous business founder foregrounded the benefits of these types of activities: "I went to a weekend
long hackathon, and I met pretty much everyone working in immersive
tech in Sydney over that weekend. I honestly think hackathons and game
jams are an amazing way for anyone that's interested in getting into
whatever space, just to go and get together with people that know how
to make these things and just make something quick."[19] An anonymous
TV and VR producer in the United Kingdom talked about their own
positive experiences as a participant of a hackathon, but also revealed
how it demystified the immersive production process:

> I did a hackathon a year ago and I was shocked at how quick it
> was to create a piece of immersive content. We did something in
> 48 hours. It's a little bit like taking a car to the garage! You com-
> mission a creative developer to make content for you, but it's all
> smoke and mirrors. They suck in air, "Gosh, this is going to take
> us a good couple of weeks and it's going to cost you £30,000."
> And I can shrug my shoulders and have no idea if that person
> is telling the truth. . . . [T]hat's frustrating and daunting, it's sti-
> fling the industry.[20]

The above producer's account reveals how the hackathon process
debunked the illusion of the complexity and complicated nature of the
innovation process. This also resonated with Amelia Winger-Bearskin,
who talked about the establishment of the "stupid hackathon," of which
she is the founder. She explained the genesis of the idea, which responded
to the oversaturation of hackathons in 2013–15:

> They would have hackathons that would solve incredibly com-
> plex problems, such as everyone coming to the UN hackathon
> where you're supposed to solve water scarcity with JavaScript in
> 24 hours. . . . It [the stupid hackathon] really ended up being quite

a lot of artistic content that was hilarious and that poked fun at male-dominated culture or unbridled capitalism or the VC funding of insane ideas. It harnessed all of that, and it was a tremendous amount of fun and it became very popular. People started doing them all over the world. Even now, when I say I invented the stupid hackathon, people will say, "No, that's just a thing. It's like a phenomenon that exists all over the world." I know that. But I also founded it! . . . I also got an enormous amount of backlash in Silicon Valley because I was a woman. I even had two guys who created a derivative hackathon, try to sue me to stop because they said I was making them look bad because they couldn't get women to go to their hackathon and it wasn't fair. They wanted me to shut down my whole operation because it made them look bad, and I thought, "Well, first, you stole my idea and secondly, you're doing it terribly." . . . It was very funny that it struck a nerve—we had 60% women at our hackathons.[21]

Winger-Bearskin's account once again highlights the frequent marginalization of women's contributions to spaces of technological innovation, as well as a notable lack of women's presence in the more traditional, institutional, and commercial spaces. Many of our participants quoted illustrative figures around the paucity of funding and investment that went to women-led companies. For example, Van De Keere stated: "In the UK, for one pound of investment, one pence goes to female founders. Worldwide, it's 3–5%, which is something that obviously has an impact on the VR industry and that will reflect how the VR industry will evolve in the future."[22]

Lina Srivastava (2016), a strategist and producer, quoted another earlier illustrative piece of data: "It's amazing. It's only 9% of women-led companies that go in for VC funding actually get funding. . . . It's super low. There has to be a lot more investment in women-led companies or minority-led companies. I'd love to see those things happen sooner than 5 years. Funders and investors really need to take that seriously."[23] Our own research undertaken in 2019 revealed that only 14% of UK VR companies have any women directors on the board.[24]

Amandine Flachs, an emerging tech specialist and VC scout, expressed the need for definitive and reliable data to point people toward.

To illustrate the notable lack of funding, she talked about an online data-base called Diversity VC: "It's not just about guides and practices, but it's also a lot about data. It's a good way to convince a lot of different types of people. Some people will be more attracted to small takeaways to apply to their own businesses; others will be more interested in hearing the facts."[25]

This same point—the need to draw from consistent and reliable data in order to convince and persuade others of the need for action—was underscored by Vassiliki Khonsari (2022), cofounder of iNK Stories:

> As a part of this group called the Women's Impact Network, we created the "Ms. Factor Toolkit," and I loved it because it was so actionable, and what it did was, it basically aggregated all the statistics and information and box office numbers of female-lead drama and female-directed content. . . . [A]s an online resource, it really allowed producers to counter with hard facts and say, "Actually, if you look at the top ten grossing films . . ." So you could counter that misinformation flow in an informed way.[26]

From the discussions so far—it is clear that the funding landscape is fraught for our participants, with barriers, resistances, and attitudes weighted against them. Martina Welkhoff of WXR explained how she set out to address the issue of getting funding to women and women-led projects in response to the feedback that they were receiving from their creative communities:

> We sent out a survey to everyone, asking [them] to rank [their] top needs, and the top need by far, not even a close second, was fund-ing. The next was corporate resources. [Jump Canon], which is in San Francisco, focused on underrepresented founders in emerging tech, so a lot of overlaps with women and XR, but a bigger fund. . . . [T]he way that we're positioning both WXR and Jump Canon is first and foremost as an economic opportunity and then as a social impact piece as a secondary benefit. That's where I think there's real power in this moment and in investors shifting their con-sciousness. I know a lot of investors who see very clearly based on the data that we have and the research that continues to emerge

that companies with diverse leadership and different genders and different perspectives represented on the core team outperform homogenous teams time and time again. Companies with women leaders unfortunately tend to be undervalued in today's market. Anyone with an opportunistic mindset can see that there's a huge economic opportunity there.[27]

As we progressed with our research in 2019–20, the talk of blockchain and cryptocurrency was starting to take hold in the creative industries. Non-fungible tokens (NFTs) became a new discussion point with many of our participants working at the forefront of Web 3.0, and women communities emerging in support of their use and advancement of these technologies, particularly during the COVID-19 pandemic—including Women in Web3 (WiW3) and the Black Women Blockchain Council. There were varying levels of excitement and optimism expressed by our participants. Tiffany Shlain, founder of the Webby Awards, spoke in support of the potential of these technologies: "[T]he NFT world is exciting because it's creating a new revenue source for art. There's a lot of silly money out there, but it's also like the Wild West, which I love. I'm a Californian, and I love that period of being a pioneer where there aren't a lot of rules."[28]

Sara Lisa Vogl, a performing artist working within virtual worlds and social VR, explained the imminent potential of Web 3.0 when it comes together with immersive technologies from an individual artist's point of view: "As soon as we have virtual reality, social spaces that are running on a blockchain, we are basically looking at the seamless 'in-game economy,' which enables us to make transactions in real life—people can just tip me by throwing an emoji—that's actually not that far away."[29]

Amelia Winger-Bearskin describes her interest in the future potential of the blockchain, while also highlighting some of the pitfalls:

I've been into decentralization since the late '90s as a crypto anarchist. We had a lot of values around privacy, security, and non-amenity, which really chimed with me as a woman because I could really be a full member of this online community. . . . Being able to be part of these international movements and having your privacy secured was a value I really believed in. Decentralization was something that we thought would free people from the oppressive governments and financial structures. . . . [I think someone who is Indigenous sees it firsthand how codified the laws are to make sure] we are never allowed to have generational wealth or make sure we're never allowed to have sovereignty or dominion over our own lives.

I thought the possibilities of decentralization meant that we could have some form of self-governance and we could have ways in which we could share and pull our financial resources or gain or trade them in a way that could allow Indigenous people to have sovereignty. . . . [T]here are possibilities there for understanding how through DAOs [decentralized autonomous organizations] you can take large amounts of money, which would be a small amount from each individual and make powerful collective decisions. . . . It's natural to hope that Web3 could be a really good alternative. However, there's just a lot of issues right now. It's a space that's very difficult to talk to people about my hopes and dreams in the space. Because there's so much fraud. There is still a lot of the very rich getting richer and it's a very white male–dominated space.[30]

Artsy Marie, an independent creative, talked about the potential benefits of the blockchain and NFTs to individual artists who need support with the business aspects of monetizing their creative output: "I think what is most transformative is that instead of a gallery selling it as a one-off to somebody and having no tracking, no history of where it has gone and where it has been sold to, and no connection back to the original artist—the blockchain and the NFT allows that to happen, so the artist can always be compensated no matter when it changes hands."[31] Another independent digital artist, Mimi Ọnụọha, also foregrounded the key benefit of selling digital artwork on the blockchain: "The ability to not have gatekeepers, it's really unusual. It frees you from the bureaucracy of getting paid. There's so much work [of] being an artist that is just admin and finding people to sell it. It takes so much time. I have friends who are now generative artists or NFT artists."[32]

Digital artist Juliana Loh similarly acknowledged the benefits to individual artists while also highlighting the barriers that creators will inevitably face:

> We're still seeing a lot of male-dominated NFTs. It's difficult for a lot of women to have that kind of visibility. . . . [W]e women are fighting for inclusivity and accessibility, but there's barriers like the UX [user experience] on all the platforms—they are really difficult to work with and you need people that help, you need agents. There are so many people . . . not even in place yet because it's a brand-new system. . . . It's the gambling and speculative aspect that attracts a certain crowd and that creates opportunities for some and barriers for others.[33]

There were certainly mixed views around the potentialities of Web 3.0 technologies across our participants, with some expressing reticence around their intentions to move into these spaces. Much of the discussion so far has involved individuals and artists and those leading SMEs and start-up organizations, where issues of funding are the most prominent. But some of our participants were working in established industry environments where process-based challenges rather than funding were at the forefront of their working realities, and this is where we now turn our attention.

Workflows and Workloads

In this section we offer the perspectives of those who work in established organizations, such as studios, postproduction houses, VFX companies, and virtual production studios. Whereas in the previous chapter, we considered how these spaces impacted our participant's working experiences, here we look at how different working practices and processes have been both experienced and influenced by our participants. We will first examine the ways our participants have sought to intervene and improve recruitment practices in order to diversify the workforce.

Kaya Jabar, a virtual production supervisor from Framestore in London, recounted an experience where "you had a male candidate that was much more extravagant, much more confident, but probably not as experienced—people just gravitate towards that [because] 'they talk the talk.' That was an instance where I had to say, 'Let's try the quiet person—they're female—but I have a feeling that they know exactly what they're doing. They just need a bit of help with confidence.'"[34] Here we see the fundamental importance of intervening in processes in order to counter the entrenched biases of others.

A managing director of a UK-based creative SME described the diversity challenges that she faces in her own organization:

> We only have one other member of the production team who's a woman and that's a junior 3D artist. In three years, I've never had an application from a woman developer, for instance. . . . [O]n a personal level I'm very committed to the idea of much more diversity in all sorts of ways. We're certainly not able to fulfill that ambition at the moment, possibly at the consequence of needing to fill roles too quickly to be able to do that responsible searching. . . . I assume it's because outreach in the industry is not effective, and it's hard. I wouldn't know, for instance, where to put a job ad that would give me access to women or ethnic minorities.[35]

This participant went on to express the infrastructural challenges as a barrier to supporting a diverse workplace: "I want an organization that really helps me concretely address the lack of diversity rather than just meeting up and talking about it. Whether it's jobs boards or recruitment events or genuinely tangible ways to address diversity issues."[36]

Carrie Lozano, a documentary filmmaker and journalist, described her own experience of working in Al Jazeera and expressed a very clear and lucid strategy as to how diversity in the workplace can and should be achieved:

> The ethos was the newsroom has to be diverse and there has to be a lot of women and people of color. Thus, that's who we hired, and thus, we had a diverse newsroom. . . . [I]t was really simple; if that's what you value, you will do it. The people in power have to care, and they have to do it. . . . I hate those discussions: "Well, does that mean we're going to have poor quality?" It's ridiculous. I think it's really simple, and so in some ways I'm almost tired of the conversation. If you care about it, you'll achieve it. If you don't, you won't.[37]

Other participants expressed challenges in retaining a diverse work force due to the nature of the work. Nancy Xu, a virtual production producer, described one such environment that does not lend itself to supporting women as a result of laborious industrial VFX work processes:

> FX was a factory environment. If you can imagine an assembly line, but somehow in one of the most creative fields. . . . I had to deliver 200 shots every week for *Lion King* with a group of 100 artists—that's a lot of shots! It takes hundreds of hours to do, so it's a really tough environment. I will say the leadership style is [such that] there's no room to nurture and coach and ensure well-being. It really is at the forefront—do or die—get me those shots. I did that for six years of my life and that was a very difficult position. . . . There are gender issues in VFX—you will not meet many women. The crazy work hours that they have to put in because of all the short windows we're given to deliver projects, and it's not a surprise if women want to have kids, they quit VFX.[38]

Transmedia work processes within the film and media industry have been described as similarly laborious and challenging for those juggling other life demands and caring responsibilities. Kamal Sinclair (2017) spoke about her 2012 work as a transmedia producer at 42 Entertainment, where she worked on several key industry transmedia campaigns, including J. J. Abrams and the *Amazing Spiderman* campaign: "It was wonderful, but at that time I was divorced and a single mother, so the 100 hours a week was a challenge. Because you're working on a global transmedia campaign, it is not the same thing as a film or anything else, because you've got PAs [production assistants] in London doing drops on a totally different timescale, and you're one of the elves in the workshop making sure all the magic happens—it's a sleepless job."[39]

During our research when the COVID-19 pandemic hit, virtual production really started to take off.[40] "Virtual production," said Vicki Lau, "has such strong ties to virtual reality and mixed reality—it's specifically in that area of development—because of the technology updates that came from there—it's led to a more nuanced virtual production system that we have today, and all the jobs that come with that."[41] Working in virtual production with nascent technologies that are still in development could be challenging, and Kaya Jabar discussed the impact these challenges had on working processes and workloads:

> We started creating these methodologies for filming very compli-
> cated effects elements and breaking down complicated shots. It
> was a balance because it wasn't purely about how to export data
> to motion control rigs. I needed to know about composition and
> cinematography and about how people are doing things on set so
> that you became this person who looked at the shot as the sum of
> its parts. Then you could figure out which parts needed to go to
> which piece of equipment in order to inform the crew about what
> they were doing—the volume of work we had to do was insane.[42]

Jabar's account reminds us of the multiple multiskilled roles participants
had to play, which we identified in chapter 3. Wearing many hats is a
necessity in start-up and indie contexts and also in the transitional context of emergent spaces, where roles can be ill defined across venues,
resulting in excessive workloads and stress. Neilda Pacquing described
the challenges of working in a start-up environment:

> When you're an entrepreneur, especially in a start-up, a 40-hour
> a week, nine to five, doesn't exist. It's almost 24/7, whatever your
> business needs. It's almost like raising a baby, so it requires quite a
> bit of attention in making sure that the team that you have . . . is
> aligned and knows exactly what they need to do to reach the next
> milestone. . . . [T]here definitely are [crunch times]—especially
> being part of the accelerator where you have metrics, and you need
> to report on the progress every single week.[43]

Similar issues of exhausting labor conditions also emerged within
the independent production sector. Taryn Southern spoke about the
impacts of the demanding labor required to sustain a career as an independent content producer:

> I built a small production team and constantly rolled out con-
> tent on my channel and for other channels. In 2013 I had several
> employees that worked with me for several years. We made over
> 1,500 internet videos for lots of different companies as well as my
> channel. We made series for Snapchat, Instagram, and YouTube
> and also for sites that had their own original content needs, Condé

Nast, Marriott, Movietickets.com. . . . Ultimately, I got to the end of 2015 . . . basically my three-year mark. I was exhausted. I was really happy that I had been able to do it, but I felt what a lot of other content creators were feeling, which was just this exhaustion from the constant strain of making content and that there were just more and more emerging platforms to keep up with and recognizing that your audience grows. You're always worried about losing them or not evolving with them.[44]

Gendered Labor

Other elements of working processes were identified as being highly laborious and often uncredited too. Catherine Allen spoke about the inequitable gendered dimension endemic in writing and preparing funding applications:

> There's a pattern I've observed of women doing funding applications tirelessly for VR projects, getting the funding after often years of trying, then because they need a production company or a developer to work with, they find another company to partner up with. And then this development company will get two-thirds of that budget. Development companies tend to be mainly men. That specialist work swallows up most of the budget. Women don't get paid for any of that early concept development or business development time. That business development time doesn't get accounted for anywhere.[45]

Lina Srivastava (2016) also talked about the gendered dimension of emotional labor—and why this very often fell to women: "You have to balance a number of different people's needs. If and when you're actually going to make social change or if you're in the middle of putting together a project. It's also the things that are not funded. We're often responsible for the emotional labor, the caretaking to a certain extent of teams. You add the layer of that for people of color."[46] Other forms of labor included self-branding. Many of our participants described the sheer exhaustion of having to constantly explain and justify one's position. Jessica Clark, founder of the Dot Connector Studio, cofounder of Immerse.news, and coauthor of the *Making a New Reality* book and toolkit explained: "This is the playbook where people tell you what you need to do is have a personal brand and be an entrepreneur . . . and there was definitely a gendered aspect to that because there are more hurdles for women starting businesses. There are ego hurdles, there are perception hurdles, there are capital acquisition hurdles, and our self-image hurdles. We're not necessarily taught to be aggressive, self-aggrandizing, and bold."[47] Amy Rose, cofounder of Anagram, added her own experience of the behaviors that Clark described: "There's something about bravado that matters—about how you describe yourself, what you say about your project and what it can do, really getting comfortable with blowing your own trumpet and I sometimes thought that is a gender thing. I would come across very overconfident men who would feel quite comfortable with making some fairly mediocre VR and still really sell it as if it were the answer to poverty."[48]

An anonymous filmmaker and producer working in journalism explained the impact her gender has on the perception of others toward her: "I have been underestimated in the field, and sometimes I really quite enjoy that because you get much better access when people underestimate you. People are much more careless when they underestimate you. I'm good with that."[49] These attitudes are reaffirmed in various exchanges and settings. May Abdalla recounted one particular experience: "We were shooting a music video we had incredible RED cameras and I needed to get a cable for this RED camera rig and I went to COMET to ask the guy for this cable which I'd seen online and he was really skeptical that I needed this cable, and he said to me, 'Could you call your son and just ask him what he needs?' I almost choked. I'm very competent with kit and cameras and I don't even have a son."[50] These types of everyday discriminatory exchanges can also occur in interactions with other women, as Abdalla went on to describe: "We were presenting at Parliament and somebody came up to me and said, 'Are you a researcher at the BBC?' I mean she was a lady and I'd never really said anything, so I said, 'No—I run the company that coproduces the project.'"[51]

One of our participants, who wished to remain anonymous when providing this particular account, also spoke about how it was another woman who undermined her expertise:

I still feel like it is a very male-dominated space and sometimes there are women who are perpetuating this. I was once at an event [where] I met a woman from [a tech company] and I was talking to her about my project and she asked who had made it for me. I told her I didn't understand the question—"What do you mean? *I'm* making it"—and she said, "But who's making it *for* you?" I found out later on that she approached colleagues of mine and she asked other women makers who I knew if they had heard of me and if what I was saying was true. I thought it was funny that it was a woman who was questioning my ability to make things or do them myself, and, of course, I can't separate my race from my gender. Who knows if I was a white woman, if she would have been asking the same questions. I did find that bizarre because she worked for a big tech company.[52]

These are just a few of the many accounts our participants shared with us about the impact of their gender on their work and the biased attitudes of others toward them. Our interviewees revealed that they are very often subjected to these exchanges, attitudes, and resistances. As a woman, Winger-Bearskin stated in chapter 5, "you get challenged 1,000 times a day." Regardless of these day-to-day experiences, we see tremendous resilience from our participants, through the formation of different working practices and alternative processes designed to circumvent these barriers. We look at a representative range of examples in the following section.

Emergent Feminist Working Practices

We identified a number of common themes that centered on how our participants approach their work and the supporting of one another, including collaboration, mentorship and allyship, self-teaching, archiving, and the sharing of best practices. Many of our participants cited the importance and centrality of collaboration in their work. As an individual artist, Mimi Ọnụọha was keen to foreground this: "I consider myself in conversation and collaboration constantly. I try in my work to really pull back the curtain and say the people who helped me, list them with the creation of the work. I think the art world is terrible at that."⁵³ Katerina Cizek, coauthor of *Collective Wisdom: Co-Creating Media within Communities, across Disciplines and with Algorithms*, underscored co-creation as a feminist practice in our interview: "Over my 25 years, women or women-identifying folks tend to draw to co-creation a little bit more than men, not solely, but there is an appreciation of co-creation. . . . I do think co-creation is part of the gender issue too—it's a profound acknowledgment that we can't do this alone. . . . Not one person or not one organization or one discipline really [has] all the answers. We have to find radically new ways of organizing and doing it quickly to deal with the major issues of our time."⁵⁴

Many of our participants including Jenn Duong, an immersive director and producer and cofounder of Women in VR/AR and SH//FT, were keen to acknowledge and celebrate the mentoring support that they had received from other women. "It was at RYOT [VR company] that I really started to get great mentorship from Molly Swenson, who is now their CMO [chief marketing officer]. Just having her as a strong female figure in my career and having her help me navigate the space of negotiating and understanding business deals and the culture of what it meant to be a strong woman in an industry predominately run by men."⁵⁵

Kaya Jabar flagged a particular instance when she was supported by a woman: "My supervisor vouched for me because I hadn't done the thing before—my entire set crew was male—there were no women on that crew."⁵⁶ A senior producer working in immersive spoke of the importance of mentorship to her own development: "The most effective support I've had progressing my career in this space has been informal mentorship from other people in general—men and women—but some of the things that I value the most have been other women in the area, other peers, other people more experienced than me. I have found that to be a very useful resource."⁵⁷

Jennifer Palais, creative strategist and digital producer, described how accessing mentorship online and via social media channels was incredibly useful, echoing our earlier discussions in the previous chapter related to the value of online support groups:

I felt very much like I wanted to empower people because that's how I felt when social media came, I felt empowered. Whereas,

when I worked in media before, I felt very disempowered. . . .
I didn't have any mentors at the time, and it just felt like a really
big business world that I didn't understand. . . . No one had a voice,
unless you had millions of dollars, whereas once social media
came out it was like everyone can have a voice now. . . . The web
also felt very much friendlier to me and for women in general. I
really felt that I didn't have to hide or behave in a different way.
I could just connect with people in a real way.[58]

Sara Lisa Vogl talked about the importance of allies and who they
should be, and she offered an example of a negative impact if they are not
in place: "Having an equal ratio team, that's the most basic thing—having
an equal ratio conference. I was just so sad—Somnium Space—the platform that I'm spending most time on—they had their 'Somnium Space
connect' and I could only see white males on the stage."[59]

In our interviews, we also uncovered the incredible lengths many
of our participants went to in terms of their own self-teaching—to
improve their skills, to enhance their prospects, and to augment their
art-making practices. Neilda Pacquing talked through her own self-
development activities, which augmented those which she would have
been developing in the workplace: "In 2016 I took a VR development
class. It started as a weekend course where I learned how to make my
first VR experience using the Oculus SDK, and being able to use Unity
and prototyping, and testing the experience, and then eventually I
started taking evening classes. I realized that because the knowledge
wasn't very accessible . . . I wanted to take advantage of any opportunity to learn how to do it myself."[60] Self-teaching is a far more central aspect to the work of our participants who were resourceful and
entrepreneurial self-starters. As Taryn Southern explained: "I always
want to know how things are made. . . . There's a lot of different skill
sets I've picked up as a result of this from internet marketing to even
just filmography, how to shoot, how to properly film, how to light, how
to think about your scripting and your dialogue, especially for digital
media. It's very different. It's very quick and snappy. The internet has
been my friend—when I can't figure out how to do something, I just
Google it."[61] This also includes Artsy Marie, an independent social VR
architect. Speaking in 2022, she stated:

I taught myself how to use Unity 3D, the game engine, I taught myself SketchUp, an architectural rendering program. I had no previous experience, no background in 3D. . . . Then other people wanted what I was building, so I decided that I needed to learn how to build everything from scratch. That's what I did, and I turned it into a fully-fledged business. . . . I've built a nightclub, storefronts, and boutiques. . . . I've built over 200 templates. . . . There are over 4,000 worlds in alt space that have my logo on them. I was the first worldbuilder to monetize the platform.[62]

She also reflected on how she has benefited as a result: "When I first came into VR, I was struggling financially because of the pandemic and trying to sell my art. . . . I never had a job, I always work for myself and sold my art. I've probably made more in VR than I have in any other venture. . . . I got hired by NFT Oasis recently and I'm working on a collection of dream houses for their Dream House drop."[63]

Danielle Brathwaite-Shirley talked through her own process of self-teaching and the motivations that underpin her approach:

I had come from video games, so I'd often used video games as a medium to test out transitioning, to buying a character design to a home in Sims, to designing my first trans character. I remember . . . a game called *Dragon's Dogma* that allowed me to play a trans character and also have my original dead face follow me around. . . . I began very slowly modeling in Blender—excruciatingly slowly—I would use Blender as a diary to archive part of me and my process. It was much more about trying to remember and archive a moment, than trying to do a good 3D model. That explains my approach to all things tech—I'm not trying to do the best thing with the tech—I'm trying to use the tech in order that it does the best thing for the people I'm trying to remember and archive.[64]

Brathwaite-Shirley introduces an incredibly pertinent process here—archiving—a theme that was frequently raised in our discussions. In chapter 4, we discussed the issue of platform obsolescence, the corollary issue of which is the challenges of archiving and accessing content that has specifically been made for platforms that subsequently become obsolete. This was mentioned by several of our participants. Helen De Michiel, an independent producer, writer, and director, expressed a strategy for sustaining projects and platforms:

> Because the internet has advanced so quickly in directions that could not be planned for, they became really old, really fast and without being taken care of and nurtured. Technologies online started to decompose in many cases. . . . [R]ather than create a luxury vehicle, we have to start thinking about ways to make very small life adaptable vehicles that can live longer or live for a certain amount of time. That's what I would say is for the future is to be very light, very experimental: write about it, iterate it, and get it out there, and somehow archive it.[65]

Siobhan O'Flynn (2016) echoed this point and compared the insufficient archiving of limited access to transmedia and interactive projects to that of computer gaming—an established mainstream industry:

> Some of the projects that were really influential for my thinking and understanding [of] how the form was evolving I have almost no records now. . . . I think this is going to be a major factor in the future since many of the really interesting and cutting-edge projects over the last 10–15 years have come out of marketing and advertising, and they don't necessarily archive. . . . [T]here are a lot of these key, touchstone past projects that have informed the way individuals think and that informed the way the industry exists now. Because there's no record, it's very hard to trace that back. . . . It's dissimilar from games. The people who will talk about first playing Zelda or first playing Mario Brothers or first playing Atari, that's well-documented, and a lot of it [them] can go back and still play.[66]

Stephanie Dinkins, an artist working with AI, expressed less concern about the potential loss of her works. Rather, she accepted that it is an innate characteristic of the media that she is working with:

In some ways, the artist in me wants to be someone who is remembered. Like most of this stuff, nobody's going to be able to decipher it in the future. And then the stuff that it gets played on . . . I already have projects that are breaking down because the dependencies that they rely on are going away. They're just disappearing in front of my eyes. In one sense I think, "Oh no," but in the other sense, it's kind of beautiful. . . . And I'm sort of OK with that. I don't know that the provenance of the object is super interesting to me, but the permanence of the idea or the pervasiveness of the idea.[67]

In 2016 Sarah Wolozin also reflected on the inherent issues of archiving important creative projects for future access:

The fundamental problem is that our media is being curated, edited, and distributed by big tech companies. They decide what we see. They are all owned by men. . . . We are doing a big conference in May [2022] about preservation and this issue of making all this work on technologies that are unstable. Losing your work, being beholden to these big tech companies, and whatever they want to do. They can cancel Flash—it's not lucrative for them anymore, but it means our projects can no longer be seen.[68]

Jan Libby talked through her own archival strategies and processes: "I have a little bit from each project that I've done. It's just the nature of the beast. Unless there's someone taking care of it, it's just not going to stay up . . . I've learned over the years. I've tried to grab them when they're up there because I've missed a couple. Sadly, the one that we did for the Ford Focus rally was on Hulu, but the minute that Hulu went over to subscription, they pulled that down, so that's gone forever."[69]

The fragility and ephemerality inherent in digital media works undoubtedly have a profound impact on the future history of these creative technologies and their output. As we suggested in the cycles of innovation model (see chapter 1), these losses and erasures are more likely to negatively impact the documentation and historicization of how women's contributions are recognized and referenced. Despite these prospects, what emerged from our discussions is the importance of tracking and documenting creative production processes. We conclude this chapter on how the working processes, principles, and practices of our participants have been documented, archived, and crucially shared by many of our participants.

Sharing Best Practices

Many participants have either led or engaged in projects focused on the creation and dissemination of materials and resources, and we uncovered numerous initiatives that had been designed to help and support the progress of others. We highlight a small number here, centering on those that have produced shareable documentation or resources, but there are many more. These include XR Inclusion, a democratic, volunteer-based initiative led by a diverse and global group of XR professionals, diversity and inclusion experts, lawyers, human resources professionals, artists, and researchers. This organization produced its own report in 2020 based on survey data from 190 XR professionals (over half of whom were North American).[70] This speaks to the need for further research, including studies that involve a more diverse range of respondents and which are globally oriented.

Many of our participants clearly valued sharing their practices and processes in order to learn from others and build on their own work, and many embraced inclusive and collaborative processes. These include Kamal Sinclair, who with Jessica Clark and Carrie McLaren, produced an openly accessible set of online resources, *Making a New Reality: A Toolkit for Inclusive Media Futures*,[71] and Kat Cizek who coauthored with William Uricchio the book *Collective Wisdom: Co-Creating Media within Communities, across Disciplines and with Algorithms*; an open online version of *Collective Wisdom* was made available for community review and discussion.[72]

Three of our interview participants (Ingrid Kopp, Jessica Clark, and Sarah Wolozin) cofounded Immerse.news—an online technology publication dedicated to the creative discussion of emerging nonfiction storytelling. Immerse regularly publishes blog posts, features, and articles and has an international reach of around 10,000 readers. Jessica Clark described their focus: "It's an unusual thing because it's a technology publication led by women, and it features a lot of women and people of color who are working in this space because we think inclusion is part of the innovation dynamic."[73]

Jessica Clark was also responsible for developing "the Impact Pack" card deck in 2017 through a collaborative research project with documentary filmmakers, journalists, and interactive producers. It enables participants to think through their goals, weigh the merits of various platforms, and define their relationships with audiences. Since its launch, the deck has been adapted into digital form using the Miro platform to enable remote participation and collaboration among creative teams.[74] Another one of our participants, Karine Halpern, founder of Transmedia Ready, created an education card game. The project is "a non-profit organization based in France to do advocacy for the transmedia concept," she said. "Meaning, I'm not making any money. It's an intellectual project. It's a creative project."[75] What all these endeavors have in common is the clear motivation to elicit positive change and to make an impact; interestingly, these are all nonprofit initiatives, with some relying on volunteer labor. Sara Lisa Vogl coestablished Women in Immersive Tech Europe, which has also curated some useful resources, including a self-generated directory of European-based women XR speakers who were willing to add their details to a publicly available database.[76]

Whereas these are grassroots, community-led initiatives based on willingly volunteered labor, others are resourced through publicly funded sources. Siobhan O'Flynn talked about the Transmedia Multiplatform and Convergent (TMC) Resource Kit, which she developed in collaboration with Anthea Foyer: "The TMC resource kit came out of constantly prepping and presenting case studies at different industry events. It felt like there would be a value in hosting and archiving a lot of the case studies around successful works, because it would then serve as a resource within the Canadian context for content producers trying to figure out how to get into this space. It was CMF [Canadian Media Production Association] funded, and the CMF saw a marked value for this."[77]

Best-practice initiatives such as these are all underpinned by a drive toward collaboration and sharing, through which our participants are paving the way for others to follow in their footsteps, to benefit from their learning and to diversify participation in these spaces.

Conclusion

We have drawn out the following key points in relation to process in this chapter: Access to funding is the main barrier our participants face, and lack of secure investment impedes their progress. Some choose to no longer pursue certain types of funding since they perceive they will have little chance of procuring it. However, many of our participants have chosen not to prioritize commercialization. Workflows and workloads are characteristically heavier and more intense across a range of emergent media sector contexts—ranging across independent, artistic, and commercial realms—sometimes as a result of our participants having to occupy multiple roles demanding multiple skills. We identified numerous emergent feminist working practices that circumvented, avoided, and overcame the barriers that our participants have faced. These included mentorship and allyship for enabling their advancement in creative spaces of innovation. Both self-support (through self-teaching activities) and support of one another through a drive to proactively share best practices is one of the key characteristics that defines our participants' positive experiences of emergent media. Ensuring that there is a free flow of information, spaces of support, and opportunities for collaboration are common priorities.

Having now considered the platforms, places, and processes of our participants and the numerous barriers and challenges that they have had to overcome, chapter 7 moves toward a detailed consideration of the productions that they have brought to successful fruition.

7

Production

Aesthetics and Ethics in Emergent Media

Production, the outcome of labor, provides a fitting last topic for our book. Within this chapter, we will see the confluence of our participants' hard work, leadership, and tenacity in overcoming challenges in their finished productions and artworks. The participants interviewed for this study represent a diverse array of creativity across art practice and media production—with work that fills a spectrum from abstract and experimental art to social justice and documentary projects and employing without prejudice cutting edge technology, analog materials, performance, and hybrid forms.

Forty-four of our participants identified as independent artists. We have not been able to include examples of all their work in this chapter, but we have endeavored to reference them as much as possible in the discussion. Our approach to the chapter is to draw together and synthesize the creative contributions of the participants and to identify shared areas and commonalities in the principles and approaches they have evolved through their practice.

Given the varied range of our participants' creative output, compounded by their crossover interests in other fields—such as science and technology, cultural critique, anthropology, and community building—much of their work is not easily classifiable within tidy categories of media, entertainment, or art. And digital work has faced difficulty in gaining acceptance as a legitimate form within the institutions of the art world, as many interviewees expressed.[1] We uncovered a stark example of this. Lynn Hershman Leeson, whose five-decade history of radical media work across multiple platforms, which has incisively interrogated issues of technology and its impact of culture and identity, was nevertheless largely ignored by the art establishment until a major ZKM retrospective in 2014. Astonishingly, her first solo show in New York was in the summer of 2021.[2] Hershman Leeson attributed this remarkable oversight in part to both gender and regional bias (her West Coast locale), but there was the additional problem of the platforms that her work employed: "I think the fact that it was media that wasn't considered an art form until just very recently. In the United States, maybe there are two or three museums that have media curators, which is ridiculous. It's just catching up, and I have no doubt that I will have a firm place in art history with regard to media art and to works like *Lorna* and *Roberta* and the films. But I was excluded until just very recently because they excluded everything."[3]

Even in our highly mediated world with technology at the forefront of our cultural conversations, Hershman Leeson noted that the art establishment still has boundaries: "It's slowly changing but not fast enough. I did a project with Harvard last year with scientists where we created a way to transform plastic from water and erase it, eradicate it. It was so successful that the people at Harvard quit their job and started a company to do it. It actually worked. That premiered at the New Museum show, and it's going to be in Basel, but very few places would show something like that."[4]

Christiane Paul, professor at the New School, director / chief curator of galleries at Parsons School of Design, and adjunct curator of digital art at the Whitney Museum for more than 20 years, confirmed the institutional challenges digital artists face. Paul commented that the primary difficulty she encountered in her curatorial practice was with the acceptance of digital work as a legitimate art form:

> Where the challenges really came in was the medium. And they have been radical. I've been at the Whitney 22 years and it's only in the past 5 years that I've really gained momentum there and have my own acquisition committee. And it's radically different right now, in terms of the voice I have in the institution, particularly since NFTs. . . . [N]ow I have much more of a voice in all of that. I would say there has been massive medium discrimination. Visitors have been, even on the exhibition floors, so offensive and angry. I know that artists in the '60s like Manfred Mohr once told me how they threw tomatoes at him. Because he was working with computers. I've seen a lot of that. I'm not saying only within the

institution but also from the public: "What is this? This doesn't belong into museums." "Here's Christiane who deals with all the highfalutin stuff"—that was a quote.[5]

Hershman Leeson and Paul's experiences reveal that the use of emergent media within the domain of digital art complicates any discussion of the basic qualities, practical strategies, and social/cultural outcomes of projects that fall within this designation. As we have seen with naming conventions for emergent forms and their associated practices and roles (see chapters 3 and 4), our understanding of the possibilities will be fluid, contested, and even murky. In this chapter, we will explore how artists, curators, campaigners, strategists, and thought leaders in emergent media spaces we have identified (transmedia and multiplatform, VR, AR, and immersive) imagine both the aesthetic parameters and the ethical boundaries for these creative areas through the productions that they create and commission.

Several topics arose within our interviews that have informed the structure of this chapter: the affordances of particular artistic mediums; the status of digital art; the desired outcome of creative work; the role of the audience; the larger social context of how art is made and experienced, by and for whom; and the work's impact on our understandings of past, present, and future. Within these concerns, we look at some of the consistent aesthetic factors our participants have highlighted as driving their work, such as process/action, representation, presence, participation, immersion, embodiment, temporality, space- and place-making, and narrative forms. These elements in turn intersect with the myriad social and cultural concerns that are central to the artistic practice under discussion. While specific social and political issues of gender, racial, environmental, and economic justice were critical focal points within our interviews, the conversations often turned to more holistic commentaries that encompassed such topics as well-being, community engagement, technology, self-reflection, futurism, and hope. The structure of this chapter reflects the interlocking areas of aesthetics and ethics given the ineluctable connection of these dimensions in the productions that we explore.

The Art Object

As discussed above, digital art/media has been, until fairly recently, seen as a medium outside the established art world. While in some part we might attribute this to the comfort of conventional forms and art history and curation that reinforces this bias, there is a further complication. Christiane Paul notes in the introduction to her edited collection, *A Companion to Digital Art*, that the challenge to defining the aesthetics of digital arts begins with the multiple, shifting, hybrid, and ephemeral forms of projects.[6] Katja Kwastek traces a shift in our understanding from early twentieth-century avant-garde to digital and interactive artworks. In this new landscape, there is a move from an aesthetics with a focus on an *object* to one of *process*—with many digital media artists' work focused on an action or process orientation.[7] The art form as variable, or platform agnostic, as we have previously discussed in chapter 4, and outcomes that are more critically than materially located, were repeatedly pointed out by our participants as characteristic of their projects.

For Lauren Lee McCarthy, an artist working across various media, the element of performance is crucial as a medium and a key idea under investigation within her work. Her series, *Lauren* (2017–), uses a variety of human-AI interface scenarios to consider the scope of machine-driven personal tasks, from party host to smart hosts, and asks us to consider how identity is shaped in an increasingly mediated landscape. McCarthy discussed the centrality of performance in her work:

> I'm working across a lot of different media ranging from performance to film, software installation, photography, sculpture, an internet intervention community, more like social practice organizing. The core for me is usually performance. That's not always obvious to everyone that sees my work, but for me I'm thinking about the performance of ourselves. So going back to a lot of these social dynamics. . . . Also, beginning my practice around 2009, I noticed that so much of the art and technology work was very tech driven, it was made by mostly men, but there wasn't a lot of expression in terms of thinking about the psychological and emotional social experience of interacting with technology.[8]

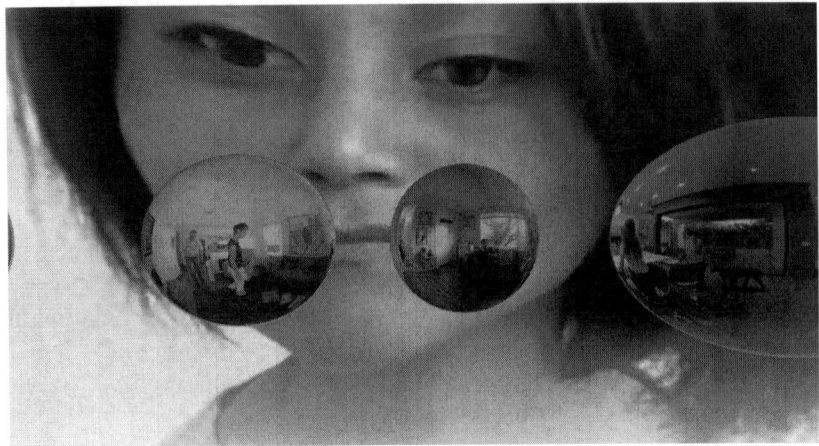

Figure 7.1. *Lauren*, installation and performance. 2017. Lauren Lee McCarthy.

Digital artist and theorist micha cárdenas pointed to her studies and activism at university as formative to her creative practice with an attention to ideas and iterative turns in writing and making: "My process is driven by conceptual questions. Sometimes I make a thing to try to get at those questions, and then I learn something from making that thing and then learn something else from writing about it."[9] Her 2008 performance mixed-media piece, *Becoming Dragon*, followed this iterative process as prose and poetry written during her yearlong hormone replacement therapy. These were included in the work, and a scholarly essay on her research and practice followed.[10] She told us:

> I lived in Second Life for 365 hours straight as a durational performance. . . . I wanted to challenge this real-life requirement that you're supposed to live for a year as your chosen gender before you are allowed to get surgery. Could I live for a year in Second Life and then get species change surgery? Partly to undermine the ridiculousness of asking someone to live for a year as a woman, what does that mean? Am I supposed to wear makeup every day? Do I have to wear a dress every day? Such, it seemed to me as an oppressive outdated requirement. A lot of my work continued that

thinking how technology could be used for social justice, for trans people, for trans people of color, and immigrants.[11]

While the art establishment presented its own set of access issues, Hershman Leeson noted that pervasive cultural bias against women in technology and art also presented challenges throughout her career. She recounted the resistance to imagining a woman working in media and technology today, even within commonplace settings, and then described the serious long-term impact such prejudices held for her work:

I just went to get an iPhone. I said I wanted to get something that was 4K and I wanted to get an external mic. He said, "Oh why?" I said I want to do some videos. He said, "Yeah, you gonna to do something about recipes?" That's what I got all the time. . . . It took me 25 years to show *Lorna*. Nobody would show it other than in the first month. The same thing with my *Breathing Machines*. [They] were taken out of a museum when I first showed them, and I had to wait 52 years for anyone to see them. I made them in 1965. They weren't shown until 2014. Then I found out that they were the very first works anybody had ever done with sound and the very first media works, and because they had no history, nobody knew what they were, and they kept telling me it wasn't art. I was constantly either talked down to or degraded or berated. I couldn't get a gallery. I couldn't get exhibitions.[12]

Obstructions caused by institutional gatekeepers who decide what gets to count for art and who can make art came up in several interviews. Rebecca Allen described how this lack of fit for her interests in emergent media extended in two directions—the blending of artistic experimentation with technological innovations—over the course of her 40-year career. She detailed her efforts to expand her art studies into computer animation, which required getting permission from Rhode Island School of Design to take a class at Brown University:

They said artists can't work with computers. But I ignored them. I did it anyway. When I reflect back, that's been from both sides. To watch over the decades how people, particularly in the art world, try to justify why digital art or computer art isn't really art. From the other side, because I had to be in a very technical environment—it would be artists can't work with computers, because they aren't computer scientists. This has been a world I've been navigating to the point where I feel like part of my role has been a performer. I always felt like I was infiltrating these technical environments.[13]

Toni Dove, whose renowned and radically experimental storytelling practice of more than 40 years blends responsive technologies, installation, and performance, similarly noted her lack of fit in the art world due in part to technology but also to the absence of an object to monetize. To illustrate, a 2018 retrospective of Dove's work at Ringling Museum of Art featured an interactive robotic dress installation, *The Dress That Eats Souls*, which tracked viewer movements to prompt short films, thereby enabling an experience of the garment through different periods of time. The multimedia interactive dress does not sit easily within conventional art practices, nor does it produce the physically contained art "commodities" of sculpture, painting, or photography.

I skate around at all these different places. You pay for that in a lot of ways. If you're not in a place that has an institutional validation system, it makes it difficult to create a critical mass of attention. I have definitely felt that, but at the same time, it gives me the freedom to do the things that I want to do without having to adapt myself to the various genre recipes that any given field purveys. My work wouldn't quite fit into the art world—at least it wouldn't have for a long time. Maybe it would more now, because they're opening up a little bit more of the technology, but probably not because it's not very object oriented, it doesn't lend itself well to creating value. I can see that from doing a retrospective, you can box up the dresses, you can do all this kind of stuff. And it looked like this incredible show full of stuff that could easily be for sale, but it's a different focus.[14]

The art object that cannot be monetized and does not fit into the capitalist flow of media of high-end production is reminiscent of the "poor image" that Hito Steyerl maps out in the 2009 article "In

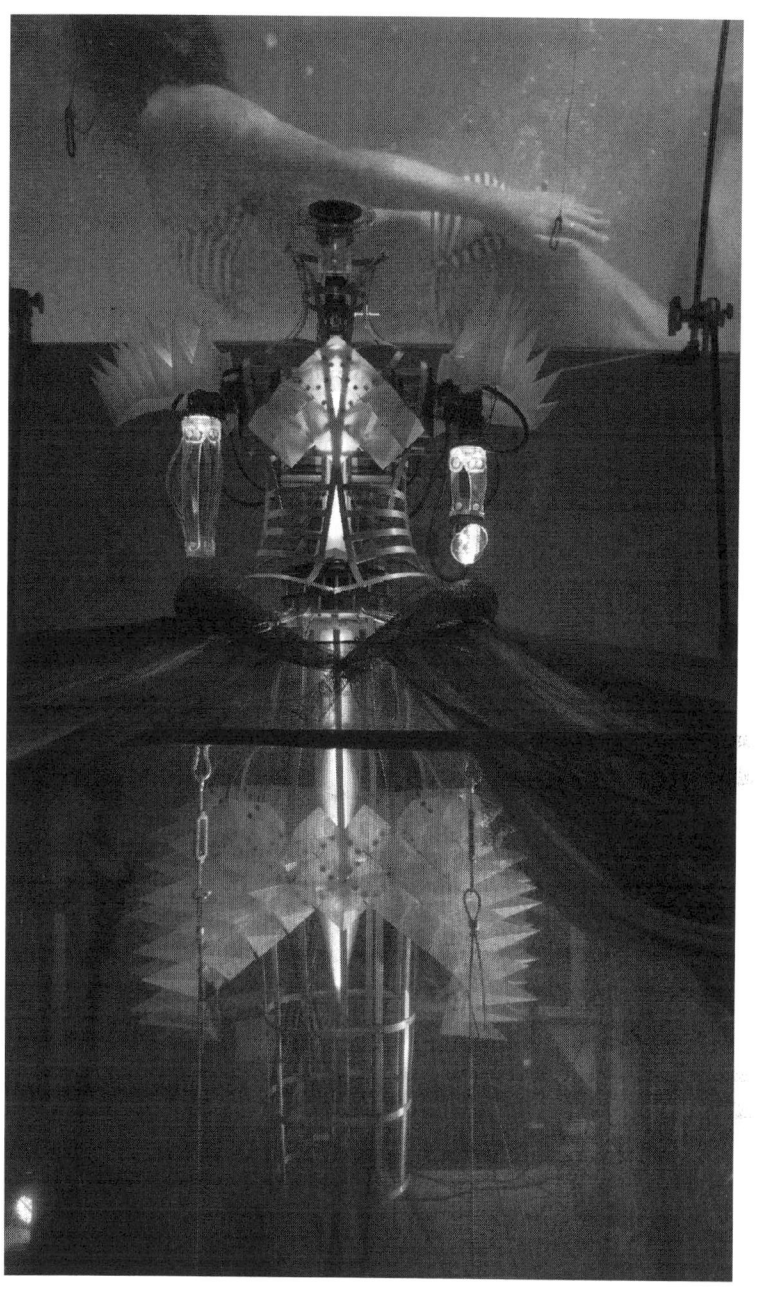

Figure 7.2. *The Dress That Eats Souls*, interactive cinema installation. 2018. Toni Dove.

Defense of the Poor Image." The attention to the high resolution, the mimetic, establishes a hierarchy of value, which the "poor," the remixed, reappropriated image, cannot ascend. Steyerl notes in this global monopoly of culture, the essayistic, experimental, and the noncommercial disappear, in favor of a "rich" image aesthetic. To invoke these "poor" images can in some sense be a point of opposition to authorship, commodity culture, and global media. For Steyerl, digital technology assists in the degradation of the image, through reproduction, circulation, and appropriation, and thus can reinforce the hierarchy of global "rich" media or can be a site that disrupts authorship, commodity culture, and mimetic, closed forms of representation.[15]

In our interview with Illya Szilak (2016), she discussed the significance of transmedia as a narrative strategy and the central role of appropriation in *Queerskins: A Novel*. Her remarks are suggestive of Steyerl's "poor image" as resistant to the artwork and artist as global commodity. This aesthetic and ethic is founded on a multiperspectival commitment seen throughout the multipart *Queerskins* project, beginning with the novel as a transmedia space of collective artifacts/stories:

> The idea of originality, of a genius artist who makes this magnificent, singular, exalted thing, is just not what I wanted. I always wanted the work to have a conversation, even if it was displaced in time and space with the collective crowd around me. . . . What I ended up doing was curating from Flickr Creative Commons, people's vacation photographs, and home photographs. I found this treasure trove of photographs from rural Missouri, there's no people, they're all active sets, but for me it was important to bring material that was already circulating into the work so it wasn't just me—that's another real trans aspect that's absolutely critical to the kind of work I do.[16]

Again, we see that the fragility of the media object as a fixed entity is enhanced by the vicissitudes of digital technology as elements degrade and become obsolete (see chapter 6).

Many of our participants articulated the aesthetics of their work in terms of their experiential, rather than tangible, qualities. For example,

Nancy Bennett (2022) discussed her *Performance of Your Life*, a very personal piece that utilizes one of the final performances of her late brother (William Bennett) with the San Francisco symphony. Bennett had discussed the many technical improvements with VR but noted that it was still predominantly a game space that had not yet made the most of its storytelling potential. With *Performance of Your Life*, Bennett hoped to extend the idea of perspective into a rich aesthetic and emotional experience: "When you do anything at the top of your game, you hit a flow state. I wanted to immerse people in what it's like to be a virtuoso player and to transcend into that flow state . . . being able to play the different parts in the orchestra, be in those seats and feel that. I'm a musician—so when I play any instrument, there's a feeling of being inside that instrument. That's really part of the flow state where you become the sound and that's what I want to try and give people a sense of."[17]

Representation and Participation

The shift away from the preeminence of the object and authorship within emergent digital media is matched by a parallel growth in work that employs participation and co-creation of the work. In some sense, this move connects to an understanding of the limits and problems of representation given the insufficient access for diverse voices and experiences in the production of contemporary media. As May Abdalla, documentary filmmaker and cofounder of Anagram, noted in speaking of her experiences of both watching programs as a young person and then matching that experience with her beginnings in television documentary production and thinking critically about the role of media in knowledge production:

> I remember watching the documentary about the Tutsis and the Hutus and at the time I really felt that the person who was telling me that stuff was all powerful and all knowledgeable. And I kind of had this shock entering the production process; it was like—who are these people? . . . [I]t was like the *Wizard of Oz*—you're putting on this booming voice and you're hiding behind this curtain. It was

complete smoke and mirrors, of creating the illusion of authority. I was a bit shocked by that; it was like the manufacturing of author-ity way before the manufacturing of stories or information.[18]

For Carmen Aguilar y Wedge and Ece Tankal (2022), cofounders of Hyphen-Labs, the genesis for their interactive studio was the desire to expand the understanding of who gets to make stories and to foster a culture of visibility whereby diverse participants are engaged, seen, and imagine themselves at the production table. As Tankal related: "When we looked around, there are no women in this space. Why are women not driving these spaces? Why aren't we really represented? I'm from Turkey, Carmen's from California and Cozumel. . . . [W]e wanted to see people that looked like us in these spaces so that we can encourage other people to also be in that space—to open this platform so people can see themselves doing these sorts of things. . . . [T]hat's how we started Hyphen-Labs."[19]

The complications of representation—the lack, absence, or one-dimensionality of on- and off-screen visibility—were addressed by many of our participants. Their conversations challenged us to consider ques-tions of visibility beyond a varied demographic checkbox and delve into the nuances and specifics of diverse experiences. Stephanie Dinkins, an artist working across emerging media, including AI and XR, explores the limits of expression through language and received history. Dinkins's *Not the Only One* (2018) employs AI that has been trained using oral histories from underrepresented communities to create a multigenera-tional memoir of an African American family. *When Words Fail* (2020), a WebXR project, explores those experiences and feelings that are inade-quately considered, limited, or obscured by language by requesting and including online audience collaboration. Dinkins discussed the central role of visibility in her work and the limits of what and how we see:

I think the question of value of invisibility is really one of my deep-est questions. That's a specifically American question. How do we get to a point where value and visibility isn't a sliding thing, but all humans get the same?—get to be valued and get to be seen on an equal footing. That's truly my question. . . . I'm always trying to fig-ure out, what do I need to do to get you to see me? Like, really see

Figure 7.3. *Not the Only One*, deep-learning AI installation. 2018. Stephanie Dinkins.

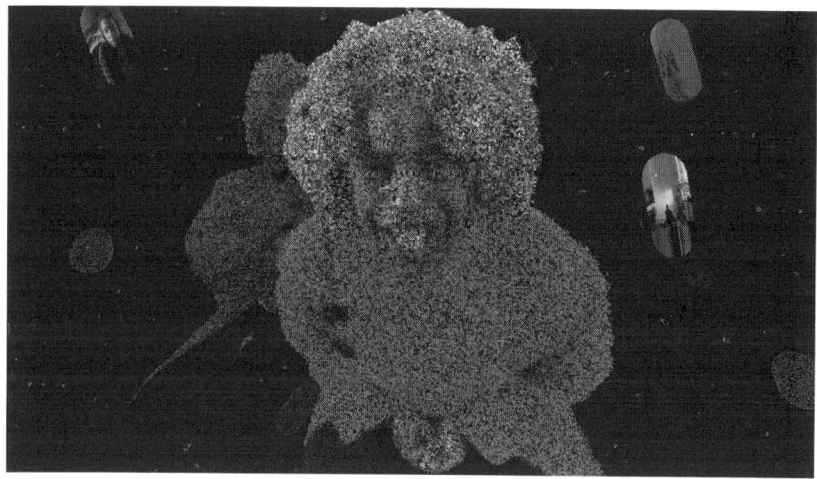

Figure 7.4. *When Words Fail*, WebXR experience. 2020. Stephanie Dinkins.

me? Not in the way you want to see me, but as I am? I don't think that's a question for white folks because I think it's a question for Black folks, how do they see because people often want you to fit in a certain box. . . . But what I know is that we don't see most of what we encounter, and we don't actually want to see it.[20]

micha cárdenas spoke to the dual-sided challenges of visibility for marginalized, particularly trans communities, and how she tries to address this in her work. She discussed her work on the Critical Realities Studio project, *Sin Sol / No Sun*, an AR game that explores the intersections of personal and environmental trauma and examines the unequal effects of climate change on immigrants, trans people, and disabled people:

With *Sin Sol*, I was thinking about demands for visibility from trans communities and how to complicate that or how to add something to that conversation, because for many decades what we think of as the LGBT movement has demanded a visibility and an acceptance into mainstream society and things being on television. In

Figure 7.5. *Sin Sol / No Sun*, ARG. 2020. micha cárdenas. Kristine Eudey, 2019, micha cárdenas, *"Sin Sol,* Prototype" as part of *Arch,* Leslie-Lohman Museum.

2014 Laverne Cox was on the cover of *Time*, this article called "The Transgender Tipping Point."[21] Then soon after that, *Pose*—this TV show from the guy who made *Glee*—came out and people were talking about it as a moment of change when there would be less violence against trans people. And the results? More violence. The number of murders of trans people in the US went up 30% and has continued to go up every year since. So partly I was writing and thinking how to complicate the conversation about visibility and how, what we need is not *more* visibility, because being on TV is not helping us, but the ability to control our visibility. I was looking at theorists writing about holograms. Achille Mbembe is a South African theorist who was writing about apartheid and Palestine, and he also writes about holograms as being part of the way to think about visibility today. That it's not as simple as just being visible or invisible.[22]

For many of our participants, co-creation was a critical tool to redress the homogeneity of voices and the singularity of storylines that dominate media (see chapter 4, where the multivocal affordances of transmedia and multiplatform are discussed); jesikah maria ross, mixed-media documentarian understands community storytelling as a key instrument for social impact. Her background as an activist during the time of the Iran/contra scandal led to her shift to media activism and community media / public access work. A skepticism about mainstream news and her experiences in grassroots and public media set a course for her methodology founded on engaging with multiple voices and perspectives. Her *Saving the Sierras* and *Restore/Restory: A People's History of the Cache Creek Nature Preserve* are projects illustrative of the mix of documentary and social change employed. For ross, the goals, outcomes, and stories are neither singular nor simple:

> My storytelling is based around creating processes and spaces for people to speak and be heard. Sometimes that's about healing. Sometimes that's to address justice issues. Sometimes it's just about inspiring hope. . . . I also think that there is a different sound and feeling that comes from it because I am creating a context for the storytelling to happen. That context always starts on the

Figure 7.6. *Sin Sol / No Sun*, ARG. 2020. micha cárdenas. Kristine Eudey, 2019, micha cárdenas, "*Sin Sol*, Prototype" as part of *Arch*, Leslie-Lohman Museum.

> ground and face-to-face, in developing relationships. The stories come out of those relationships because the stories are based around what we want to do together and why we want to do it, and how we can help each other. . . . I think that there is an art to crafting these processes so that people feel valued and respected and safe and motivated and curious.[23]

Like ross, the artist Kim Stringfellow looks at the connections between place and community. Her Mojave Project is what she sees as a "serial project," based on deep field research with different components exhibited over time—the project has been ongoing since 2014. Focused on revealing the cultural, physical, and geological landscape of the region, the project uses interviews, photography, audio, and video documentation to tell the complex stories of the region.[24] Stringfellow underlines that both the long duration of the Mojave Project as well as specified "fixed" times for other work underscores that these "histories aren't static. None of these projects are."[25] There is a speculative component to the possibilities for the region, and Stringfellow weaves the local stories with intersecting critical political, economic, and environmental issues. She described her approach as

> looking at environmental impact like industrial, solar, wind. We have this upcoming administration [Trump] that is taking a stick toward climate change. The desert, these environments are going to be drastically affected if they have their way. There have been people that have looked at the desert Southwest as a place to preserve for its own beauty, but it's mostly been seen as an extractive space or a space to stage military testing. It's been heavily harmed through these activities. The Mojave Desert, about a third of it is militarized landscape. So, speculating on what that future may be depending on how we continue to address these situations and presenting that for people, I think, is really important. There's a lot of geopolitical aspects that I'm also interested in, but I'm interested in people's stories.[26]

Sharon Daniel began work in participatory documentary by using image and text with the goal of facilitating online communication for community engagement with communities and nonprofit organizations in Argentina and Buenos Aires. As technologies advanced, she became interested in how to use these tools with more expansive goals: "I started building projects that were focused on participatory tools for self-documentation for communities that didn't normally have access to media and information technologies. This was in 2003–4, before YouTube was really established and before cell phones had good media acquisition built into them. Before they were very extensively used within marginalized communities . . . designing and developing a platform for self-representation."[27] As social media developed with increased access of tools and communication, Daniel became interested in the possibilities of database-oriented documentary work. Her focus was still on access and issues of self-representation for marginalized communities but with the attendant objective of critical insight into systemic injustices. Daniel discussed her approach for the projects *Public Secrets* (2007) and *Blood*

Sugar (2010), which look, respectively, at the prison industrial complex and the nexus of poverty and addiction in the United States. She began her fieldwork for these projects in 2000–2001.

> In terms of designing a project, the problem that I'm addressing is a site, it's a large territory—like a hundred square miles. I want to populate that hundred square miles with the multiple stories and statements of a fairly large number of people who are impacted by the same structural inequality dynamics. Then I want to organize the relationships between their statements and stories based on the arguments that they want to make about the situations and circumstances that they encounter. Then, rather than building a road across that territory, I want to drop the viewer down into the middle of the territory. Give them a little bit of an introduction to it, and then let them find their own way.
>
> Through that process of choosing what they're going to look at and listen to, based on quotes, or clues of some kind, that are provided by the interface, they have the same transformative experience of coming to understanding the recognition that I have in my research or fieldwork encounter. Where I'm investigating the problem by being in in-depth conversation over a long period of time with the most impacted individuals.[28]

Daniel's commitment to sharing multiple voices and storylines as the foundation for our pathway through complex social and political problems steps outside of established conventions for documentary work, even within these emergent spaces. Daniel challenges us to think of the rigid models we use for documentary, the affordances of platforms we select and why, and what the larger objectives at stake are for a work. In her words:

> What really bothers me is when there's a notion that there needs to be a monolithic approach. Which I think is happening now, and I think it's very problematic, around the character-driven narrative in documentary. Both in single-channel film documentary and in the realm of interactive documentary. I argue for plurality, but also try to get people to think about if you want to do character-driven

narrative, film is the perfect medium for that. It's got a narrative arc, you can focus on one character, it can be very compelling. I just don't think it's the best way to seriously address concerns around issues of structural inequality. . . . I don't even think of myself as a storyteller. The people that I'm interacting with, engaged with, and encountering are telling their own stories.[29]

Like Daniel, Stringfellow, and ross's commentaries above, Rosemarie Lerner and Maria Court share a similar approach to documentary, based on a participatory media ethos. Lerner and Court's *Quipu Project*, is an audio-based, online collective memory archive of the Indigenous people who underwent forced sterilization by the Peru government in the 1990s, which turns attention to survivors' stories.[30] Almost 300,000 people, mainly women from rural areas, were forcibly sterilized, with little visibility on this crime for two decades. Although there were some journalistic accounts of the sterilization program, Lerner and Court, learned past representations had been an extractive process, with scant transparency or impact on the women's lives. They knew their approach must be different, so they began a long process of community outreach, research, and ethical design for the project. Court pointed to the challenges they initially faced:

It was really hard to gain access to these groups, because they were very reluctant to speak to the media, especially journalists, because they had given many interviews, but they felt that they were always giving away: people came, took from them, and they saw no results. . . . [Reporters] didn't even send them the pictures back, or they didn't have ways to see what they were collaborating with. . . . [W]e had one really amazing contact, that was the human rights lawyer who actually uncovered the issue, who was an activist—Giulia Tamayo. She put us in touch with the leaders of the organization. . . . [S]he had actually gone and spoken with the women for years, and she knew what the fight was actually about.[31]

Their work, Lerner said, was not a documentation of the past but rather a form of participation in a larger process: "It wasn't just about how these women were sterilized in the '90s but the ongoing stories that these groups of women have been fighting for 15 years, and they're still fighting. We wanted to see how we can actually show this fight that has been going on. It wasn't about us creating something out of nowhere, but seeing the situation and how can we contribute to a process that's already started."[32] Lerner outlined their objectives and role in the project:

> The first objective was more than achieving justice or changing the law; it was to start building a community, and not only for them to have a chance to tell their stories in their own voices but also to listen to one another and to know that they are not alone. One of the interesting things about the sterilization policy is that it happened all across the Peruvian territory. . . . [T]hey had no idea this had happened outside of their communities. When they heard that this had happened to hundreds of thousands of people, they were in shock. Nowadays more is known because the issue came back again in the last presidential elections. . . . The first idea with a project for them is local, to start creating a stronger community so that their fight is stronger. We are just two [people] that help an ongoing struggle that they already started. We are playing a communication role.[33]

Court and Lerner reflected on the ethics of their process, including an important framing of the project, which pointed to the agency of the women:

> Since the beginning, we completely removed the word "victims" from the project. We decided we would never refer to them as victims, but as activists. We didn't want to concentrate on the horror of the past, but [instead on] the ongoing fight for justice and the fact they are amazing women. They are really resilient and not losing hope after what has happened to them. They have been continuously violated, they don't get justice, and another government turns their back to them, and they're neglected by their communities. Some of them have been abandoned by their families, but they keep going. It's really amazing. That is the core of the story more than what's happened in the past, and it's a catalyst for a lot of these women to change their situation in society.[34]

For many projects directed to social advocacy goals, the single story is not the main site of activity; rather, it is the community that is the central locus. Lina Srivastava (2016), a strategist and producer, who has worked on numerous campaigns for social change, noted:

> Multiple authorship is the point—you can't make social impact with one story or one voice. I think that's one of the problems I've had often with working with film . . . we're going to make this movie and it's going to change the situation. It might move the needle forward in a really big way—for example, [An] Inconvenient Truth created an entire vocabulary around climate change that we've built upon and . . . you look at how he [Josh Fox] was able to leverage Gas Land to really create a network and this amazing anti-fracking community. The movie becomes one of the hubs. It's the reason to start creating community. It's humanized. . . . It's the lived experience. . . . [I]t's the communities who are doing this work. It's civil society organizations, or these community organizations, that we're providing tools for and we're able to collaborate with them to enhance the work that they're already doing.[35]

Many of our interviewees spoke to the need for more diverse representation and inclusive participation in projects, often with an articulation of their working processes and the outputs they were motivated to create. A shared set of concerns regarding the inclusion of multiple voices, co-creation, and community-focused ethos emerged from the accounts. The expressive and experiential limitations of a linear narrative, centered on a lone protagonist, spurred many of our interviewees toward an expansion—or even abandonment—of story structure and a move toward forms more conducive to their goals of social justice and community building. As we will see in the next section, the experiments with story and storyworld continue as a means to spark audience engagement, enhance insight, and initiate connection and cultural imagination.

Narrative/Story/Storyworld

In our conversations on transmedia and emergent media, numerous artists discussed their attraction to these forms due to the opportunity to disrupt conventional narrative and sites of storytelling. Illya Szilak, working with her longtime collaborator, Cyril Tsiboulski, on the multipath, nonlinear story *Queerskins: A Novel*, designed strategies to destabilize the centrality of authorship and create a space for audience engagement, including the project's use of multiperspectival story threads and public domain imagery of "everyday" settings. Although the drive toward co-creation was not formally realized for the first part of *Queerskins*, later iterations created in VR (*Queerskins: A Love Story* and *Queerskins: Ark*) were accompanied by in-person and virtual installations that paralleled the world of the story with period imagery and artifacts. Throughout these different installations, spaces were produced for the audience's memories, creativity, and performance. As Szilak (2016) explained:

> I always wanted stories to be told in different ways and for people to access them in different ways. It wasn't so much that I was going to get more audience if I did it through multiple platforms; it was really that I feel like there's many different ways to tell these stories. . . . With *Queerskins*, there was a hope that we would actually do a crowdsourced version of it, where we would put out diary entries and then people could respond with their own images. . . . I thought it would be great to activate that through crowdsourcing, so in lieu of people being able to actually see him and hear him [Sebastian, a key character]. . . . If he had been alive, what would they have wanted to hear or see?[36]

Maya Zuckerman, whose writings on regenerative narrative and the "collective journey"[37] explore the connections between alternative narrative forms and new social formations, underlines the need for "transformational media" or stories that help us evolve individually and collectively and imagine outcomes and strategies for environmental and social justice. The narrative bind of the singular hero savior, often gendered as male, disconnects communities' ties and does not provide empowering role models nor the insights needed for change. Zuckerman discussed her project in development, Em's Theory, a young adult sci-fi story, which spoke to her need for new storytelling models beyond staid story arcs and content. She found particularly tiresome "the hero's journey perpetuated until infinity" and bemoaned the lack of "positive stories about the future besides *Star Trek*."

> Em's Theory takes a lot of ideas from *Star Trek*. . . . There's almost nothing like that in popular narratives now. There's only dystopia. There's only *Mad Max* and *Hunger Games* and *Divergent*. All of it is bad . . . [and] we're going to go there if we don't change the narrative. That's scary. We're in such a predicament now with climate change. . . . We don't have time for false narratives. We actually need to create a world that we can live in. That's where the power of the creators and writers is. To paint a world where we can actually go to. . . . Em's Theory is waking up to the fact that you have amazing powers to see the future, finding others like you.[38]

For many of the participants, the expansion of narrative, beyond plot and character, includes the different elements used to tell a story. Lily Baldwin, a mixed-media artist, whose work ranges across and blends multiple forms from film, performance, installation, VR, and audio/soundscapes shares a similar devotion to an expanded palette. *Through You*, a live-action VR piece codirected by Baldwin and Saschka Unseld, is a magical realist exploration of a couple's love over several decades, a story told primarily through dance. Said Baldwin: "We need to expand what we think of as a story. . . . Stories that don't need a ton of dialogue. Stories that maybe have more than one meaning. I use the word 'dreamscape' as a way to help people feel safe with that—a dream world where multiple beats occur. It isn't a dark or fantastical soliloquy—it's a dimensional dream world where what can't fit into words can happen with bodies."[39]

Embodied interaction and viewer participation are themes and approaches that have infused virtual arts practice since 1995 and were first explored in Char Davies's seminal VR works (see chapter 3). Toni Dove, like Davies, and Baldwin after her, sees the body as a central component of her practice. Dove's media work began at first with a mix of slide projectors, laser discs, and found footage, and in early 1990s VR, Dove was drawn to the idea of building "these instruments that human beings play."[40]

For the last 20 years I've been working with new tech. I make human-operated machines that tell stories. I'm a visual novelist, and I work with different kinds of technologies to create responsive environments. I started out early on working with motion sensing, so that a viewer's movement would connect to a character on the screen or create movement and respond to body movement. I've been interested for a long time in embodied interface and the idea that we can use the proprioceptive and perceptive apparatus of the human body as a navigational tool for media in ways that are similar to the way we use it in life as a navigation tool.[41]

Dove commented that her work has long blurred the lines of performer and audience. Her project currently in development, *Sunjammer 6: A Tale Told by a Solar Breeze*, which uses machine learning and artificial intelligence, is intended as an instrument to bring these two areas closer together. She described the activities of her lead character, Hypatia, through which to provide insights into her own creative process:

[Hypatia] responds by either speaking, mirroring people's movements, or selecting various different kinds of animation and

Figure 7.7. *Sunjammer 6: A Tale Told by a Solar Breeze*, installation in development. 2022. Toni Dove.

motion behaviors. She can select who she's going to react to. She can follow people around the room; she can motivate people to get them to do things. We're in the early stages now of building the brain; we've got a labeled database of motions we've developed. One of the things that we were working on during the early part of the pandemic was getting the look of the character, getting this wire frame character that's a ghost, and getting the look of the whole sensibility of the piece. Now I want to work on the interactivity—usually I'm working on the interactivity and the story at the same time.[42]

Interactivity

As the possibilities of emergent media technologies evolved for participation and co-creation, our participants began to interrogate the levels of involvement and ways in which to deepen the engagement of the audience, whether regarding social impact, critical reflection, or emotional power. May Abdalla, documentary filmmaker and cofounder of Anagram, who earlier noted she had issues with documentary strategies of representation and voiceover techniques, nevertheless was drawn to the genre and the integrity of process, which is the same for so many working in the area. She was inspired by Susana Ruiz's serious game, *Darfur Is Dying*, to think about new storytelling options for documentary:

> There was something in the possibility of what might happen if we had to think extremely creatively about the things that we knew we wanted to do, but from the perspective of who was actually trying to understand it, as opposed to necessarily who's telling it. What's the way that you might tell the story in a way that it would be heard, or embodied or embraced, or absorbed or [so that] the reality of what you were saying would be really felt . . . this is exciting. I also thought that was something categorically about agency that has always interested me. This wasn't really represented in the world of interactive documentary.[43]

Amy Rose, Abdalla's Anagram cofounder, has a background in documentary film but also has for many years organized outdoor camps for children, which came to shape how she imagined the possibilities for documentary storytelling:

> We would do a lot of interactive games. It was really impactful on my professional life because it gave me this license to play and to experiment in a way that was all about participation and about something fun and engaging. If something's boring for children, they just walk away. . . . [E]ven though I was always really passionate about documentary, I felt like there was something missing from the developing interactive documentary industry; it was all very screen based. We would go to festivals, like IDFA [International Documentary Film Festival Amsterdam] and Sheffield [DocFest], and the interactive work was mostly on computers. The types of ideas were "choose your own adventure" and things that were quite perfunctory in their approach.[44]

With *Door into the Dark* (2015), Anagram's Abdalla and Rose created an interactive/immersive experience that shifted away from monitors and prompted physical actions from the audience. Participants enter alone and blindfolded. Holding on to a rope and guided by audio and touch, they are tasked with navigating a 6,000-square-foot labyrinthine space. While doing so, they hear the voices of three individuals who recount their real-life physical and emotional challenges and loss.[45] "We just don't think clicking stuff on a website will ever feel enough," Abdalla said. "Like you've got [to have] skin in the game. . . . Going to the cinema means that you are going to watch the film until the end, even if you feel tired, it is a commitment. Sometimes commitment is rewarding, because people eventually will want to give it, and they will get something out of it."[46]

A physical act by an audience member, even seemingly slight movements, can have quite powerful impacts on participants. Lynette Wallworth, an artist who works with a variety of immersive media, such as VR, installation, digital full dome, and interactive video, discussed the role of gesture in her work. Wallworth had a traditional art school background and was particularly drawn to installation because of her interest in audience engagement, and then in working with a variety of forms, she realized she wanted to make projects that were more "social," with the viewer directly involved. Wallworth's work is deeply embedded in the critical issues of our times—Indigenous rights, global warming, survivors of violence—and her ethical framework is founded on creating encounters of potential connection. In 2001, with the immersive installation *Hold*, which had been commissioned by the Australian Centre for Moving Image for its opening, Wallworth wanted to shift the ground on what we often define as "immersive." "I was interested in achieving a state of immersion in oneself, so, I would say participant focused, as opposed to passive participant, or passive viewer," she said. "I was trying to create the state of immersion in the viewer, as opposed to creating immersive space."[47]

In *Hold*, the viewer considers the delicate ecosystem in which they live and the close connections between humans and the environment. In a darkened space, *Hold* centers the participant in the installation, as it is their role to activate the experience. Three beams of light fall into a bowl, but the imagery does not appear in focus until the participant holds it correctly. The focused lights project microscopic imagery of astronomical and oceanic life. The act of holding the bowl connects the viewer to the environmental crisis, but it also initiates profound interpersonal connections. Wallworth explained:

> Everything that I wanted to say was contained in the materiality of the work. You could drop this thing; you could shatter it. It was precious, and it needed to be held in a particular manner. Gesturally, what happened was that people would wait in the room and then hand the bowl to a person coming after them. . . . [Y]ou had this beautiful moment that happened, where people would stay and would do this almost ceremonial passing of the bowl to the person who was coming next, which added a whole other layer of meaning for me in the work. That's the most important central consideration in terms of environment: How are we going to gift this to the people coming after us? What state is this environment going to be in? I then became interested in one-gestural interfaces. What are these universal gestures that connect us and how can I create an ecosystem for the work where the viewer is implicated by being a participant?[48]

Hold Vessel I and II, 2001 and 2007 Lynette Wallworth

Figure 7.8. *Hold Vessel I and II*. 2001 and 2007. Lynette Wallworth. Photo credit: Colin Davidson.

An interactive gesture might also be in the form of spoken language as Tamara Shogaolu's 2021 AR installation and multiplatform project *Un(re)solved* demonstrates. *Un(re)solved* is an ambitious and wide-ranging multiplatform project for the US PBS series *Frontline* and includes, in addition to the emergent media noted, a film, podcast, curriculum materials, events, and a web-based and AR installation.[49] The project looks at the US government legal efforts in 151 still-open cases of racially motivated murders as part of the Emmett Till Unsolved Civil Rights Crime Act. Shogaolu described the key action the audience must make to initiate the interactive dimensions of the installation:

> I designed it in a way where you have to say the name of the person to access their story. In testing it, I started collecting responses, and we did it in different environments in the US and other places. Usually, it was white men who felt uncomfortable with having to say the names three times; they felt annoyed by it. People of color said that they realized in saying the name so many times that it was a person and that they had an emotional reaction to it. We could have made it so it worked with saying the name one time,

but I realized that in the testing of it, there was a realization that was happening. Each time you said the name or the first time it can feel like a gimmick; the second time you really start listening to the name. The third time is when it really it hits you that this is a person that was murdered, and that's what was making particularly white men, in the testing sessions, uncomfortable with saying the name the third time because they realize this person was murdered because of their race, and it was probably by a white man. I decided to keep that level of interaction. I think that in the design process, you have to look at the variety of the audiences and what is the emotional impact of what's happening.[50]

As already highlighted in previous chapters, Nonny de la Peña has been a leading proponent of setting the audience at the center of the story and questioning how to "tell stories through the body as much as through the eyes and the ears."[51] De la Peña (2016) discussed her development of emergent tools from virtual worlds to VR, including a touchstone project *Gone Gitmo* (2007–12), coauthored with Peggy Weil.

Figure 7.9. From *Un(re)solved*. Courtesy of PBS *Frontline* ©2024 WGBH Educational Foundation.

Figure 7.10. From *Un(re)solved*. Courtesy of PBS *Frontline* ©2024 WGBH Educational Foundation.

De la Peña had previously made a documentary project, *Unconstitutional: The War on Our Civil Liberties* (2004), which examined the impact of the Patriot's Act on civil rights and included a segment on detainees held at Guantánamo Bay. Seeing a MacArthur digital grant opportunity for extending a film project into the digital world, de la Peña reached out to Weil with whom she had previously collaborated. With a 24-hour deadline, she told Weil she wanted to make a project on Gitmo that "put people in the sensation of being there."[52] Weil suggested they try Second Life as a platform, which at the time was unknown to de la Peña. Speaking of this pivotal moment in her career, de la Peña said:

> I still remember the feeling of walking through my Second Life patch of land, where other artists were working, to build my virtual Guantánamo Bay project. That piece ended up being pretty significant. I was able to take a lot of the research I'd done on my original *Gitmo* and put in video and photographs, material that the Defense Department had stopped releasing because it turned out to be so controversial—it became a library and repository.
>
> We also took control of your computer and all you saw [were] these lights filtering through, as if you were wearing a hood, and you heard this airplane sound. Everything was taken from what real detainees and soldiers described. We had classrooms from all over the world doing tours. I remember saying that this piece was effective because this place was off-limits and virtual but gave us a sense of what the real prison was like to walk around. I thought we can do this for all kinds of journalism. I began to coin the phrase "immersive journalism" and began to think about how we could use embodied experiences for telling new stories.[53]

While a research fellow at USC, de la Peña began working on the first VR documentary, *Hunger in Los Angeles*, which premiered in the Sundance New Frontier program in 2012 (see chapter 3). The project, which used animated figures and real audio taken from a food bank in downtown Los Angeles, was a powerful indictment of hunger and the health care system in the United States. De la Peña followed the New Frontier success with a series of documentary VR works, placing the viewer at the center of many contentious issues, such as criminal justice, abortion rights, climate change, homeless youth, and LGBTQ discrimination. With this content and with expansion to other immersive forms, such as AR, her focus is still very much on the body and on the diversity issues she has prioritized consistently in her work and workplace. As she commented on her new role as founding director of the Narrative and Emerging Media program at Arizona State University in 2022, her ambition is "to create what [she calls] an Institute for the Body, [which] privileges the body at the center of everything it does, and then, for example, thinking about haptics for inclusion."[54]

Empathy and Ethics

A discussion of emergent media, particularly with VR, has often been accompanied by heated debates about the role of empathy in these new forms, especially as employed in documentary. In no small part, a firestorm has circulated about empathy and VR since the oft-cited TED talk by Chris Milk in 2015, "How Virtual Reality Can Create the Ultimate Empathy Machine."[55] While many of our participants saw potential for powerful storytelling, others were skeptical about seeing this as an "empathy machine." Sadah Espii Proctor, sound designer, new media artist, and dramaturg, who directed the 2019 VR piece *Girl Icon* and was part of the creative team for the 2022 VR gallery *Ancestral Futurism: Unapologetically Melanated; A Virtual Exploration of the Mythic and da Truth!*, discussed the problem with the notion of the "empathy machine" in the documentary space. Espii wondered to what extent many of the works in the genre generated more than short-term outcomes. Was there a real call to action in many of these works or simply a transient emotional response?

> In my approach to work on the VR documentary [*Girl Icon*], looking at other documentaries has made me realize the lens that it's been told through [is] very much of a savior lens. . . . I have slowly grown to dislike empathy in VR because there is this idea that yes, you put on this headset—you see this experience and you can really feel how that person feels. You can laugh with them, and you can suffer with them, et cetera. Not so much as a woman but as a person of color, I almost find that extremely insulting. That despite

this virtual environment, you'll never fully understand what it's like to be me. It's not to say that my story isn't worth telling. You can imagine for those five minutes, however long that experience is, . . . what it's like. But what I need as a person of color is not so much for you to feel my pain—you should be able to hear my voice and stand with me in whatever issues that I'm going through and not necessarily have to indulge in my suffering. . . . Documentaries have had that problem, so it's not a new one, but because of VR that problem is now magnified. Now I'm no longer looking at a frame or snapshots of your life. Now I'm literally sitting inside of your shoes. This idea that you're allowed to indulge in my struggle is hard.[56]

Although she had worked on several projects in VR, Lina Srivastava (2022), reconsidered when and where to employ the format. Her preference was for more aesthetically oriented experiences, and she expressed serious doubt about using it in the social change context except with deliberation and care:

VR—unless it's for pure art—leaves me cold in a lot of ways. I think it was tainted. . . . [T]he whole notion of VR as an empathy machine makes no sense to me. . . . It's so heavily mediated and it's so removed, and you're not actually being placed in somebody's shoes. The voyeurism of it is enhanced . . . I remember talking to somebody about the climate change implications. If you can do a 360[-degree] or a VR or something that enhances the way you experience climate devastation without having to fly there, without creating, increasing your carbon footprint, there's something to be said about that. . . . But I remember someone asked me if I would work on a project where they would follow Syrian refugees who are trying to get into Hungary, and they would do a VR thing about that journey. It's such poverty porn, it's just awful.[57]

Lynette Wallworth, who often works with underrepresented communities and focuses on environmental issues, created the VR project *Collisions* (2015) in response to an invitation by the Indigenous Australian Martu tribe to film the story of the tribe's activist-artist elder, Nyarri

Nyarri Morgan, who had witnessed the 1950s atomic testing conducted by the British government in the South Australian desert—his first contact with Western culture. Wallworth discussed the limits and possibilities of empathy in our interview:

> There was this intense discussion around empathy and VR, and people having this emotional responsiveness because of the sense of presence. I still think just feeling something is worth very little. Feeling something that's attuned to someone and comprehending their state, and actually wanting to improve their state, that level of compassion, is more powerful for me than empathy.
>
> It annoyed me that suddenly empathy became a commodity. Suddenly, empathy is this thing of value, when there are largely women who've been working with this technology in this way for decades and for us, the fact that people had intense empathetic responses to work meant little. It was a given until male technologists started to talk about empathy, empathy was not a valuable commodity.
>
> What I think is there are some of us, both male and female, who bring the quality of empathy not into the experience of the work, but into the making of the work. . . . [W]hat I'm interested in is how that heightened sensitivity might be crucially important in bringing virtual reality into places where someone wants to share a story. My interest is in knowing how this community wants to be seen, what this community wants to share. In order to know that I have to be able to have empathy for where they are, I have to be able to be tuned in enough to them that I am not standing outside to such an extent that I am exploitative of the capacity that virtual reality gives me to basically take in a whole world in 360 [degrees].[58]

For Wallworth, a key objective in her work, as noted earlier, was illuminating connections, making links across stories, experiences, and ecosystems. She discussed an upcoming project, *Awavena* (2018), which was completed after our conversation and initiated by an invitation and in collaboration by the Yawanawá people in the Amazon. *Awavena* shares the story of Hushahu, the first woman shaman of the Yawanawá and the bridge her work provided with the past and insights of Tata, the elder shaman, to the future of the community. The project was initiated at the invitation and in collaboration with the Yawanawá people. Wallworth discussed the way emergent media could facilitate points of intersection:

> What's exciting me is merged reality and the possibility for a VR/AR work, because I think one of the challenges with virtual reality is how you bring people back from an experience where they feel themselves to be somewhere else.
>
> The stories I'm interested in telling, the communities I'm interested in supporting with my storytelling are people who often live in what we would call remote places, depending on where we are in the world. But those people have stories they want to share, have communications that they want to give, that virtual reality is extremely useful for them, but I don't want to intensify a sense of distance or difference, so I'm looking, as I always am, for connection, for where we can find the threads that join us and that help us feel connected to one another.
>
> Augmented reality, because it layers onto my reality or yours, then seems to me the next natural, powerful progression for me to use for such storytelling. So I can go to the Amazon, where I'm going next, but through augmented reality find a means of bringing back into our reality a touchstone that means that that connection is in some way placed back into this reality, and that's what I will explore.[59]

Carla Borrás (2022), senior producer of special projects and innovation on PBS's *Frontline* is an individual whose expansive oversight gives her an informed and acute sense of trends and developments in the emergent media field. She recounted attending the 2021 South by Southwest Conference and Festival and commented on the prevalent trends, such as the development of AR, which she noted significantly increased audience access to projects via the employment of mobile devices. She also gave her thoughts on the XR project *Breonna's Garden*, which includes both AR and VR experiences. *Breonna's Garden* was a project developed by Lady Pheønix, in collaboration with Breonna Taylor's family and many artists, as a space of healing.[60] Taylor was shot and killed by the

Figure 7.11. *Awavena*. 2018. Lynette Wallworth. Production shot. Photo credit: Greg Downing.

police during their illegal entry into her Louisville, Kentucky, home in March 2020. Borrás stated: "The AR experience is much more moving and magical, because it brings my own reality into the experience. It can be programmed for any park that you're in. It really melds where I am in my real-world situation, with the storytelling, and it's done in a simply beautiful way—you're exploring your real-world space, to find the beauty of Breonna's story and these flowers that emerge and build upon the layers of the space you're already in."[61]

Borrás's comments are mindful of the complicated decisions of where and how to use emergent media. Janet Murray, in her provocative 2016 "Not a Film, Not an Empathy Machine" essay, set out some design guidelines for creating work in VR and warned against misguided thinking of imagining VR as an "empathy machine." As Murray notes, VR is a medium still in development, and it is useful to remember "de la Peña's first rule of VR design: Begin by thinking of your body in the space. The focus of VR design is not the camera frame but the embodied visitor."[62] For Murray, all the images and sounds must be part of the diegetic space, and edits must be consistent with conscious actions of the participant, understanding a "sense of agency is the single most important design value in any digital artifact."[63] She pointed to the progression in de la Peña's projects from *Hunger in Los Angeles* (2012) to *Across the Line* (2016), where the participant shifts from observer to enactor, as an example. In *Across the Line*, the enactor must navigate a hostile crowd of anti-abortion protesters to enter a women's health care clinic as a patient. As Murray noted, neither a headset nor imagery by themselves generate empathy, and she advised that rather than "overhyping the inherent empathy-value of VR documentary, we should look for the specific moments that point to the genuine promise of the medium in creating compassionate understanding and build on those."[64]

The heated conversation around empathy can in many ways be seen as part of the larger discourse around the hype cycles surrounding tech more generally, which are more about achieving market share than generating social good. As Lynette Wallworth noted above, it is the reduction of a vital issue to a commodity—the notion that we can extract the concern, exploit it for a quick and intense emotional response, and then turn a profit—that is so distasteful. This process of objection, the extraction, is one that strips the person, environment, or event, from its *context*. The alternative language suggested by Murray's "understanding" or Wallworth's "compassion" does not presume that spending five minutes in a headset might be equivalent to an individual's lifetime of cultural marginalization or of a specific traumatic experience; rather, it assumes a desire to understand a specific historical/cultural context and to develop new insights.

Empathy is but one part of a larger ethical query we need to undertake with regard to technology and, specifically, emergent media. As de la Peña commented, immersive storytelling is in many ways in its early stages, particularly with the developments of Lidar (light detection and ranging) technology for mobile devices. She pointed to the ethical questions raised by this expansion of technology:

> The fact you just walk around through your phone and capture your world volumetrically and share it, how is it going to get shared? What kind of stories? Those are all the things that we need to be thinking about. Also, the ethics: Are you going to let people step over the bodies? How are we going to produce this content in a way that tells the truth without traumatizing people? I think those are the ethical issues. Not whether it's this objective experience which is the sort of thing that a lot of these organizations could worry about. . . . Martha Gellhorn, who was a World War II reporter, called it "the view from the ground." So this idea that

we're going to give the view from the ground, in this immersive way, it's just starting.[65]

What is needed is a clearer vision of the development and implementation of technology for harm and health; like empathy, we need a better context, a more informed history and critical insight. Nedra Kline Weinreich works with public agencies, nonprofits, and other organizations to address various public health issues using social marketing and behavioral design. Working with the Entertainment Industries Council and the California Mental Health Services Authority, she created "Social Media Guidelines for Mental Health Promotion and Suicide Prevention," a first of its kind. Weinreich stressed the need to strike a balance with social media and an acknowledgment that "the tools themselves are neutral."[66] Social media, she said,

> can bring people together for positive things, give people social support, help people collaborate towards a goal. That means that we shouldn't just throw it all out and dismiss it all, which I think a lot of people are in the process of wanting to do at this point. It involves a shift in how people think about the tools and especially in schools, I think media literacy is so important, now more than ever.
>
> I think that social media literacy and internet literacy, in terms of how do you know if something is true or not, when [is it] appropriate to pass along information, those kinds of questions, are a matter of education. We need to change that idea that a lot of people have, which is that if it's on the internet, it must be true.[67]

For Heidi Boisvert, interdisciplinary artist and creative technologist whose academic research investigates the interactions of cognition, the body, and technology, the ethical challenges with emergent media are complex. She argues that much of contemporary media works against critical insight. She returns us to the body and the importance of movement and physical activity as a critical factor in countering the effects of media. Boisvert sounds a warning that tech without critical thinking does more than destructively, or falsely, "mimic" a sense of empathy but may in fact harm our ability to feel connections and compassion. In our interview with her, she noted the change in her own approach to working with technology particularly in the context of using media for social change:

> I was making social change projects using emerging technology and pop culture to advance these different issue areas and the idea was to galvanize audiences to be moved to act in some way and by doing that, we want to access empathy. I started to realize that the very tools themselves that we've become dependent upon to tell our stories were actually eroding the empathy that we were trying to cultivate. I went to RPI [Rensselaer Polytechnic Institute] and worked with the cognitive neuroscience department to understand how the brain is affected by various types of technologies, as well as media. . . .
>
> Before we could create change in the world; we actually had to restore our capacity for critical feeling. This led me down the road to try to understand how cognitive and affective cues, within games or transmedia storytelling, how do all of these things affect certain brain regions. . . . I started looking at what I call "intelligent technology"—internet wearables, mobile devices, immersive displays, whether it's VR or AR, actually affects certain regions of the brain called the amygdala and the hippocampus, which are responsible for emotion activation and regulation. What's happening is that the gray area in our brain is actually being eroded by these technologies. . . . [I]ntelligent technology is essentially a slow form of violence that's rescripting our nervous system. I'm thinking about that both now, but also epigenetically, that it's actually changing our nervous system. That movement, to some extent, can become an antidote to that human connection, which is the one thing we're losing.[68]

While the empathy debate—in its current form as one conflating a transient headset experience with complex cultural identity—had exhausted much interest from most of our interviewees, there was clearly a sense that technology still could be used positively for social impact—to tell stories marginalized from history, to build community and organize activism, to raise awareness and promote cross-cultural connections and understanding, and to inspire critical thinking. To achieve these goals, it was clear from our conversations that methodologies, project design, and the development of the tools themselves need more context and critical insight, from constituencies ranging from technologists/developers, creators/practitioners, collaborators/co-creators, and audience. Of course, none of these objectives is possible without improved access. Access, a recurring theme in our conversations, is a complicated issue with many moving parts in its own right. We began to explore accessibility in chapter 4, in relation to technology platforms, hardware and interfaces, and will extend these discussions in our next section.

Access

With the rapid expansion and availability of emergent media, how we tell stories is key, but ethical questions extend to asking who gets access to these stories, who gets access to write them, and who has the skills and funding to create the works. Many of our participants, when asked about impediments to more equitable media, immediately pointed to issues of access. For example, micha cárdenas expressed the real economic challenges that counter the notion of easy availability of emergent tech:

> I've tried to make access not an afterthought, but a central design parameter. With *Local Autonomy Networks*, I made these wearable electronics pieces and then showed them to trans people of color who I was hoping might use them. They said, "This is too expensive. If I had a hundred dollars, I'd buy a smartphone, I would not buy this weird hoodie." . . . [S]o we thought about this as a prototype and changed direction, how could we make it free or inexpensive. . . . [A]fter *Local Autonomy Networks*, I made a web-based game, which I felt was more accessible. It had a different kind of accessibility because people could see it online for free and thousands of people have seen it instead of just the hundred people at a live gallery performance or museum performance. In some ways, the web-based game is more accessible to more people—in some ways, it's less because not everybody has internet and not everybody has a computer.[69]

Lauren Lee McCarthy gave a detailed response to the question of access, especially given the variety of challenges facing creatives. McCarthy began with the complexities of access in the unique context of art and technology through various academic and corporate institutions. She pointed to the opportunities but also many facets of privilege that shape access:

> An institution . . . limits [access] to the people that gain admittance, which we know is not an equitable system. It's based on a lot of factors around your background and identity. Then just to use the technology costs a lot of money, to own the tools or to engage with them or to buy the licenses. Similarly with the way the work is funded, when the funding comes from tech companies, there can be certain limits on how much you are able to question the technology if it's being funded by Google or Microsoft. So I think those are problems unique to art and technology. And then you look at the space of people working in it and it's very white, it's very male dominated. . . . [Y]ou're entering a space that's already set up to be less inclusive towards you. I also think a lot about disability and the further we get into interactive systems, the more assumptions it's making about the abilities and the disabilities of the people using them. Also thinking geographically—and I saw that a lot with p5.js [client-side graphics and interactive experiences library]—so many of the tools and communities are English based, US centered.[70]

One artist, who wished to remain anonymous, came at the complicated issue of access with respect to the ongoing development of the tools themselves, particularly with VR and AR:

> Part of it is accessibility with being able to get new tools, but also having the ability to catch up on all the little bugs and nuances that a program has. Then the amount of time that it takes to learn how to use a program. If you're not in school, you have to do it by yourself. That's a lot of time, especially if it's not paid. Even for things like the Unreal Fellowship, if you're not within

the industry and you're still looking to learn, there are videos and things that someone can download and be able to use, but there's not really compensation for that, unless it's a job. There's still a lot of barriers.[71]

The inequities of access is evident in many contexts, including funding, educational background, gender/racial/ethnic/disability bias, resources of tools and training, and user experience. Many of our participants integrated efforts to address the inequities of access, whether by collaborative and participatory media practices (e.g., Wallworth, Srivastava, cárdenas, Dinkins, Daniel, ross, Lerner and Court), training and hiring (de la Peña), or teaching and mentoring (most of our interviewees expressed how they have played this role). Many of our participants also have been involved in some type of community building, whether formally or informally, as part of a project or as a larger commitment to this question of access (i.e., access to tools or knowledge or funding). Both Mimi Ọnụọha, cofounder of a People's Guide to Tech, and Lauren Lee McCarthy, who established the p5.js open-source coding group, are representative of the many artists committed to building inclusive communities around learning specific tech skills.

Self-Reflexive, Critical Making

For many of those we interviewed, there was a clear sense of teaching the audience to interrogate technology or the systems in which the technology is embedded as part of their work. As noted earlier, several artists were interested in stepping back from some aspects of emergent media, some toward more live and analog elements, signaling an effort to demystify technology and to provide a more critical turn. Lauren Lee McCarthy described the goals of her own work: "I'm using technology, but it's really not about the tech—it's trying to open up these systems that we're operating within both the technical ones that we're building, but also the social ones that govern our behavior. Then how do you create glitches or breaks in that, or performative frames where we can do a different performance to the one we do in our everyday lives, to put a lens on that and see what are these implicit systems that are shaping us and do we want to shift them?"[72]

Carmen Aguilar y Wedge and Ece Tankal both spoke to a concern about the speed and fetishization of technology in contemporary culture. As Aguilar y Wedge commented:

> We're living in this super temporal 30-second Instagram selfie focused life. . . . That really feels like it degrades the audience and the artist because things need to be bite sized. Our audience has become used to being told what they're seeing, and we want to get to a place where we're encouraging audiences to think for themselves and ask, why am I feeling this way? . . . How is this experience specific to my experience? How does that connect me to the other people in the audience? That's where I'm curious about exploring—using theater and light—and having a collective experience where we put our phones away for an hour and pay attention to this story and have that enrich our lives somehow, rather than this very quick scrolling through . . . and having those pieces that people work for months on just be consumed rather than appreciated.[73]

Ece Tankal also addressed our need for a more critical approach to technology and even a move away from emergent tech:

> What are the promises of the tech and what they're not delivering? That's what I'm interested in, because I think for the past four or five years we've been promised a lot of things with emergent tech and then they've all always been falling short. Look at the metaverse now—all of these things are trying to solve a problem, but they don't even know what the problem is. I'm interested in trying to figure out what makes people even start thinking about these technologies. Is it the science fiction that was written 60 years ago by a white man? Is it the need to actually switch our realities . . . sever our realities and then distract us from what is actually going on? . . . So, I think right now, I am trying to gear our practice into more analog things.[74]

Throughout her career, Hershman Leeson's artistic practice can also be seen as having a pedagogical energy, interrogating the tools' mechanics, and asking us to consider technology's impact on humanity, the self, and identity. Her latest works, *Shadow Stalker* (2018–21) and *Logic Paralyzes the Heart* (2021), are about the effects of AI, digital surveillance, data mining, and other forms of algorithmic injustice inflicted on us.[75] The two works are film installations, and Hershman Leeson is imagining a third future work to show alongside them: "I would like to make it a trilogy about a technology that's trained to replicate all of your personality and have them exist. These technologies, email, the language you use—they know your choices when you Google, and basically, it's you, except it's a program that's designed to be your false identity. I think these are the issues. I want to do things that are the issues of our time."[76] She went on to address algorithmic violence specifically in response to a question regarding the current state of technology and her long record as feminist artist of examining issues of identity and gender:

> I think that they are more subtle and more lethal. Things happen
> to us without our knowing it. With surveillance cameras, we'd see

Figure 7.12. *Shadow Stalker.* 2019. Lynn Hershman Leeson. Installation view, *Manual Override*, 2019–2020, The Shed, New York. Photo credit: Gregory Carideo. Courtesy The Shed.

Figure 7.13. *Logic Paralyzes the Heart.* 2021. Lynn Hershman Leeson. Still. Featuring Joan Chen dressed by Nina Hollein, digital video, 13 minutes 53 seconds. Collections: Carl & Marilynn Thoma Foundation; Nevada Museum of Art, Reno. Courtesy of the artist; Altman Siegel, San Francisco; and Bridget Donahue, New York.

cameras and we'd know when things are being stolen, but now there are these invisible sources that are affecting our profiles and limiting our freedom. We don't know who's behind them. We don't even know when it's happening. You can get turned down for a loan and not know why, and it's because of a false report somewhere that somebody's filed. That's a difficult problem because it's not as obvious and you can't track it as freely.[77]

Carla Borrás returned us to the importance of the body and gesture, especially as a teaching device in the documentary genre. She discussed an insight from *Greenland Melting*, a 360-degree VR film made in collaboration with PBS's *Frontline* and *Nova* along with Nonny de la Peña and Emblematic Group. Originally, the plan for the film was to have participants use controllers to take them below the surface of the water to see the effects of climate change on Greenland's glaciers and surrounding environment. During the testing, however, the controllers did not work as planned and the participants had to move physically to make the film transition to the underwater space. They realized the transition through the physical move had more impact for the participant. "You remember the information that's given to you much better," Borrás said,

> because you had to do a physical gesture that's going to help remind you, sit up, pay attention. We then said, "Forget it. Let's not fix it. Let's actually have that be what you have to do." And the narrator tells you to go below the water surface to see what's happening. . . . [I]t's this idea that learning through doing can be very powerful. That's not a new concept. . . . [I]t was an awakening moment for VR and journalism, which is, in theory, trying to educate and inform that if you can have a physical experience of doing, that's going to be stronger for making the information stickier. To be thinking about that, that every action you're asking someone to take has to be intentional. That's when you'll have the most powerful reaction for your viewers.[78]

Hope, Healing, and Future Opportunities

The issue of hope was eloquently addressed throughout many of our interviews, whether during the tense run up to the US 2016 election, its crisis ridden aftermath, or in the somewhat "post" COVID-19 pandemic period in 2022. Kamal Sinclair (2022), author of *Making a New Reality* series,[79] a project that reset the conversation on equity and inclusion in emergent media, provided her thoughts on hope, considering some of her recent work:

> We did over a hundred futurist writers' zones over the last year, and we did it with different communities that don't necessarily intersect. The things that kept coming up, and it's not a surprise because of the pandemic, but wellness, nature, rejection of the future context of robots and everything metal, beautiful visions of where we can be, more human and more connected to the planet, but still having the almost invisible technology benefits of, but not having it be so in our face and driving our mental world. And that to me is my hope that in five years we actually find a mental health, physical health, and social health balance with these technologies so that they are really designed for our well-being. They're very much designed for addiction right now. . . . It's about wanting

more balance in our work and our life and our relationship to technology. There were a lot of wonderful visions that came through that process, and I thought, "I can see that. Can we amplify this vision?" So people don't see it as just an either/or binary, but they can actually see a well-balanced integration. That would be ideal for me.[80]

Artist Lily Baldwin also addressed the need to move past the either/or binary with emergent media and tech and its relation to the body/human:

I'm not interested in disconnecting the viewer from their body. I'm interested in using technology to humanize their bodies. We live in a technical world. It can shut us off from our bodies . . . major digital disconnect. It doesn't mean that to find my body I need to go away from that, because then it means there's a divisiveness here. A division that I would like there to not be. I'd like to not disembody with the technology. . . . What are stories that enhance humanity and what the viewer's seeing, which is why I like to work with older protagonists and Marni Wood was 86 at the time, the last dancing member of the Martha Graham company and just full-on in VR [*Through You*]. Let's have a body that is close and older and articulate. And then, what does it feel like to be seen by that body, in this space?[81]

Jessica Clark, founder of Dot Connector Studio, shaped the discussion of technology and emergent media using the language of opportunity, one grounded in an explicitly futurist outlook. (Several of the artists interviewed were working with a futurist aesthetic, and we will follow up on the theme of futurism in the closing remarks of our final chapter.) Clark expressed her ideas of futurist work as a series of opportunities:

I conceptualize it as a field of experimentation. If you stipulate that technology is going to continue to change, and there's nothing that we can do about it, we're not going to stop time, and you welcome it as an opportunity to try to intervene at each level, each new platform, each new invention. To both use the new affordances of that technology to tell stories and then involve people in a different way. And to ensure that the people who are making that actual technology itself are diverse, then you have a chance of shifting it away from the capitalist imperative or the militaristic or pornography imperative and having it being able to discover other ways that we can relate to each other and learn things and make things happen in a political arena. If you're ready for change, and you're not attached to any particular technology, and you're able to find other people who want to play with you on whatever new ground is evolving, then it's more fun, and it's less psychologically damaging than constantly feeling as though everything that you've built is being dissolved by whatever the next new thing is.[82]

The comments from Sinclair, Baldwin, and Clark point to ways in which we might break the mold that seems to bring repetitive cycles of hype and dread to each new iteration of technology. AI and ChatGPT are recent examples where we might take on Sinclair, Baldwin, and Clark's suggestions to move past the binary of "abolish or binge" and instead experiment with the technology's possibilities with a critical awareness on how these new tools are defined and who gets to contribute to their definition, framing and application.

Conclusion

It was striking in our conversations to hear the clarity with which participants addressed the intersections of aesthetics and ethics in the emergent media ecosystem. Many of our participants' works focus on issues of social change, although the content and strategies varied widely. The conversations on social change often centered on building a sharper understanding, or literacy, of the inner workings of media and storytelling and the structures within which they operate. A broader effort to educate and empower audiences and build community could be seen by shifting from a more passive consumer model to one of more active, creative producers. The larger cultural ethos that can be drawn from that shift would be toward, in short, a participatory design for a more equitable, sustainable, and healthy future. In this vision, technology is neither the savior nor the demon, but simply another tool in the box, which our participants strive to understand how best to employ.

Our participants thought expansively about how to use this tool and whether indeed to use it at all. There was a feeling that—particularly among those interviewed post–COVID-19 pandemic, where the world of Zoom replaced much of our public and private space and large swathes of our communication—we needed a deep reassessment of where and how much we rely on technology. But a healthy skepticism toward technology by our participants—both pre- and post-COVID—sent out warnings on the harmful impacts of media, and our interviews saw concerted efforts in their work to uncover and address these effects despite the dubious cover of "empathy," hailed especially with VR. Instead of the hype of VR, we saw participants thinking through techniques regardless of the technologies employed—or absent—that would enhance, as Lynette Wallworth thoughtfully noted, our "connections" and draw attention to our responsibility for care for one another and the earth's resources.

In many ways, the work and the approach in this chapter inverts our opening dilemma, where digital art / emergent media faced a lack of recognition due to its failure as an identifiable "art" object or, more importantly, as an object for sale. Our participants design work not for profit but to tell us something about ourselves and our relationships to material culture, to the planet, and to one another. These may be "poor," ephemeral objects as commodities, but they offer us rich possibilities for our future. In chapter 8, we will hear more about the history lessons that our participants shared with us and what we might imagine going forward.

8
Conclusion

Having brought together the rich accounts and sharp insights into the lived experiences of our 140 research participants, we have been able to identify numerous strands of compelling commonality. Although our participants live and work in different parts of the world, and many of them are unknown to one another, the ideas, issues, and experiences that they have shared are incredibly similar and, in some cases, almost identical. Through a focus on the emergent spaces of transmedia, multiplatform, VR, AR, and immersive, our research has shown that these mixed spaces—blending "old" and "new" media industries and practices—have inherited problems of the past, including systemic exclusion and profound funding inequities. The COVID-19 pandemic and the uncertainty of arts exhibitions and funding produced both a reimagination and reconsideration of the possibilities and limits of our digital lives and virtual worlds. Our chapters trace an arc of history and a future that challenges the boundaries of what the intersections of gender, media, and technology might mean for human and earth-centered design, aesthetic and archival forms, and structural inequality.

We frequently heard from groundbreaking artists, technologists, curators, programmers, and futurists that the challenges and the opportunities presented by moments of innovation and technological transition are rarely about the tools themselves but rather how the ideas put in play through technology can teach us something about ourselves, our everyday lives, and our communities. Time and again, our participants' innovations in technology, media, and storytelling are driven by methods and outcomes incompatible with economic models that depend on speed, disposability, and profitability. We see our participants working at the margins in uneven and inequitable circumstances, with less pay and without the status to break these rigid models in the media industry and technology. By synthesizing these accounts and foregrounding the contribution of our participants, this volume has offered a sense of

the possibilities that could be realized through alternative power structures, equitable economic imperatives, and inclusive practices. Our book
can be considered an extended experimentation lab or a kind of worldbuilding on past, present, and future possibilities, contributing to the
histories that will be written, the communities that can be built, and
the future that can be imagined.

On our journey through this mixed reality of innovation, struggle,
and resilience, our lens in chapter 3 was focused on the efforts of our
participants to create, organize, value, and document a range of artistic and storytelling practices. Taking on roles on the inside of large
organizations that often obscure or minimize their contributions left
our participants in many ways working in the margins and bumping
up against the so-called glass ceiling—although there is evidence that
changes are occurring in response to larger cultural shifts and the tenacity of those who, despite adversity, continue to excel at their practice
while educating their colleagues. We also saw participants who decided
to strike more entrepreneurial or independent paths, guided by visions
that did not fit into established models of the art world, journalism, and
documentary or the film, television, and the extended media industrial
complex. Some participants inverted the foundation of these forms by
placing community building and participatory models of engagement at
the very center of their practice, rather than as a marketing or audience-
building strategy. Chapter 3 was shaped by those curators, archivists,
and programmers whose commitment to opening up the possibility
of media histories—from discovery, development, amplification, and
preservation—has been critical to making a new—*and equitable*—reality.

We aimed to work in concert with their efforts through the inclusion of detailed profiles of four of our participants—to highlight, contex-
tualize, and historicize their important contributions to the evolution of
immersive virtual world creation. Our participants, we learned in chapter 4, were at the vanguard of platform experimentation. As platforms
evolved and became commercialized, our participants recounted how
access to them became increasingly exclusionary and how the organizations for which the platforms were designed often failed to accommodate a diverse range of participants with varying types of accessibility
needs. Once technologies reached the commercialization stage, we
could see how our participants moved deftly and nimbly to the next,

adapting and developing their approaches and practices but still carrying forth the principles, values, and working practices that they have developed through engagement with the former technology. The stage at which technologies are open, accessible, and uncommercialized—when there is ample opportunity for experimentation and innovation in storytelling, media making, and artistic creation—is what attracted many of our participants to their fields. If we revisit the model that we envisioned in chapter 1, we can see how both the transmedia and VR domains could be mapped onto the continuum of the cycles of innovation (see figure 8.1).

Our research showed that many of our participants have been working and thriving within spaces of organizational and logistical complexity, such as the characteristically multidisciplinary fields of transmedia and multiplatform. These are fields where projects require careful and close management across a diversity of people, specializations, skill sets, and departments. One way to account for their notable and visible participation was the sectorial need for project managers and producers; whereas in previous cycles, it was the feminized labor of machine work and secretarial work that was deemed essential, here we see *organizational* labor being foregrounded, and as we identified in chapter 1, historically more women have been present in production management roles in the film and TV sectors. As transmedia formats evolved within mainstream contexts, its growing popularization and dominant association with huge Hollywood cinematic franchises has meant that it came to be increasingly associated with male figureheads, both in popular media discourse and in academic research. However, what we revealed was that our participants were far more active and visible in leadership and influence within documentary spheres of practice— experimenting and innovating in documentary forms, significantly influencing process, practice, and aesthetics (as we saw come to bear in chapter 7). Likewise, in our observations of the commercialization of the VR sector, the demands of the sector involved the bringing together of disparate domains of expertise, again requiring individuals who were able to manage a diverse range of people and complex projects. We can see that as the headsets and hardware became commercialized and fetishized, the actual production of content became a secondary concern of dominant mainstream media discourse and became sidelined in the history that is currently being recorded (with the exception of

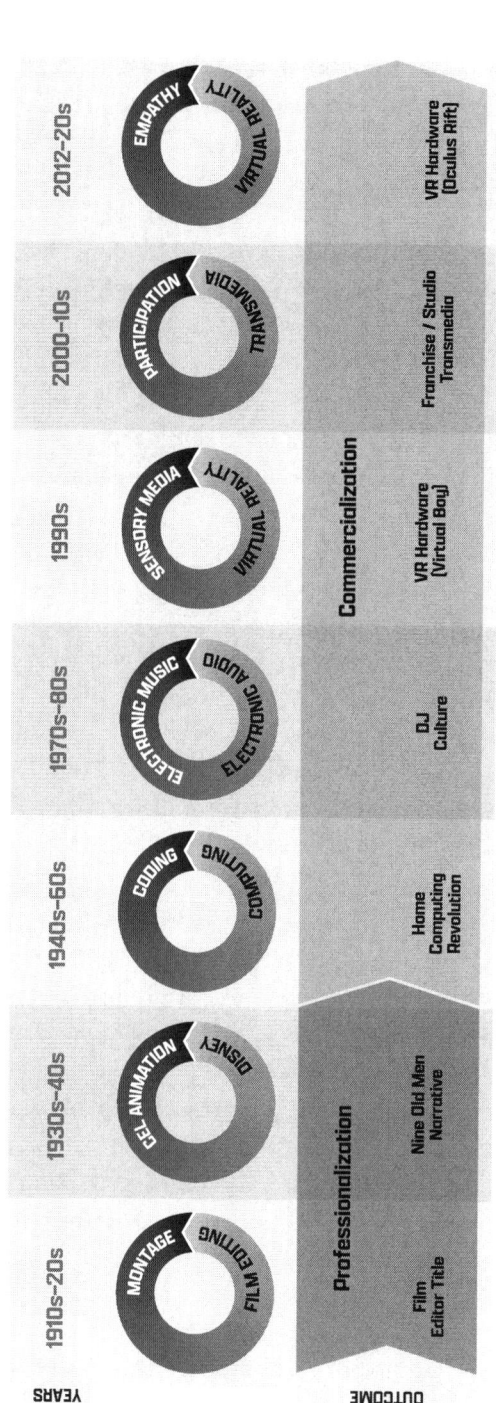

Figure 8.1. Cycles of innovation model (1910–2020), including transmedia and VR. The model shows multiple moments of creative experimentation with different technological mediums that are characterized by gender diverse participation before they become commercialized or professionalized. Graphic design by Bullet Creative.

computer gaming, a sector of the creative industries that has seen the most significant uptake of VR hardware technologies). However, it is those very spaces of artistic and documentary content creation and aesthetic innovation that have informed the requirements of the hardware through challenging the limitations of existing systems.

Places of creative technical production, as we explored in chapter 5, have historically been male-dominated spaces where our participants found themselves working among very few women or sometimes as the only woman. The early discoveries made by women within these spaces have generally been ignored, often overwritten by a more dominant "institutional" narrative. Within tech-focused work cultures, our participants' experiences ranged from everyday microaggressions and exclusions to more extreme forms of harassment. Despite these challenges, they have continued to propose and develop numerous strategies to circumvent these barriers, including establishing their own working cultures, businesses, support groups, and gender-diverse places and events.

Funding, as detailed in chapter 6, continues to be the main barrier for women to access, progress, and secure investment, and many of our participants who de-prioritized the commercialization of their work saw no chance of receiving funding and therefore stopped pursuing it. A 2019 report revealed that for every pound of venture capital investment in the United Kingdom, all-female founder teams received less than 1 pence, whereas all-male founder teams got 89 pence and mixed-gender teams got 10 pence, and by 2022 there was very little improvement.[1] Although these figures specifically relate to venture capital funding, we see this has been perpetuated across all types of funding and is a major area in need of systemic change. We revealed how workflows and workloads are characteristically heavier and more intense across a range of mixed-reality sectorial contexts: spanning the independent, artistic, and commercial—sometimes as a result of our participants occupying multiple roles and subjectivities. Numerous feminist working practices surfaced that responded to these challenges in order to circumvent, avoid, and overcome barriers to access. These strategies included mentorship and allyship as incredibly important support mechanisms for the advancement and success of our participants working in these spaces of innovation. They also included both self-support (through self-teaching activities) and support of one another, as well as a drive to proactively share best practices through volunteered labor.

Artists and practitioners have faced numerous challenges in emergent media, as discussed in chapter 7, including navigating the ambiguous terrain these new forms inhabit and the gatekeepers from established fields. The blur between the domains of "art" and "media" and between "high" and "low" culture complicates where work resides and who evaluates it, and that digital work is ephemeral, often with no tangible object attached to it, and not obviously monetized, presents additional challenges. In response, our participants have created new genres, communities, and values that often centralize a critique of the tools and the larger systems in which industry, culture, and identity are shaped. Their work not only challenged gender norms but also questioned who tells and frames the stories, bringing to light the changing relationships between maker and participant. As these forms shift, we also see the outcomes and impacts of the works shifting, from profit to sustainability, connection, and healing. The works present us with speculative forms of expression, generative models of knowledge, and counterhistories for us to consider.

Our interviews brought to light some established patterns, entrenched behaviors, and systemic and institutional discrimination—grinding day-to-day experiences that have become an *expected* and, in some cases, *accepted* way of working for women in tech spaces. These insights confirm the worst of what we already knew. On the one hand, it is incredibly dispiriting and discouraging to hear the same experiences over and over again and to feel that nothing has actually changed despite the decades of effort, campaigning, and advocating for reform. On the other hand, drawing attention to these persistent experiences across a broad spectrum of contexts, by documenting and presenting them alongside the many successes, discoveries, and innovations that our participants have been responsible for, reveals the commonality of hardship that elevates these successes to a more profound level of achievement. Women forging their way in spaces of technology will always inevitably be a two-sided story, one that can be told and fully understood only through the foregrounding and amplification of their successes and achievements while also laying bare the barriers, resistances, and challenges they have faced along the way. As scholars continue in the project of uncovering and revealing the many missing and misrepresented histories across a multitude of domains, we hope to have underscored why this important work matters. Histories *can* be revisited, rewritten, corrected, *and* captured at the time of their making by placing them in the hands of those who can carry them forward.

The Emergent Media Landscape

Having concluded our interviews in July 2022, two years after the onset of the COVID-19 pandemic, we can now look back and appreciate how the global health crisis accelerated the development of the virtual and immersive technology industries. For example, social VR became an increasingly popular way for people to socialize and build communities in the lockdown era, and in response to the need for social distancing, virtual production technologies were rapidly adapted and adopted for use in film and television production settings.

In the context of this process of necessity-driven rapid innovation, application, and further commercial exploitation, there is evidence of many immersive technologies already becoming obsolete. This was most apparent as we compiled our glossary, which demonstrated just how many VR platforms had been re-versioned or entirely withdrawn from use. These included the discontinuation of headset production of the Oculus Go, the Oculus Rift, and the Samsung Gear—along with the withdrawal of all Samsung's support for their XR services, applications, and access to their video content. This era of rapid obsolescence was captured by Vicki Lau's comment on the much-hyped AR start-up Magic Leap: "What happened to Magic Leap? That's actually a legitimate Google search entry now."[2]

This rapid obsolescence also affected our ability to access projects published on platforms that are no longer supported. There is a real loss to media history when key works of emergent media are no longer accessible and have no archival home. It is especially troubling when these losses are sustained by artists and communities who are already operating at the margins of media industry and history due to race, gender, and class inequities. By way of three widely acclaimed examples, Sharon Daniel's *Public Secrets* (2007), a cross-platform work that shared stories of women incarcerated in the California prison system; Lynette Wallworth's VR documentary *Collisions* (2016), which examined atomic testing by the West on Martu land; and Nonny de la Peña's VR project *Out of Exile: Daniel's Story* (2017), dealing with issues of LGBTQ homeless youth, are not accessible for viewing at the time of our writing.

The ephemeral nature of digital media has had a more detrimental impact on the women / gender nonbinary / genderqueer and under-represented communities whose works historically have been outside those projects which are more mainstream, profit driven, or critically accepted and recognized. Rapid obsolescence has arguably been the case with any nascent content-delivery mechanism throughout history (as documented by the many infamous "format wars") and has been the inspiration of many historiographical media archaeological projects in screen studies. For example, since the invention of the stereoscope by Charles Wheatstone in 1838, stereoscopic home-viewing devices have rapidly evolved, only to be cast by the wayside and consigned to the annals of "novelty" optical technologies, and now VR headsets may well take their place among them. However, what is unique at this particular moment is not just an accelerated obsolescence of digital content—the access to which is lost as companies, vying for market share, withdraw support for a platform—but also the exceptional proprietary nature of the hardware, whereby content access is limited to specific formats, with significant and cascading cultural impact. We might argue that we have seen a similar pattern throughout cinema and media history, but the pace and implications for access and shared community and culture, particularly for groups historically underrepresented, are devastating. We see a parallel phenomenon in media streaming platforms, whereby audiences are fragmented across a multiplicity of streaming services and channels—never has the fragmentation of content been so acute. The history of these technologies is just one part of the story, but it is one that has shaped both women's experiences and the representation of their participation and contribution. This is the story we have focused on in this book, with the knowledge that there is much more historical and theoretical groundwork to be done.

Now we find ourselves at another transitional media moment, riding the wave of the latest hype cycle, which is dominated by talk of the metaverse and Web 3.0 and the promise of their emancipatory and democratizing capacity. We can already see the similar patterns begin to appear. Alongside the dominant narrative (shaped by a limited number of voices), we can begin tracing the alternate version.

The concept of the metaverse, conceived as it was in the context of an influential dystopian science-fiction novel,[3] appears to be no different in this regard. Many of our participants cut straight through the latest hype of the metaverse as somehow being a "new" revelation. Char Davies's position is that the metaverse is "accessible only through a corporation that seeks to track us all in order to sell more advertising [while] keeping everyone entertained on an overheating planet where all the nonhumans are dying. I warned about this more than 30 years ago, in 1991."[4] Others were very reluctant to engage in the concept, including Toni Dove: "I keep hearing about the metaverse right now in the world of commerce. It sounds like a horrible place. . . . This vision of hell—it just seems like you're doing that again. It sounds like the holodeck; it sounds like the nineties. . . . The metaverse is essentially a corporate sales mechanism."[5]

Dove's insight points to the parallel narrative of women / gender nonbinary / genderqueer individuals quickly identifying the pitfalls of a particular platform and wanting to divert to a different trajectory. For example, Nonny de la Peña drew some interesting insights and observations to other Web 3.0 technologies and the potential to subvert them for good:

> There may be a really interesting, useful application of blockchain technology. . . . [W]ith deepfakes, it's the same thing—people freaked out—but Witness [the human rights and media organization] did this very interesting piece on Chechnya where they [filmmaker David France] made deepfakes of their witnesses who were interviewed so that their identity was protected, but they could still participate in a documentary [*Welcome to Chechnya*] about abuses. So I still remain optimistic about these kind of practices and their potential for good without being naive about their potential for evil.[6]

We are already starting to see key interventions being made by women in Web 3.0, as noted in chapter 6. Other examples include Afro-Caribbean artist Itzel Yard, who became the highest-selling NFT artist in 2021 when selling her digital artwork for $2 million, and Everyrealm, a metaverse real estate start-up that achieved one of the largest Series A funding rounds in 2021 for a company with a woman CEO. But while there are many other women / gender nonbinary / genderqueer leaders, innovators, and entrepreneurs influencing and engaging in the opportunities presented by Web 3.0, their contributions are already being occluded by the mainstream privileging of accounts of male pioneers, such as by Mark Zuckerberg's colonizing advances in the metaverse. Similarly, the domain of "worldbuilding"—which is a key underpinning concept and practice for the creation of the metaverse and virtual worlds—is an area of academic inquiry that has largely privileged and elevated the work of white male fantasy authors, such as J. R. R. Tolkien. Women's contributions within this field are largely marginalized. For example, in proposing a canon of 25 worlds in a 2017 publication, only one was created by a woman.[7] However, worldbuilding is an embedded working practice at the core of many of our participants' work. Meow Wolf's Joanna Garner explained how this is central to their work:

> What we do is really deep worldbuilding. We want to create worlds that feel lived in and complex. Part of that is having lots of characters and lots of storylines, so that you can walk into a world and feel like, not everything has a purpose, because that's how the real-world works. Not every mailbox you look at is connected to this greater story of your life, and so given that challenge, which is fun and awesome to get to go down all sorts of rabbit holes, how do you also guide an audience through a story experience if they choose to follow it? I do think that's where technology like utilizing your phone and RFID [radio frequency identification] and moments of AR and VR, can all help to create that.[8]

Some of our participants are leading critical thinkers in the area of worldbuilding, already offering alternative ways to challenge extractive worldbuilding practices and approaches. According to Monika Bielskyte:

> The future is not just about building, but more importantly it's about growing and how we could move away from that building

paradigm to a growing paradigm. . . . [W]hen people talk about flying cars and drones, I say that the most futuristic thing that we can do for our cities is not make space for flying cars and drones but to make space for birds, for wild species. Rewilding our cities is the most futuristic thing that we can do. That doesn't mean that there shouldn't be flying cars or drones for some very specific cases—such as urgent organ transplants, urgent ambulances tackling particular disasters or cataclysmic events. There's space for these new technologies, but they should not be to cater [to] the minds of the rich and idle.[9]

As Bielskyte implied, the concept of worldbuilding has been dominated on global platforms by male figureheads and speakers. Jessica Clark, like Bielskyte, is a futurist, and she explained what this means in terms gender:

It's very, very technocratic. A lot of it is influenced by the business and military sectors, which are also, of course, male dominated. There's a tactical focus, there's lots of shiny-toy conversations. So part of what Kamal [Sinclair] and the Guild [of Future Architects] had been trying to do is to model a different, more participatory, more inclusive way of imagining futures that represent what people want and need. . . . So how do we create an empowering humanistic future in practice that is welcoming and allows for peoples lived experience to shape our visions for what could come next?[10]

What Clark is proposing is an alternative possibility to the dominant metaverse discourse, which is currently being shaped by a narrow range of voices in mainstream media. Sara Lisa Vogl, working at the forefront of immersive technologies, participation, and performance in virtual worlds and social VR spaces, captured this sentiment: "I strongly disagree with anything that Tony Parisi put into his 10 [sic] rules of the metaverse—especially that there is only one—there's never just one—there's never one space and no other—there's always underground clubs—there's always the darknet. There's never going to be just one metaverse."[11]

To echo Vogl's point, neither should there be just one history of the metaverse—or of any sociotechnological phenomenon—as we have shown in this book. These histories will always be revisited, rewritten, and recast by the many perspectives who have shaped it. This volume, which has captured, documented, and contextualized the creative contributions of our participants and their specific roles in moments of innovation and transition, tries to rectify the erasures of the past and to begin the process of detailing a more gender-inclusive history of the significant and consequential contribution to these emergent fields of production. Our volume is just a beginning, and we hope to see significant work that builds on these stories and identifies further contributions and significant innovations. As we advance headlong into the era of AI, now more than ever we must examine our present and current patterns of innovation to highlight the need for and value of including a greater diversity of voices, stories, models, and futures.

Appendix 1

Projects

Allen, Rebecca. *The Bush Soul*. 1997–99. Immersive VR with haptic interaction.
——. *Coexistence*. 2001. AR installation.
——. *MyoPhone*. 2003. AR.
——. *Swimmer*. 1981. 3D animated graphic.
Anagram. *Door into the Dark*. 2015. Immersive experience.
——. *A Face to Open Doors*. 2020. Interactive installation.
——. *Goliath: Playing with Reality*. 2021. Animated VR experience.
Baldwin, Lily, and Saschka Unseld. *Through You*. 2017. 360-degree film.
Brathwaite-Shirley, Danielle. *BlackTransArchive.com / We Are Here Because of Those That Are Not*. 2020. Installation.
cárdenas, micha. *Becoming Dragon*. 2008. Performance, mixed-media piece.
——. *Local Autonomy Networks (Autonets)*. 2011–15. Performance, online and offline network collaborations, handmade wearable electronic fashion.
——. *Sin Sol / No Sun*. 2020. Augmented Reality game.
Cizek, Katerina. *HIGHRISE*. National Film Board of Canada, 2009–2015. Multimedia Documentary series.
Daniel, Sharon. *Blood Sugar*. 2010. Online interactive documentary.
——. *Public Secrets*. 2007. Interactive multimedia.
Davies, Char. *Ephémère*. 1998. VR installation.
——. *Osmose*. 1995. VR installation with breathing/balance interface vest.
De la Peña, Nonny. *Hunger in Los Angeles*. Emblematic Group, 2012. VR installation.
——. *Out of Exile: Daniel's Story*. Emblematic Group, 2017. VR.
——. *Project Syria*. Emblematic Group, MxR Studio, 2014. VR.
——. *Unconstitutional: The War on Our Civil Liberties*. 2004. Film.

De la Peña, Nonny, Brad Lichtenstein, and Jeff Fitzsimmons, dirs. *Across the Line*. Emblematic Group, 371 Productions, Custom Reality Services, 2016. VR and 360-degree video.

De la Peña, Nonny, Catherine Upin, Julia Cort, et al., dirs. *Greenland Melting*. *Frontline*, *Nova*, Emblematic, Xrez Studio, Realtra, 2017. VR and 360-degree video.

De la Peña, Nonny, and Peggy Weil. *Gone Gitmo*. 2007–12. Installation in Second Life.

De la Peña, Nonny, and Sharon Yamato. *A Life in Pieces: The Diary and Letters of Stanley Hayami*. Emblematic Group, 2021. VR and 360-degree video.

Dinkins, Stephanie. *Not the Only One*. 2018. Deep-learning AI installation.

——. *When Words Fail*. 2020. WebXR experience.

Dove, Toni. *The Dress That Eats Souls*. 2018. Interactive cinema installation.

——. *Sunjammer 6: A Tale Told by a Solar Breeze*. In development. Visual novel, film, a human operated machine.

Espii Proctor, Sadah. *Girl Icon*. Oculus VR for Good Creators Lab, Malala Fund, and Milaan Foundation, 2019. 360-degree video documentary.

Hershman Leeson, Lynn. *Breathing Machines*.1966–67. Sculpture.

——. *Lorna*. 1983–84. Interactive video art disc.

——. *Logic Paralyzes the Heart*. 2021. Video installation.

——. *Shadow Stalker*. 2018–21. Live interactive installation.

——. *The Roberta Breitmore Series*. 1973–78. Mixed media, installation, performance.

James, Valencia. *Suga': A Live Virtual Dance Performance*. 2021. Virtual dance.

Lady Pheønix, dir. *Breonna's Garden*. Produced by Joanna Popper, Lady Pheønix, Ju'Niyah Palmer, Big Rock Creative, YesUniverse, 2021. XR, VR.

Libby, Jan, Jenni Powell, Mary Feuer, et al. *lonelygirl15*. 2006–8. Web series.

Lichtenstein, Brad, Janicza Bravo, and Jeff Fitzsimmons, et al., dirs. *Ashe '68*. Produced by Jeff Fitzsimmons, Keller Fitzsimmons, Renée Frigo, et al. 371 Productions, 2018. Documentary film and VR experience.

McCarthy, Lauren Lee. *Lauren*. 2017–. Installation and performance.

ross, jesikah maria. *Restore/Restory: A People's History of the Cache Creek Nature Preserve*. 2012. Oral histories and Online interactive documentary.

——. *Saving the Sierras*. 2007. Online interactive documentary.

Ruiz, Susana, dir. *Darfur Is Dying*. Take Action games, 2006. Online video game.

Shogaolu, Tamara, creative lead. *Un(re)solved*. Ado Ato, Frontline, Story Corps. 2021. Multiplatform experience.

Szilak, Illya, and Cyril Tsiboulski. *Atomic Vacation*. Cloudred, 2017. Transmedia narrative game, online and VR.

———. *Queerskins* series (*A Novel*; *A Love Story*; *Ark*; *Fly Angel Soul*). Cloudred, 2012, 2018, 2020, 2024. online novel, VR, film.

Szilak, Illya, Cyril Tsiboulski, and Pelin Kirca. *Reconstructing Mayakovsky*. Cloudred, 2008. Hybrid media web-based novel.

Tharp, Twyla. *The Catherine Wheel*. 1982. Dance performance.

Thiel, Tamiko. *Atmos Sphaerae*. 2021. 360-degree VR time-based experience.

———. *Gardens of the Anthropocene*. 2016. AR installation.

———. *In the Land of Babari-an*. 2006. Live dance performance with interactive 3D stage.

———. *Reign of Gold*. 2011. AR installation.

———. *Sponge Space Trash Takeover*. 2020. Online VR art installation.

———. *Unexpected Growth*. 2008. AR installation.

Thiel, Tamiko, and Manifest.AR. *Shades of Absence: Public Voids*. 2011. AR installation.

———. *We AR in MoMA*. The *Shades of Absence* AR series. Guerilla AR Art Exhibition. 2010. AR.

Thiel, Tamiko, and Zara Houshmand. *Beyond Manzanar*. 2000. Interactive VR large-screen projection.

Thiel, Tamiko, and /p. *Evolution of Fish*. 2019. AR large projection.

Thiel, Tamiko, and /p. *Lend Me Your Face!* 2020. Participatory deepfake AI video installation.

Thiel, Tamiko, and Teresa Reuter. *Virtuelle Mauer / ReConstructing the Wall*. 2008. Interactive 3D VR large projection.

Wallworth, Lynette. *Awavena*. In collaboration with Hushahu and the Yawanawá people. 2018. VR.

———. *Collisions*. In collaboration with Nyarri Nyarri Morgan and the Martu tribe. Sundance New Frontier-Jaunt VR Residency, 2015. VR experience.

———. *Hold Vessel I and II*. 2001 and 2007. Interactive installation.

Weil, Peggy. *LIPSYNC*. 1980. Frame buffer animation with Votrax and typed input.

Zuckerman, Maya. *Em's Theory*. 2017. Project series, multiplatform series.

Appendix 2

Participant Biographies

We include a biography from each of our participants who agreed to be identified as part of this research. These are brief due to word count limits—the many important contributions that they have made to their respective fields extend far beyond what we have been able to include here. We strongly encourage you to look up their work!

There are five participants who wished to remain anonymous, and while we are sorry not to be able to include their profiles here, we extend our sincere thanks to them for their valuable contributions.

May Abdalla is executive director and cofounder of Anagram. She is also a documentary filmmaker with numerous projects for BBC, Channel 4, and Al Jazeera. Since 2016 Abdalla has been executive director of BBC Arabic Digital, Investigations, and Documentary. Partnering with Amy Rose at Anagram, *Goliath: Playing with Reality* won best VR immersive work at the Venice Film Festival in 2021 and *Door into the Dark* won the 2015 Storyscapes Award at the Tribeca Film Festival.

Carmen Aguilar y Wedge is a Latinx structural engineer and artist synthesizing design and technology to develop immersive-transmedia experiences. She cofounded Hyphen-Labs, an international team of women engineers, scientists, and architects turned designers and artists who blend themes of speculative design, humanity+, the environment, and social issues in the context of architecture, robotics, VR, fashion, computation, new media, music, and smart materials.

Catherine Allen is a leading expert in immersive technology. She founded Limina Immersive—a VR events and research company in the United Kingdom dedicated to bringing immersive tech to broader audiences. She worked on the BAFTA-winning iPad app Disney Animated and led the creation of two of the BBC's first VR experiences. As an expert in creative immersive technology, Allen has authored several public reports including for Innovate UK and Digital Catapult.

Rebecca Allen is an internationally recognized digital artist. Her work is part of the permanent collection of Centre Georges Pompidou, Whitney Museum, and Museum of Modern Art. In her career, which spans more than 40 years, she has collaborated with Kraftwerk, Peter Gabriel, and Nam June Paik, and she has worked in design and research for Nokia, MIT Media Lab Europe, Intel, Virgin Interactive, Nintendo, and Apple.

Artsy Marie is a social VR architect and illustrator. She established Artsy in VR where she has created over 2,100 VR environments. She 3D models, designs, and builds structures, environments, and furniture from scratch, including storefronts, art galleries, nightclubs, mansions, roof top lounges, luxury lofts, dream destinations, and obstacle courses. She became a designer in residence at NFT Oasis in 2022.

Tonia B. is an experience designer collaborating on immersive media projects for Universal Studios Japan, Sesame Street at Sea World (Beaudry Interactive), Tender Claws, and Oculus Next Gen Symposium. She is cofounder of Browntourage, a diverse media collective and media agency spanning curatorial projects, experiments in interactive media, brand collaborations, and platform for media and design moments that are forward thinking and socially conscious.

Lily Baldwin is an artist, filmmaker, and performer. Originally a contemporary dancer, Baldwin works with hybrid forms spanning film, documentary, VR, mixed reality, and performance. Her works have screened at major festivals, including Sundance, South by Southwest, Berlinale, and the Venice Biennale and have been exhibited around the world. Baldwin is creator/host for podcast *Stories of the Stalked*, nominated for a Peabody Award. Baldwin has been a juror for the Tribeca Film Festival and is a Sundance Institute New Frontier fellow. Baldwin is the founder of Stop Stalking Us, a nonprofit that unites people impacted by the dangerous, often invisible, crime of stalking.

Nancy Bennett is a creative artist working at the nexus of groundbreaking technologies, cinematic storytelling, and creative design. Bennett is an Edmund Hillary Fellow to New Zealand and also a Sundance New Frontier Lab Grantee. She cofounded Two Bit Circus, using innovative technologies to blur the lines between physical and digital playgrounds. With more than 20 years of experience in XR, film, television, music videos, commercials, marketing, and start-ups, Bennett collaborated on the first episodic series in stereoscopic VR (NFL, Google 2016); the first synchronized film viewing in VR (*Collisions*, 2016); and the first live-action, multi-user VR experience (NFL/Samsung, 2014–15).

Robin Benty is a digital strategist with 20 years of entertainment experience. At Fox Broadcasting, she is responsible for the strategic oversight of digital media content for more than 30 Fox-scripted television series as well as development of ancillary digital revenue streams. She was executive producer on the *Sleepy Hollow* VR experience which won an Interactive Emmy Award for VR.

Monika Bielskyte is a futures researcher, futurist, and futures designer exploring futures in more than 90 countries. Working at the intersection of science, tech, culture, and politics, she has collaborated with Google, Nike, Universal, Disney Marvel, BBC, and Microsoft and is a regular public speaker at international forums in the immersive media space. Bielskyte is founder of Protopia Futures, a platform for research and creative collaborations that challenge and offer alternatives to dystopian/utopian stereotypes.

Heidi Boisvert, PhD, is an interdisciplinary artist, experience designer, creative technologist, and academic researcher who interrogates the neurobiological and sociocultural effects of media and technology. Boisvert has been mapping the world's first media genome while taking great care with its far-reaching ethical implications. She founded futurePerfect lab, cofounded XTH, and collaborated with David Byrne on Theater of the Mind, an immersive theater piece.

Carla Borrás, senior producer of Special Projects and Innovation for PBS's *Frontline*, has worked on numerous award-winning documentaries, such as the immersive web interactive *The Last Generation* (2018). With *Frontline*, Borrás produced, in partnership with Nonny de la Peña and Emblematic Group, the VR project *Greenland Melting* (2017) and, with Tamara Shogaolu and Ado Ato Pictures, the multiplatform initiative *Un(re)solved* (2021).

Danielle Brathwaite-Shirley is an artist working in animation, sound, performance, and video games. Her practice records the lives of Black Trans people, intertwining reality and fiction to create participatory work. Her work has been exhibited at David Kordansky Gallery, Los Angeles; arebyte Gallery; and Science Gallery London, among many others.

Caitlin Burns is the story director for Palm NFT Studio, leading teams of creators who build new experiences for original and major franchise intellectual property using NFT platforms. A globally recognized expert in franchise storytelling, experience design, and brand strategy, Burns has spent more than a decade creating multiplatform content strategies for well-known intellectual property, including *Pirates of the Caribbean*, *Descendants*, *Tron Legacy*, and *Avatar*.

Becca Caddy is a journalist and author specializing in consumer technology, popular science, and the future. Her work includes bylines in Metro, OneZero, Inverse, *The Observer*, Insider, Wired UK, New Scientist, Gizmodo UK, How it Works, MSN, TechRadar, and many others. Her first book, *Screen Time* (2021), is a guide to help people find a better balance with everyday technology.

micha cárdenas, PhD, is an artist, writer, and scholar in the Performance, Play, and Design and Critical Race and Ethnic Studies programs at the University of California, Santa Cruz, where she directs the Critical Realities Studio. She is the author of *Poetic Operations: Trans of Color*

Art in Digital Media (2022) and a member of Electronic Disturbance Theater 2.0, and her artworks have been presented in MoMA, ZKM, and the Centro Cultural del Bosque.

Katerina Cizek is a documentary film director and artistic director of the Co-Creation Studio at MIT Open Documentary Lab. Her films include the *Seeing Is Believing: Handicams, Human Rights and the News* (codirected with Peter Wintonick, 2002) and *The Dead Are Alive: Eyewitness in Rwanda* (1999). Her other projects, supported by National Film Board of Canada, include Webby-winning *Filmmaker in Residence* (2004) and the Emmy-winning *HIGHRISE* (2009–15).

Jessica Clark is founder/director of the Dot Connector Studio, cofounder of Immerse.news, and coauthor, with Kamal Sinclair and Carrie McLaren, of the *Making a New Reality* book and toolkit. Clark led the Future of Public Media Project at American University's Center for Media and Social Impact, 2007–11. She has a research affiliation with MIT's OpenDocLab and is currently a Futurist in Residence at the Robert Wood Johnson Foundation.

Maria Ignacia Court is a Chilean documentary maker, producer, and academic exploring the intersection of documentary and new media. She cofounded Chaka Studio in London, leading and codirecting the award-winning interactive documentary *Quipu Project*. She is director of Mucha Media in Chile, which specializes in storytelling on multiple platforms that mix narrative, design, and technology to create a positive social, cultural, and environmental impact.

Carrie Cutforth is a creative producer and writer who tells stories across a range of media, including interactive, digital, web series, film, VR, AR, transmedia, ARGs, live events, and text. Carrie cofounded several community-building organizations, including Transmedia 101 and the Independent Web Series Creators of Canada. She coproduced TO WebFest's inaugural year in 2014.

Sharon Daniel is a media artist and scholar in the Film and Digital Media Department and the Digital Arts and New Media MFA program at the

University of California, Santa Cruz. Daniel's work in participatory documentary explores social, economic, environmental, and criminal justice issues. Her creative work has been shown at ISEA/ZeroOne, Ars Electronica, Lincoln Center Festival, and Corcoran Biennial. Daniel's essays are included in the anthologies *Context Providers* and *Database Aesthetics* and also in *Cinema Journal* and *Leonardo*.

Char Davies, PhD, is a Canadian artist who is internationally recognized for her pioneering immersive virtual artworks *Osmose* (1995) and *Ephémère* (1998). These works, which use early stereoscopic head-mounted display technology and motion-tracking breath and balance sensors, have been shown around the world. She was a founding director of a world-leading 3D software company, Softimage, in the mid-1980s.

Nonny de la Peña, PhD, is the founder and CEO of Emblematic Group, producers of VR, AR, and mixed reality. De la Peña's *Hunger in Los Angeles* (2012) was the first VR documentary, premiering at Sundance in 2012. In 2022 de la Peña received the Peabody Field Builder Award and elected to South by Southwest Hall of Fame. Noted for her work in "immersive journalism," de la Peña also has worked as a documentary filmmaker and as a writer for *Newsweek*, the *New York Times*, and the *Los Angeles Times*. She is the founder and director of Arizona State University's Narrative and Emerging Media program.

Helen De Michiel is a filmmaker, writer, and educator whose media-making work moves across independent film and television to media installation and transmedia projects, which are included in museum collections across the USA. She produced *The Independents* and *Alive TV* for public television, has created several innovative community media projects with youth, and writes about issues in the public media and arts field. With Patricia Zimmermann, De Michiel coauthored the book, *Open Space New Media Documentary* (2018).

Christy Dena, PhD, is a writer-designer-director of multi–art form and interactive projects. She has worked on installations, apps, live games, tabletop, ARGs, VR, films, theater, and TV shows. Her original interactive fiction projects have won and been nominated for awards, and her work has been exhibited internationally. She founded Universe Creation 101 studio in Melbourne, Australia, in 2009 to create original and commissioned interactive and multi-art form projects.

Stephanie Dinkins is a transdisciplinary artist who creates platforms for dialogue about AI as it intersects with race, gender, aging, and future histories. She holds the Kusama Endowed Chair in Art at Stony Brook University. Dinkins's art practice employs lens-based practices, emerging technologies, and community engagement to confront questions of bias in AI, consciousness, data sovereignty, and social equity. Past residencies include Sundance New Frontiers Story Lab and Nokia Bell Labs.

Toni Dove is an artist who has been producing unique and highly imaginative embodied hybrids of film, installation, and performance since the early 1990s. In her works, performers and participants interact with an unfolding narrative, using interface and interactive technologies, such as motion sensing. Her installations feature female characters from different eras who are subjected to the economic and technological determinants of their time.

Jenn Duong is an immersive director and producer. She has directed and produced a range of projects from short form VR docs to VR music experiences. She cofounded Women in VR/AR one of the largest channels for resources, opportunities, and collaboration in her industry. She has become a leader and advocate for women and underrepresented groups in the emerging technology space.

Sadah Espii Proctor is an XR director and sound/media designer working in live, digital, and virtual forms of storytelling through multimedia theater, audio dramas, VR/AR, and immersive experiences. She was recognized by American Theatre Magazine for multimedia storytelling in the "Six Theatre Artists to Know" series, and she also received a Barrymore Award for outstanding media design.

Maureen Fan is CEO and cofounder of the award-winning Baobab Studios, the world's leading interactive narrative animation studio. Maureen has held leadership roles in film, gaming, and web, and she was vice president of games at Zynga, where she oversaw three game studios, including the FarmVille's. She worked on Pixar's *Toy Story 3* film and is an active member of many organizations for minority groups and women.

Mary Feuer is an award-winning writer for film, television, and the internet, where her work includes the seminal web series *lonelygirl15* and her original series, *With the Angels*, created for the online network Strike. TV, which was honored with Streamy Award nominations for writing and directing. She was supervising producer and head writer of the TV series *Dante's Cove* (2004–7).

Caitlin Fisher, PhD, is a researcher, writer, and practitioner at York University, she cofounded Future Cinema Lab and is the director of the Augmented Reality Lab. In the AR Lab, she is working to construct and theorize spatial narrative environments and build expressive software tools for artists. Fisher is the author of the hypermedia novella *These Waves of Girls* and *Andromeda*, one of the first poems created in AR.

Amandine Flachs is an emerging tech specialist and VC scout. She has been supporting start-up founders for more than 12 years in France, the United States, and the United Kingdom, helping them launch new innovative products, build communities, and bring teams together to kickstart new projects and approach new markets. She cofounded WildMeta, an AI start-up based in London, with the aim of helping video game developers create more human-like game AIs.

Anthea Foyer is a strategic leader, creative strategist, narrative designer, and city builder. At the Interactive Digital Media Office, Toronto, she supports the creative interactive media industry in the city focusing on AR, VR, MR, e-sports, gaming, immersive media, and emerging media. Foyer has created, produced, and advised on a wide array of critically acclaimed projects, including graphic novels, interactive installations, online narratives, wearables, participatory theatre, and multiplatform experiences.

Shari Frilot is chief curator for New Frontier at the Sundance Institute since 2006 and also senior programmer for the Sundance Film

Festival since 1998. She is a multidisciplinary creative media executive and a multiple award-winning producer and filmmaker who works across platforms—including digital, television, film, immersive, virtual production, and integrated media ecosystems.

Irene Fubara-Manuel, PhD, is a lecturer in digital media practice at the University of Sussex. They research the colonial history of surveillance and its contemporary applications in racialized border policing. Their creative practice mobilizes Black, queer, and African technological imaginaries as interventions on bordering.

Joanna Garner is a playwright, musician, creativity coach and senior story creative director for Meow Wolf, an arts and entertainment company in Santa Fe, New Mexico. Meow Wolf creates immersive and interactive experiences that transport audiences of all ages into fantastic realms of story and exploration. Garner writes her own plays, designs immersive experiences, and helps companies and individuals tell their own stories.

Nettrice Gaskins, PhD, is a digital artist, academic, and cultural critic whose work utilizes machine learning and algorithms. Her portraits have been featured in the Smithsonian's *FUTURES* exhibition, Carnegie Hall's *The Black Angel of History: Myth-Science, Metamodernism, and the Metaverse*. She is the author of *Techno-Vernacular Creativity and Innovation* (2021). Gaskins is assistant director of the STEAM Learning Lab at Lesley University.

Samantha Gorman, PhD, is a writer, artist, curator, and educator. Her work combines text, cinema, games, virtual reality, and scholarship about digital media. She cofounded the indie game and art studio Tender Claws, which creates novel approaches to interactive narrative through emerging media. They created the award-winning VR game Virtual Virtual Reality (V-VR), which became one of the best-selling apps on Oculus Go.

Hazel Grian is a writer best known for *How to Build a Robot* (2017), *Star Trek Save Vulcan Alternate Reality Game* (2009), and *KateModern* (2007)— the online web series. She has worked with the band Portishead and

Aardman Animations. Her critically acclaimed virtual reality opera *We Sing in Fire and Blood* (2019) is now being developed as a live stage show.

Karine Halpern is a transmedia strategist, and producer. Founder of Transmedia Ready, Karine has been an advocate of transmedia design and strategy since 2010 and has worked in the creative industries since 1990. She induces creativity at all stages of development and dissemination with a transdisciplinary approach. She is storyteller, writer, matchmaker for talent, and a facilitator for design thinking and content production and management.

Dee Harvey is a writer-director specializing in immersive media. She is a founder of Controvert, a company focused on using immersive and interactive technology to tell stories in new ways. She cowrote and directed *IF* (2018), a VR180 film about infertility, commissioned by YouTube. She worked as an interactive producer at the BBC and in the indie sector, specializing in interactive content and social media.

Lynn Hershman Leeson is a multimedia artist and filmmaker. Over the last five decades in her work with technology and media-based practices, she has helped legitimize digital art forms. Her work combines art with social commentary, particularly on the relationship between humans and technology, identity, surveillance, and the use of media as a tool of empowerment against censorship and political repression.

Nicoletta Iacobacci, PhD, was head of Strategy and Future Media at the European Broadcasting Union until 2014. She then earned a PhD in 2015, focusing on ethics and emerging technologies. As an international speaker and event moderator, she has curated five editions of TEDx Transmedia and nine European Broadcasting Union Summits. She's a BAFTA guru and a senior adviser at Singularity University.

Jasmine Idun Isdrake is an artist, game designer, curator, and educator. As creative director at Playcentric Studios, Isdrake provides creative direction, experience design, curation, and production for games, film, stage performances, transmedia, immersive experiences, and art installations. Isdrake runs Sweden's first and only game gallery, Epic

Unidragon, exhibiting electronic, interactive, and transmedia arts, and a game/innovation/maker lab called Collaboratory.

Kaya Jabar is a preproduction supervisor at Framestore in the United Kingdom, a virtual cinematographer, and on-set supervisor leading previs, postvis, techvis, and virtual production for tentpole film and TV projects. Jabar designs sequences from scratch through effective cinematography and animation; provides on-set technical direction and planning for complex VFX; builds tools and works across departments to streamline motion control shoots; and designs workflows for better game engine integration.

Valencia James is a Barbadian performer, maker, and researcher working at the intersection of dance, theater, technology, and activism. Her work explores remote interdisciplinary collaborations with creative technologists and how emerging technologies like machine learning and computer vision might enhance creativity in her contemporary dance practice. She premiered *Suga': A Live Virtual Dance Performance* in the SIGGRAPH Art Gallery (2021) and later at Sundance New Frontier (2022).

Kirsty Jennings is a multidisciplinary producer and strategic leader who is executive producer for Anagram, working across company development and on award-winning productions. She previously worked with Documentary Campus, 104 Films, and Sheffield Doc/Fest and was business director for the internationally renowned artist group Blast Theory, producing artworks across multiple immersive forms, including politically charged immersive theater pieces, large-scale international collaborations, and a live interactive feature film.

Sarah Jones, PhD, is a senior academic leader, educator, and VR practitioner having previously worked for ITV as a correspondent and news anchor. Her research is focused on immersive realities, 360 immersive storytelling, and multisensory VR. Jones has worked with Google on a Digital News Initiative project, building a VR game around the Blitz.

Niema Jordan is a writer, director, and producer from Oakland, California. She was a health editor at *Essence* magazine and an associate producer at Trilogy Films. She writes for several print and digital publications and has worked on social media strategy for entrepreneurs, produced a music festival, and serves on the board of directors for Camp Reel Stories.

Vassiliki Khonsari cofounded iNK Stories in New York in 2006, where she is also producer, director, and writer. iNK produces immersive location-based entertainment (LBE) in VR, AR, games, interactive narrative stories, film, and episodic content. Notable projects include *Hero* (multisensory LBE VR), *Fire Escape* (interactive VR series [Daydream/ HTC]), and *1979 Revolution*, all of which have received awards, nominations, and critical acclaim. Khonsari is a Sundance Fellow and member of Women's Impact Network.

Ingrid Kopp is cofounder and codirector of Electric South, based in Cape Town, South Africa, incubating, funding, and exhibiting the work of African creators with a focus on XR and immersive media. Kopp is a member of the editorial collective of Immerse.news, a publication focusing on emerging nonfiction storytelling. Kopp previously curated Storyscapes at the Tribeca Film Festival and was director of interactive at the Tribeca Film Institute.

Vicki Lau is a VFX artist, VR developer, TEDx speaker and educator from Singapore. She has worked with more than 20 studios and filmmakers on such major productions as AMC's *The Walking Dead*, *Guardians of the Galaxy*, and *Aquaman*, while working at mobile and VR early-stage start-ups in Silicon Valley. She is the author of *Why I Do VFX: The Untold Truths about Working in Visual Effects* (2021).

Michela Ledwidge is a creative and technical director, specializing in real-time and virtual production, as well as CEO and founder of MOD Films in Sydney, Australia. MOD works with clients and partners in film, TV, games, media-tech research, VFX and branding agencies, health, arts and cultural organizations—including Epic Games, Yahoo/RYOT, Sony Interactive Entertainment USA, Microsoft Mixed Reality—to create XR experiences and games.

Rosemarie Lerner is a Peruvian documentary director and producer. She is cofounder of Chaka Studio, coproducing the renowned *Quipu Project*. Based in Lima, she is director of Lucida Media and is working on several projects including two i-docs on climate change and participatory media projects with communities in disaster risk areas.

Wendy Levy is the executive director of the Alliance for Media Arts + Culture, leading new national and international programs like Hatch-Labs, Arts2Work, and The Innovation Studio. Her creative work is at the intersection of storytelling, innovation, and social justice. Wendy was a senior consultant at Sundance Institute and also directed the MacArthur Foundation–funded Producers Institute for New Media Technologies, the first public media innovation lab in the United States.

Jan Libby is an award-winning writer who produces stories and immersive experiences for brands and media companies; she worked as a staff writer for the web series *lonelygirl15*. She wrote her own ARG, Sammeeeees; developed the thriller *36nine* with Kiefer Sutherland's East Side Entertainment; created the groundbreaking *Welcome to the Following* for Kevin Williamson's *The Following*; and wrote an immersive play for Experiment America.

Juliana Loh is a VR worldbuilder for social spaces, an XR prototype designer, and an interactive VR artist using google Tilt Brush. Her work has been featured in Burning Man VR 2021, ViFF Immersed 2021, HIFF (Film Festival), QldFreeway (Film/XR Festival), and QLD XR Festivals. Juliana's background includes brand entertainment, games, user experience, and education.

Carrie Lozano is a documentary filmmaker and journalist. She is director of the International Documentary Association's Enterprise Documentary and Pare Lorentz funds. She led the Bay Area Video Coalition's National MediaMaker Fellowship and worked at Al Jazeera America as senior producer of *Fault Lines*, where her team garnered numerous awards. She produced the Academy Award nominee *The Weather Underground* and the live cinema piece *Utopia in Four Movements*.

Jennifer "Jenni" Magee-Cook is an animated features producer at Warner Bros. Entertainment. Magee-Cook has worked as a producer for more than 20 years, including Sony Pictures Animation, Skydance, Walt Disney Imagineering, Walt Disney Animation Studios, and Disneytoon Studios. She worked as executive producer at the Disney Channel and at Dreamscape Immersive. Jenni has been a producer and production Manager on numerous feature films, television shows, and animated properties including *Mulan*, *The Emperor's New Groove*, and Disney Channel's *Descendants: Wicked World*.

Lauren Lee McCarthy is an artist examining social relationships in the midst of surveillance, automation, and algorithmic living. Her work *Someone* was awarded the Ars Electronica Golden Nica, and *Lauren* was awarded the immersive nonfiction IDFA DocLab Award. Lauren is creator of p5.js, an open-source art and education platform that prioritizes access and diversity in learning to code, with over 1.5 million users.

Debra McGrory has designed, launched, and managed highly successful data-driven software products in the immersive media space. She is recognized as an innovative leader by Fast Company and a data visualization and sonification expert by Google, and she has been a consultant to the United Nations. She is cofounder of Kinetek Inc., a generative AI company and is also an assistant professor at Parsons School of Design.

Verity McIntosh is a researcher and senior lecturer in VR and XR at the University of the West of England. Verity runs a pioneering industry-led, practice-based master's program, offering students the opportunity to develop their craft as immersive storytellers, adding VR/AR/XR to their creative toolkit, and critically engaging with the politics, business, and culture of this emerging field.

Elizabeth "Liz" Miller is a documentary maker, community media artist, and professor at Concordia University in Montreal. Miller has developed media advocacy and visual art projects with women, youth, senior citizens, and a wide range of human rights organizations. Her documentary film projects, *Novela, Novela* and *The Water Front* have been used to impact policy and educational initiatives around gender, environmental justice, and human rights.

Katy Morrison, PhD, is cofounder and producer of VRTOV—a studio exploring the emerging language of narrative VR. Morrison uses immersive technologies to put audiences at the center of extraordinary stories. Her VR projects have been honored at the Webby Awards, the Lovies, the Google Play Awards, and they have been shown in festivals around the world. She has also worked in documentary television as a researcher, writer, and producer.

Alison Norrington, PhD, is a writer, producer, and CEO and founder of Storycentral, a London-based studio that develops projects across film, television, publishing, animation, gaming, VR, and other media forms. In addition to her own work as novelist and cross-platform creative, Norrington has worked with SundanceTV, CBS Interactive, Walt Disney Imagineering, FOX International, AMC Networks on storytelling strategies. Norrington was convener and chair for the Storyworld Conference and Expo (2010, 2011, 2018).

Siobhan O'Flynn, PhD, has consulted on digital, interactive, participatory, transmedia, AR, and VR storytelling via her company NarrativeNow for almost 20 years. She is the co-creator of the online site, TMCResourceKit.com, a resource for Canadian producers moving into the digital sphere. She codeveloped Kensington Market: Hidden Histories, an interactive map and augmented reality app that reveal the layered history of key locations in the market.

Mimi Ọnụọha is a Nigerian American artist and researcher working in multimedia using print, code, installation, and video to call attention to the ways in which those in the margins are differently abstracted, represented, and missed by sociotechnical systems. Ọnụọha has been in residence at Eyebeam Center for Art & Technology, Studio XX, Data & Society Research Institute, Columbia University, and the Royal College of Art.

Neilda Pacquing is a user experience designer and prototyper, and AR/VR consultant. Founder of MindGlow, she has designed a wide portfolio of software applications spanning web, mobile, and wearables and AR+VR in teams, including EmpowHER VR, a VR application providing self-defense training for women. She cofounded Augmented Reality and Computer Vision group, a community of technologists, designers, and enthusiasts.

Jennifer Palais is director of in-product experience at Mozilla and an award-winning integrated cross-channel strategist, executive producer, content director, and product development leader. With more than 15 years of experience working with the world's top global brands, such as Apple, Netflix, Google, Hyundai and Intel, her core focus is developing data driven, deeply resonant brand strategies and integrated cross-channel campaigns with a proven return on investment.

Kate Parsons is a video artist and educator. She is the cofounder of FLOAT, a VR/AR art studio, founder of Stickney Creek, a creative outdoor recreation initiative, and founder of FEMMEBIT, a video art festival celebrating LA female artists working in video and new media. Much of Kate's practice surrounds human connection, meaning-making, and our relationships to the biological and environmental systems we inhabit.

Christiane Paul, PhD, is a writer, curator, and educator of digital art. Paul is the recipient of the Toma Foundation's arts writing award in digital art (2016), and her writings include *A Companion to Digital Art* (2016); *Digital Art* (3rd rev. ed., 2015); *Context Providers: Conditions of Meaning in Media Arts* (2011). She is professor at the New School where she is also director and chief curator of galleries at the Parsons School of Design. Paul also works as adjunct curator of digital art at the Whitney Museum of American Art, where she has curated exhibits for more than 20 years.

Phoenix Perry, PhD, is a games designer, maker, educator, academic, and speaker. She creates physical games and embodied experiences. An advocate for women in game development, she founded Code Liberation Foundation in 2012, which has reached more than 3,000 women aged 16–60 in New York and London. She also founded game studio Dozen Eyes Games, focused on games and installations that create social change.

Kim Plowright is a creative producer, digital product manager, consultant, and educator, with two decades of experience designing and delivering cross-platform projects for clients including Channel 4, the BBC, the Royal Opera House, and Wellcome. Her BAFTA and Emmy Award–winning digital projects are at the intersection of internet, art, games, and "old" media.

Jenni Powell is the producer of *The Lizzie Bennet Diaries*, *Welcome to Sanditon*, *lonelygirl15*, *Emma Approved*, and *The New Adventures of Peter and Wendy*. She was director of content and social media for VidCon; producer at Felicia Day's YouTube Premium Channel Geek & Sundry; transmedia producer for the interactive web series and ARG Blackout, and producer of immersive experience *Give Up the Ghost*.

Madeline Power is a freelance producer, having produced for the *New York Times*, the *Washington Post*, Stereogum, PBS, Milwaukee Public Radio, Planned Parenthood, and the John Michael Kohler Arts Center. She coproduced the Emmy-nominated VR documentary *Ashe '68*, which was executive coproduced by John Legend and was an official selection for the Sundance Film Festival in 2019.

Erin Reilly is an entrepreneur, educator, and strategist with 20 years of experience inventing new approaches, products, services and experiences about storytelling, engagement, and learning through emergent technology. She is professor and inaugural director of innovation and entrepreneurship for the College of Communication at the University of Texas at Austin. She has authored both academic and industry publications and was coeditor for the book *Reading in a Participatory Culture* (2013).

Sandra Rodriguez, PhD, is a creative director/producer of VR, XR, and AI experiences and is a sociologist of new media technology. She has worked on numerous award-winning interactive, web-based, and immersive non-fiction experiences and now spans her work to live performance, multiuser projection, and large-scale installations. Rodriguez is a Sundance StoryLab Fellow, a Sundance Institute, and MacArthur grantee.

Amy Rose is a documentary filmmaker and the creative director and cofounder of Anagram. For many years Rose has run wild camps for children with Forest School Camps and the food section of a small music festival called Fire in the Mountain. Partnering with May Abdalla at Anagram, *Goliath: Playing with Reality* won best VR immersive work at the Venice Film Festival in 2021, and *Door into the Dark* won the 2015 Storyscapes Award at the Tribeca Film Festival.

Mandy Rose is professor of documentary and digital cultures at UWE Bristol. She is co-Investigator on the UK Research and Innovation Strength in Places MyWorld program and was co-investigator on the EPSRC *Virtual Realities: Immersive Documentary Encounters* project. She is co-convenor of i-Docs. Mandy has worked as a TV and film sound recordist and documentary director, including for 20 years at the BBC.

Liz Rosenthal is curator, executive producer, and creative immersive and interactive content pioneer. Liz is curator of the Biennale's Venice International Film Festival's Immersive Content Official Selection and Competition, founder and CEO of Power to the Pixel, and executive producer for CreativeXR, a unique immersive content accelerator program funded by Arts Council England and Digital Catapult in London.

jesikah maria ross is a documentary media maker, who facilitates collaborative projects that help communities identify issues and develop solutions for the places they live. For the past 20 years, she has worked with schools, nongovernmental organizations, social action groups, and public media stations to create storytelling projects that generate civic participation, public dialogue, and community change.

Susana Ruiz, PhD, is an artist and educator, concerned with how the intersection of art practice, game/playful design, and digital storytelling can enable new approaches to social activism, aesthetics, and public pedagogy. She is the cofounder, with Huy Truong and Ashley York, of the game studio Take Action Games, a studio specializing in casual games for social change. Ruiz was lead designer on *Darfur Is Dying* (2006), the critically acclaimed flash-based browser, narrative-based simulation game about the crisis in Darfur, in western Sudan.

Ellen Sandor is a new media artist, and founder/director of the collaborative artists' group, (art)n. In 1983 Sandor integrated photography, sculpture, and video with computer graphics that resulted in a new medium she called "PHSColograms," which are 3D barrier-screen computer-generated photographs and sculptures. She is coeditor of *New Media Futures: The Rise of Women in the Digital Arts* (2018).

Belén Santa-Olalla is senior creative consultant at Conducttr, London, where she develops storytelling transmedia projects. She led the transmedia experience 19reinos.com based on the universe of *Game of Thrones* on Canal+. She also directs the immersion theater company Stroke114, with which she has undertaken the transmedia adaptation of the novel *El Proceso* (*The Trial*) by Franz Kafka. In addition, she coordinates transmedia meetups in Spain.

Tiffany Shlain is an American filmmaker and author. She is the cofounder of the Webby Awards and the founder of the International Academy of Digital Arts and Sciences. Four of her films have premiered at the Sundance Film Festival, including her acclaimed feature documentary, *Connected: An Autobiography about Love, Death & Technology*. Shlain is a world-renowned speaker and has given keynotes at Google, Harvard, and NASA.

Tamara Shogaolu is a director and new media artist focused on sharing intersectional stories across mediums, platforms, and virtual and physical spaces in order to promote cross-cultural understanding and challenge preconceptions. Shogaolu is the founder and creative director of Ado Ato Pictures. Her work has featured in film festivals, galleries, and museums worldwide, including the Museum of Modern Art in New York and the National Gallery of Indonesia.

Kamal Sinclair is senior director of digital innovation at the Music Center in Los Angeles and also serves on the Peabody Awards Interactive Board. Sinclair collaborated as artist and producer on *Question Bridge: Black Males*, a project recognized by International Center for Photography's 2015 Infinity Award for new media and archived at the Smithsonian's National Museum of African American History and Culture. As director of the Sundance Institute's New Frontier Labs Program, she consulted for the Ford Foundation on the *Making a New Reality* series, a landmark project aimed at furthering equality in emerging media.

Taryn Southern is a digital personality, writer, producer, director, and songwriter with more than 500 million views across her internet videos. She produced the world's first pop album composed with artificial intelligence (*I AM AI*) and wrote and produced a Streamy-nominated immersive VR series for Google/YouTube VR. Her directorial debut (codirected with Elena Gaby), *I Am Human*, premiered at the Tribeca Film Festival in 2019.

Lina Srivastava, JD, is an innovation strategist collaborating with such organizations as FilmAid, UNESCO, and UNICEF. She is the founder of the Center for Transformational Change, the Creative Impact and Experience Lab and the Transformational Change Leadership project. She has worked on impact and engagement campaigns for award-winning documentaries, including *Inocente* (2012) and *Who Is Dayani Cristal?* (2014).

Samantha Storr is an executive producer at Here Be Dragons, at the forefront of all their pioneering projects, including *Clouds over Sidra*, *Walking New York*, *The Millions March* and U2's "Song for Someone." Previously Samantha spent over 15 years as a producer, working alongside Robert Redford, Terry Gilliam, Spike Jonze, and the Beastie Boys and collaborating with Chris Milk on the world's first virtual reality film experience, *Beck's Hello Again*.

Illya Szilak, MD, is an independent scholar, writer, new media artist, and physician. She uses open-source media and collaborations forged via the internet to create multimedia narrative installations online. Shaped by her experience as a physician, her artistic practice explores mortality, embodiment, identity, and belief in a media inundated by an increasingly virtual world. Her works include *Reconstructing Mayakovsky*, *Queerskins* and *Atomic Vacation*.

Ece Tankal is a Turkish designer and new media artist based in London. She is cofounder of and head of creative design for Hyphen-Labs, a studio practice which incorporates several forms of media and emerging technologies using virtual reality, speculative object, and spatial design to embody alternative presents and futures.

Jessica Taylor has held numerous leadership positions in the creative industries. She was most recently managing director at PRELOADED, an immersive games studio, and before that, she was vice president of experience design at Antenna International, working to create innovative visitor experiences at some of the world's greatest cultural institutions.

Tamiko Thiel is a visual artist exploring the interplay of place, space, the body, and cultural identity in works encompassing a supercomputer, objects, installations, digital prints in 2D and 3D, videos, interactive 3D virtual worlds, VR, AR, and AI. Notable projects include a collaboration with Steven Spielberg, Starbright World, AR interventions at the MoMA and Venice Biennale, and *Unexpected Growth*, a digital installation.

Sarah Ticho has worked across the interdisciplinary arts as a producer, curator, and researcher. She is the founder of Hatsumi, a research and design studio that works at the intersection of arts, health, and immersive technology. She is a freelance producer with Explore Deep, an artist-led, clinically validated meditative VR experience, and a health care lead at Immerse UK.

Isabel Van De Keere, PhD, is the founder and CEO of Immersive Rehab, a digital health start-up that offers personalized and engaging neurorehabilitation programs using VR with the aim to improve patient recovery. With a background in electromechanical engineering and as a former biomedical engineering scientist, Isabel is an expert in health care technologies, digital health, and immersive technologies, with a focus using tech for good.

Sara Lisa Vogl is a VR user experience designer, creative entrepreneur, and futurist, exploring and constructing new VR and AR, as well as organizing VR events, hackathons, and investor days. She has worked to incubate the AR/VR ecosystem in Europe, cofounding the XR Base incubator and the NPO Women in Immersive Technologies Europe.

Lynette Wallworth is an Australian artist whose immersive video installations and film works reflect on the connections between people and the natural world. Her work, exhibited internationally, which often relies on activation by the viewer, uses immersive environments, interactive technologies with gestural interfaces, and narrative long-form film. The activation of the work becomes a metaphor for our connectedness within biological, social, and ecological systems. Wallworth received news and documentary Emmy Awards for outstanding new approaches in documentary for her VR narrative projects in collaboration with Indigenous communities, *Collisions* (2016) and *Awavena* (2018).

Zillah Watson is former head of BBC VR and executive producer of a number of critically acclaimed VR experiences for the BBC, including *Damming the Nile*, *Make Noise*, and *Nothing to Be Written*. She led the development of 360 VR for BBC News and is the author of "VR for News: The New Reality?," published by the Reuters Institute for the Study of Journalism in 2017.

Peggy Weil is an artist, designer, and academic. Her work spans digital urban signboards, VR, apps, and games that have been exhibited internationally. An original member of the MIT Media Lab, she has gone on to create award-winning titles, including *Gone Gitmo*. Weil founded HeadsUP!, a global competition challenging designers to create data visualization of urgent global issues for the public square.

Nedra Kline Weinreich works with nonprofits and nongovernmental organizations, public agencies, start-ups, and socially minded organizations around the world to create positive change on health and social issues through social marketing and behavioral design. Weinreich is the author of *Hands-On Social Marketing: A Step-by-Step Guide to Designing Change for Good* and was lecturer at the University of California's School for Public Health for a decade. Nedra also founded Transmedia for Good Network and is on the editorial board for *Social Marketing Quarterly*.

Martina Welkhoff is a serial entrepreneur. She was cofounder of Zealyst, a mobile gaming app that strategically connected employees; board president of Seattle Women in Tech; a World Economic Forum

Global Shaper; a venture partner at Jump Canon Ventures, and founder of ConveneVR, a VR production studio. She is a founding partner of Women in XR, a venture fund focused on women-led companies.

Amelia Winger-Bearskin is an artist and technologist. She is Banks Family Preeminence Chair of Artificial Intelligence and the Arts at the Digital Worlds Institute at the University of Florida. She has founded numerous organizations, including AI Climate Justice Lab, Talk to Me about Water Collective, and Stupid Hackathon. She also founded Wampum Codes, an award-winning podcast (*Wampum.Codes*) and ethical framework for software development based on Indigenous values of co-creation, while a Mozilla Fellow at the MIT Co-Creation Studio. Amelia is a Deer Clan member of the Seneca-Cayuga Nation of Oklahoma.

Sarah Wolozin is the director of the Open Documentary Lab at MIT, where she oversees the lab's projects, including Docubase, and collaborations with institutions such as Tribeca Film Institute, IDFA DocLab, and the National Film Board of Canada. She has produced award-winning documentaries and educational media for a wide variety of media outlets, including PBS, History Channel, and NPR.

Nancy Xu is a virtual production producer (VPP) at Epic Games' London Innovation Lab. She was previously VPP at Moving Picture Company and worked on *The Lion King* (2019), *The Jungle Book* (2016), and *Alien: Covenant* (2017). Nancy is a speaker, panelist, and advocate for the virtual production community, supporting emerging storytellers with programs at Screen Skills and BFI in the United Kingdom.

Ashley York is a journalist, filmmaker, and producer, who is committed to a feminist approach to media making. She was cofounder for Take Action Games and was executive producer for the project *Darfur Is Dying* (2006). She has worked on projects that have won top honors and premiered at the major international festivals, including the films codirected—*Tig* (2015) and *Hillbilly* (2018). She produced *My Kind of Country*, a new music documentary series by Reese Witherspoon; *Hello Sunshine* for Apple TV+; and the HBO Emmy-nominated documentary series *We're Here*.

Maya Zuckerman is a writer, entrepreneur, culture hacker, and consultant in emergent technology with experience across diverse media platforms. Zuckerman's work is focused on new storytelling models with attention to narratives promoting social change. She is founder of TransmediaSF, a network of Bay Area media and start-up creatives. Zuckerman is developing the sci-fi multiplatform series Em's Theory.

Glossary

alternate reality game (ARG): An interactive networked narrative that uses the real world as a platform and employs transmedia storytelling to deliver a narrative experience that will be determined by the players' actions or choices. This can include the use of digital devices and online communications.

Android: A mobile operating system designed primarily for touchscreen smartphones and tablets.

application programming interface (API): A type of software interface that enables two or more computer programs to communicate with each other.

Architecture Machine Group (Arch Mac): A laboratory that brought together architecture, engineering, and computing in a new vision of architectural research and teaching founded by Nicholas Negroponte and Leon Groisser at MIT in 1967. The group granted master's and doctoral degrees, the only lab at MIT to do so.

artificial intelligence (AI): The simulation of human problem-solving and decision-making capabilities by computer systems and machines. Applications include natural language processing, speech recognition, machine learning, and machine vision.

augmented reality (AR): A technology that superimposes a computer-generated image on a user's view of the real world via a digital screen-based device, thus providing a composite image which mixes the physical with the digital. This superimposition can also be auditory, haptic, somatosensory, and olfactory, as well as visual.

Bitcoin: The first decentralized cryptocurrency—released in 2009.

blockchain: A digital ledger of transactions that is duplicated and distributed across an entire network of computer systems. It is a system of recording information in a way that makes it difficult or impossible to change or hack. There are two types of blockchain system—proof of stake and proof of work. Proof of stake is a form of cryptographic proof whereby crypto-currency owners validate block transactions based on the number of coins they stake. "Validators" of a new block collect the transaction fees from the block as a reward. Proof of work verifies that a certain amount of a specific computational effort has been expended through a process known as crypto mining.

computer-generated imagery (CGI): A subcategory of visual effects—digitally created imagery in film and television that does not exist in the physical environment being recorded.

Computer Graphics Lab: A computer lab located at the New York Institute of Technology during the late 1970s and 1980s, founded by Dr. Alexander Schure.

cryptocurrency (crypto): A digital currency designed for use as a medium of exchange whereby transactions are verified and recorded on a blockchain by a decentralized system using cryptography rather than by a centralized authority, such as a bank or government.

cryptography: The computational solution of mathematical problems.

crypto mining: The process by which new cryptocurrency (e.g., Bitcoin, ether) are entered into circulation and the way in which the network confirms new transactions. It is a critical component of the blockchain ledger's maintenance and development. Mining is performed using sophisticated hardware that solves an extremely complex computational problem. The first computer to find the solution to the problem receives the next block of currency and the process begins again. Digiconomist, a site that examines the impact, primarily economic, of digital technology, estimated that one bitcoin transaction takes the equivalent of approximately 50 days of power for the average US household and that an Ethereum transaction can consume as much power as an average US household uses in more than a week.

decentralized autonomous organizations (DAOs): Originating from Web 3.0—a type of bottom-up entity—that allows communities, corporations, or any type of collective organization to be administered and governed with no central authority, using the ability of the blockchain. Members of a DAO own tokens of the DAO and can vote on initiatives.

Decentralized finance: An umbrella term for an internet-native financial system that uses blockchains and cryptocurrency.

Deepfakes: Videos created through artificially intelligent deep-learning techniques. The process involves inputting a source video of a person into a computer and then inputting multiple images and videos of another person. The neural network then learns the movements and expressions of the person in the source video and maps the other's image onto it to look as if they are carrying out the speech or act.

Ethereum blockchain: A decentralized, open-source blockchain launched in 2013 in which "ether" is the native cryptocurrency. Ethereum currently uses a consensus protocol called proof-of-work.

extended reality (XR): Refers to all real-and-virtual-combined environments and human-machine interactions generated by computer technology. It includes AR, mixed reality, VR, and the areas in between.

Flash: A multimedia software platform used to create and interact with animations, video games, web applications, mobile apps, games, and embedded web browser video players. Established by Macromedia in 1996 as a two-part system: a graphics and animation editor and a web-based player. Acquired by Adobe in 2005, the platform was officially discontinued at the end of 2020 for all users outside China.

futures literacy: A capability that allows people to better understand the role of the future in what they see and do. It enhances the ability to prepare, recover, and invent as changes occur.

futurist: A person whose specialty is futurology—the attempt to systematically explore predictions and possibilities about the future and how they can emerge from the present.

Google Daydream: A VR headset for Android first released by Google in 2016. It works with video applications (including Netflix, YouTube, and Google Play), various games, and other applications.

Google Glass: Voice- and motion-controlled eyeglasses that display information directly in the user's field of vision. An Android device that has AR and VR capabilities. No longer commercially available as a retail product, Google Glass still does exist.

haptics: Haptic technology, also known as kinesthetic communication or 3D touch, refers to technologies that can create the sensation of touch by applying forces, vibrations, or motions to the wearer.

head-mounted displays (HMDs): A display device, worn on the head or as part of a helmet that has a small display optic in front of the eyes. Uses include gaming, aviation, engineering, and medicine. VR headsets are HMDs combined with "inertial measurement units," which detect the wearer's movements and render the video/CGI in real time in response.

head-up/heads-up displays: A transparent display that overlays information and data onto the wearers normal field of vision—initially used in military aviation so pilots could view instruments and readings. A precursor to AR.

interactive documentary (i-doc): A documentary production that differs from the more traditional single-media documentaries through the application of multimedia tools and interactive digital technologies. Within an i-doc, the audience may become active agents making the work unfold through their interactions and often by contributing their own content.

leap motion: An American company that manufactured and marketed a computer hardware sensor device that supported hand and finger motions as input but required no hand contact or touching. In 2016 the company released new software designed for hand tracking in virtual reality.

location-based entertainment (LBE): A term that has emerged alongside the rise of the experience economy which refers to forms of entertainment that take place in a specific location outside of the home environment, such as theme parks, escape rooms, VR installations, and immersive experiences.

Magic Leap: An American start-up company established in 2011 that released in August 2018 a head-mounted virtual retinal display called Magic Leap One, which superimposes 3D CGI over real-world objects, by projecting a digital light field into the wearer's eye. The Magic Leap 2 headset launched in September 2022 with a starting price of $3,299.

metaverse: A VR space in which users can interact with a computer-generated environment and other users either via a VR headset or gamepad or a keyboard and mouse screen-based interaction.

Microsoft HoloLens: A pair of mixed reality untethered and self-contained smart-glasses developed and manufactured by Microsoft. HoloLens was the first HMD running the Windows Mixed Reality platform under the Windows 10 computer operating system.

mixed reality: A medium consisting of immersive CGI environments in which elements of a physical and virtual environment are combined.

motion capture: The process or technique of digitally recording patterns of movement, in particular the recording of an actor's movements for the purpose of animating a CGI character in a film or computer game.

motion platform: Also referred to as a motion simulator, a mechanism that creates the feelings of being in real physical motion. In a simulator, the movement is synchronized with a visual representation of the outside world scene—for example, a train ride or a vehicle journey. These platforms are commonly found in film and cinema-based theme parks rides.

Mozilla Hubs: A collaboration tool used to create virtual spaces that are interacted with through a first-person perspective (either via a VR headset or gamepad or a keyboard and mouse screen-based interaction).

Nintendo 64: A gaming console released in September 1996.

non-fungible tokens (NFTs): A financial security consisting of digital data stored on a blockchain—the ownership of an NFT is recorded in the blockchain and can be transferred by the owner, allowing NFTs to be sold and traded.

NFT Oasis: A platform for creative projects that combines NFTs, VR, and decentralized finance.

Oculus: Formerly known as Oculus VR, a technology company developing VR hardware for business and entertainment founded in 2012 by Palmer Luckey. Oculus initiated a Kickstarter campaign in 2012 to fund the Rift's development, raising about US$2.5 million from some 10,000 contributors. Oculus was purchased by Facebook for $2 billion in March 2014. Its hardware includes VR headsets, touch controllers, and Gear VR controllers powered by the Oculus platform.

Oculus Go: A VR headset developed by Facebook Technologies in partnership with Qualcomm and Xiaomi using an Android operating system. Released in May 2018 and discontinued in June 2020.

Oculus Quest: A VR headset developed by Oculus (a division of Meta Platforms Inc.), released in May 2019. Similar to its predecessor, Oculus Go, it is a standalone device that can run games and software wirelessly under an Android-based operating system.

Oculus Quest 2: The successor to the Oculus Quest, released September 2020, and rebranded as Meta Quest 2 in November 2021. A VR headset developed by Facebook Reality Labs (formerly Oculus).

Oculus Rift: A VR headset designed to connect to a high-powered PC to enable advanced graphics rendering. Released in 2016 and discontinued in 2021.

OpenGL: An open-source graphics library is an application programming interface for rendering 2D and 3D vector graphics.

open source: Software, source code, content, or creative work for which the copyright holder grants users a license to use, study, change, adapt, and distribute to anyone and for any purpose. Open-source assets may be developed in a collaborative public manner.

Playstation Morpheus: PlayStation VR (PS VR, known by its code name "Project Morpheus" during development) is a virtual reality headset developed by Sony, released in 2016.

radio frequency identification (RFID): Widely used since the 1970s, a wireless system that uses radio waves to passively identify a "tagged" object—which has an embedded chip. It is used in several commercial and industrial applications, from issuing library books to enabling entry into venues (e.g., hotel rooms, offices, institutions, hospitals, etc.)

real-time game engine (RTGE): A software framework that allows the user to move fluidly by flying or walking through a 3D computer environment or model and look in any direction via a VR headset or gamepad or a keyboard and mouse screen-based interaction. Examples include Unreal Engine and Unity.

rendering: The process of generating photorealistic or nonphotorealistic still or moving imagery from a 2D or 3D model through computational processing.

Samsung Gear: A VR headset developed by Samsung Electronics in collaboration with Oculus VR, and manufactured by Samsung. Released in 2015 and discontinued in 2020, when all support for XR services, applications, and access to video content was also withdrawn.

Second Life: Launched by Linden Labs in 2003, a multiuser online virtual world in which users, or "residents," can create an avatar, build their own environments, create their own content, and interact with other residents.

Silicon Valley: Located in the southern San Francisco Bay Area of California, it is the location of many start-up and global technology companies—the most well known being Apple, Facebook, and Google—and also the site of technology-focused institutions clustered around Stanford University.

Social virtual reality: A form of web-based social interaction, enabled by immersive technologies within 3D virtual worlds where individuals, represented by an avatar, can engage in real-time exchanges and shared activities.

Software development kit (SDK): A collection of software development tools in one installable package. These tools usually include a compiler, debugger, and sometimes a software framework. They are normally specific to a hardware platform and operating system combination. They facilitate the creation of applications—for example, VR SDKs provide the fundamental tools to design, build, and test VR experiences. Also referred to as developer kits, dev kits, or DKs.

Somnium Space: An open-source metaverse platform that incorporates game play, building programmable environments, purchasing virtual properties, customizing land and buildings, and trading digital assets. It is built on the Ethereum blockchain.

Steam: A digital distribution platform for video games created by Valve Corporation. It is the largest digital distribution platform for PC gaming, initially launched as a software client in 2003 by Valve to provide automatic updates for their games. It expanded to distributing third-party titles in 2005. It has since evolved as an expansive gaming community where players and developers can buy and sell games.

stereoscopic virtual reality (stereo-VR): Stereoscopic displays and viewers present a different view of the virtual scene to each eye, creating a sense of depth that makes each eye focus in harmony. Stereography replicates human vision. With 20–20 vision, each of the human eyes sees a different image. Our eyes then converge at a certain point—which provides us with our sense of depth and three-dimensionality.

tech bros: An informal term that refers to a hypermasculine man from the tech industry who is stereotypically located in Silicon Valley.

360-degree video: A spherical panoramic video recording where a view in every direction is captured simultaneously using either a singular specialist omnidirectional camera or a number of cameras—the output of which is stitched together. These videos can be viewed using either a VR headset or through a 360-degree-enabled screen interface—the former enables the user to physically look around the space by turning their head or moving their body, the latter is controlled via on-screen panning and rotation controls or keyboard buttons or by clicking and dragging the mouse.

transmedia storytelling: The technique of telling a single story or story experience across multiple platforms and formats using digital technologies.

Triple-A (or AAA) game: An informal term used in the computer games industry to identify games with very high production budgets, usually produced and distributed by major studios and publishers.

Unity: A cross-platform computer graphics game engine (redeveloped by Unity Technologies, first released in a Mac OS X game engine). The engine can be used to create 3D and 2D games, as well as interactive simulations and other experiences. The engine has been adopted other by industries including film, automotive, architecture, engineering, construction, and the military.

Unreal (engine): A 3D computer graphics game engine developed by Epic Games, first used in the first-person shooter game Unreal in 1998. It has since been used in a variety of genres of games and has been adopted the film and television industries through Virtual Production. Written in C++—a general-purpose programming language—the Unreal Engine supports a wide range of desktop, mobile, console and virtual reality platforms.

User experience (UX): Describes how a user interacts with and experiences a product, system, or service. It includes a person's perceptions of utility, ease of use, and efficiency.

user interface (UI): The means through which a user interacts with a computer system and other electronic devices. These can include: text-based UIs where the user inputs textual prompts and commands; Graphical Users Interfaces (GUI) through which the user navigates the system or device using visual icons such as arrow and hand cursors, graphical imagery, and audio prompts.

virtual production: The name given to a suite of tools that uses RTGE technologies, including Unity or Unreal Engine, in film and television production to produce content that can include CGI previsualizations of scenes and even entire films. These also include "on-set" virtual production, in which an LED wall is used as a backdrop for a set on which video or CGI rendered in real time is displayed. When the camera moves, the virtual environment on the LED wall simultaneously shifts perspective to navigate a virtual landscape.

virtual reality (VR): The computer-generated simulation of a 3D image or environment that can be explored and interacted with either stereoscopically via a VR headset or gamepad or a keyboard and mouse screen-based interaction.

virtual reality (VR) headset: HMDs combined with "inertial measurement units" that detect the wearer's movements and render the video/CGI in real time in response. Examples include all those made by Oculus, HTC Vive, and Google Daydream.

Virtual Reality Modeling Language: A programming language used to create 3D virtual space on the World Wide Web—a 3D version of HTML.

visual effects (VFX): The creation or manipulation of any on-screen imagery that does not exist or would be impractical or impossible to film, including environments, objects, vehicles, pyrotechnics, atmospheres, creatures, and people.

Vive: A VR brand of HTC Corporation that designs and produces VR headsets accessories, VR software and services, and initiatives that promote applications of VR in the business and art sectors. Released in 2016, Vive hardware is compatible with the Steam VR platform and with Windows and Linux operating systems.

volumetric capture: Also called volumetric video, a technique that captures a 3D space, such as a location or performance in real time.

VRChat: An online virtual world platform for users to interact with one another via user-created 3D avatars and worlds. It was designed to be accessed via a VR headset, although it can be viewed via a flatscreen through a gamepad or keyboard and mouse screen-based interaction. It was first released as a Windows application for the Oculus Rift DK1 prototype in January 2014 and later released on Steam in February 2017.

Web Graphics Library (WebGL): A JavaScript API for rendering interactive 2D and 3D graphics within any compatible web browser.

Web 3.0: Refers to the third generation of the evolution of web technologies. It is a new web iteration that incorporates concepts such as decentralization, the semantic web, and the metaverse. Its commercial infrastructure is based on blockchain technologies.

WebVR: An API for creating browser-based immersive 3D and VR experiences to be explored using a VR headset or navigated through a screen display using keyboard controls. Developed by Mozilla, Google and Microsoft; superseded by WebXR.

WebXR: An API that describes support for accessing AR and VR devices in a web browser.

Worldbuilding: The process of creating an imaginary world within a fictional universe that includes coherent qualities such as a history, geography, ecology, language, social structures, and political systems. It is often associated with the work of many science-fiction and fantasy writers.

Worlds, Inc.: A company founded to create online virtual worlds, which launched "Worlds Chat" in 1995.

Notes

Preface

1 For more on SP-ARK, see http://www.sp-ark.org/.
2 Sarah A. Atkinson, "Film and Audiovisual Media OERs: The Case of SP-ARK, The Sally Potter Film Archive (Topic: OER and Teaching Quality): A HEA/JISC Open Educational Resources Case Study: Pedagogical Development from OER Practice" (paper presented at the Higher Education Academy, London, 2012).
3 Sarah Atkinson, "The Anatomy of a Film: Process, Collaborative Endeavour and Archiving in the Digital Age" (paper presented at the Besides the Screen conference, Goldsmiths College, London, December 2012).
4 "Capturing *The Beast*: Transmedia, Digital Ephemera, and the Archive," with Vicki Callahan, Yvonne Welbon, Helen De Michiel, and Robert Pratten (workshop at the Society for Cinema and Media Studies annual conference, Seattle, March 2014).
5 Sarah A. Atkinson and Vicki Callahan, "TMDb: Transmedia Database" (paper presented at the Conducttr conference, London, October 17, 2014).
6 TimelineJS is an open-source browser-based visual editing tool to construct multimedia, interactive timelines. TimelineJS, accessed July 20, 2022, https://timeline.knightlab.com/.
7 Selected publications on transmedia by Sarah Atkinson include *Beyond the Screen: Emerging Cinema and Engaging Audiences* (New York: Bloomsbury, 2014); "Transmedia Critical | The Performative Functions of Dramatic Communities: Conceptualizing Audience Engagements in Transmedia Fiction," *International Journal*

of Communication 8 (2014): 2201–19; and "Transmedia Film: From Embedded Engagement to Embodied Experience," in *The Routledge Companion to Transmedia Studies*, ed. Matthew Freeman and Renira Rampazzo Gambarato (London: Routledge, 2018), 15–24. Selected publications by Vicki Callahan on transmedia include "Queerskins: Divining a Feminist Phenomenological Method," in *The Transmedia Companion*, ed. Simon Bacon (Oxford: Peter Lang, 2021), 229–38; "Where There's Smoke and the Generative Documentary: A Conversation with Lance Weiler," *Afterimage* 49, no. 1 (March 2022): 14–25; and "The Future of the Archive: An Interview with Lynn Hershman Leeson," in *Reclaiming the Archive: Feminism and Film History*, ed. Vicki Callahan (Detroit: Wayne State University Press, 2010), 418–29. We also co-delivered a transmedia-focused workshop as part of Vicki's Fulbright Scholarship: "Transmedia Storytelling: From Concept to Design and Realization" (University College Cork, October 22–23, 2015).

8 These were undertaken by USC's Viola Lasmana.

9 Thanks to the King's Undergraduate Research Fellowship awarded to Rose Doherty.

10 See Catherine Allen et al., *VWVR: A Vision for Women and Virtual Reality* (London: King's College London, 2018). The VWVR approach is more fully documented in Helen W. Kennedy, Sarah Atkinson, and Natalie Wreyford, *The Creative Collaboratory Method: Report and Toolkit* (London: King's College London, 2020), and taken forward as a case study in Natalie Wreyford, Tamsyn Dent, and Dave O'Brien, *Creative Majority: An APPG for Creative Diversity Report on "What Works" to Support, Encourage and Improve Equality, Diversity and Inclusion in the Creative Sector; A Report for the All Party Parliamentary Group for Creative Diversity*, September 2021, https://www.kcl.ac.uk/cultural/projects/creative-majority.

11 Hosted by Helen W. Kennedy, then at the University of Brighton, which funded the doctoral work of Daniel Eric Harley. See Harley's "The Politics of Consumer VR: Framing Contemporary Virtual Reality" (PhD diss., York University, Toronto, 2021).

Chapter 1

1 Kate Crawford, *Atlas of AI: Power, Politics, and the Planetary Costs of Artificial Intelligence* (New Haven: Yale University Press, 2021), 8.

2 Kamal Sinclair's *Making a New Reality* series was a commissioned research project by the Ford Foundation's JustFilms and with supplemental support of the Sundance Institute. The seven "chapter" series was published throughout 2017–18 on Making a New Reality (https://makinganewreality.org) and Immerse (https://immerse.news). With Ford Foundation's continued support, Sinclair worked with Jessica Clark and Carrie McLaren to develop a book and toolkit.

3 For more information, see Women Film Pioneers Project (https://wfpp.columbia.edu/); Women and Film History International (https://www.wfhi.org); and Oscar Micheaux Society (https://www.cmstudies.org/page/groups_micheaux).

4 These are all terms that are defined in the book's accompanying glossary.

5 T. Furness, "Helmet-Mounted Displays and Their Aerospace Applications" (paper presented at the National Aerospace Electronics Conference, Dayton, OH, 1969).

6 Safiya Umoja Noble, *Algorithms of Oppression: How Search Engines Reinforce Racism* (New York: New York University Press, 2018).

7 Char Davies, interview by Sarah Atkinson, September 27, 2022.

8 Sarah Atkinson, *From Film Practice to Data Process: Production Aesthetics and Representational Practices of a Film Industry in Transition* (Edinburgh: Edinburgh University Press, 2018), 166–68.

9 For UK instances, see Doris Ruth Eikhof, Jack Newsinger, Daniela Rudloff, Daria Luchinskaya, and Mark Banks, *Workforce Diversity in the UK Screen Sector: Evidence Review* (Leicester: CAMEo Research Institute, 2018), https://www2.bfi.org.uk/sites/bfi.org.uk/files/downloads/bfi-workforce-diversity-in-uk-screen-sector-evidence-review-2018-03.pdf (URL unavailable); Arts Council England, *Equality, Diversity and the Creative Case: A Data Report, 2019–2020* (Arts Council England, 2021), https://www.artscouncil.org.uk/publication/equality-diversity-and-creative-case-data-report-2019-20; Eliza Easton, *Creative Diversity: The State of Diversity in the UK's Creative Industries and What We Can Do about It* (London: Creative

Industries Federation; MOBO Awards, 2015); and Stephen Follows, Alexis Kreager, and E. Gomes, "Cut Out of the Picture," *A Study of Gender Inequality amongst Film Directors in the UK Film Industry* (London: Directors UK, 2016). For US instances, see Darnell Hunt and Ana-Christina Ramon, *UCLA Hollywood Diversity Report 2020: A Tale of Two Hollywoods*, pt. 1 *Film*, UCLA College of Social Sciences, accessed February 6, 2020, https://socialsciences.ucla.edu/wp-content/uploads/2020/02/UCLA-Hollywood-Diversity-Report-2020-Film-2-6-2020.pdf (URL unavailable); Stacy L. Smith, Marc Choueiti, Kevin Yao, Hannah Clark, and Katherine Pieper, *Inclusion in the Director's Chair: Analysis of Director Gender & Race/Ethnicity across 1,300 Top Films from 2007 to 2019* (Los Angeles: Annenberg Foundation / USC Annenberg Inclusion Initiative, January 2020), http://assets.uscannenberg.org/docs/aii-inclusion-directors-chair-20200102.pdf; Stacy L. Smith, Katherine Pieper, and Al-Baab Khan, *Inclusion in the Director's Chair: Analysis of Director Gender & Race/Ethnicity across 1,500 Top Films from 2007 to 2021* (Los Angeles: Annenberg Foundation / USC Annenberg Inclusion Initiative, February 2022), https://assets.uscannenberg.org/docs/aii-inclusion-directors-chair-2022.pdf; and Women's Media Center, *The Status of Women in U.S. Media 2019*, Women's Media Center, February 21, 2019, https://womensmediacenter.com/reports/the-status-of-women-in-u-s-media-2019.

10 *XR Inclusion: 2020 Annual Report*, XR Inclusion, https://xrinclusion.org/report/. This is discussed in more detail in chapter 5.

11 Natalie Wreyford, Tamsyn Dent, and Dave O'Brien, *Creative Majority: An APPG for Creative Diversity Report on "What Works" to Support, Encourage and Improve Equality, Diversity and Inclusion in the Creative Sector; A Report for the All Party Parliamentary Group for Creative Diversity* (London: Kings College London, 2021).

12 See, for example, Clive James Nwonka, *Race and Ethnicity in the UK Film Industry: An Analysis of the BFI Diversity Standards* (London: London School of Economics and Political Science, 2020); Clive James Nwonka, "Diversity and Data: An Ontology of Race and Ethnicity in the British Film Institute's Diversity Standards," *Media, Culture & Society* 43, no. 3 (2021): 460–79; Sara Ahmed, "'You End Up Doing the Document Rather than Doing the Doing': Diversity, Race Equality

and the Politics of Documentation," *Ethnic and Racial Studies* 30, no. 4 (2007): 590–609; Shelley Cobb and Natalie L. Wreyford, "'Could You Hire Someone Female or from an Ethnic Minority?' Being Both: Black, Asian and Other Minority Women Working in British Film Production," in *Black Film, British Cinema II*, ed. Clive Nwonka and Anamik Saha (London: Goldsmiths Press, 2021), 165–84; and Frances Galt, *Women's Activism behind the Screens* (Bristol: Bristol University Press, 2020).

13 See Clive James Nwonka and Sarita Malik, "Cultural Discourses and Practices of Institutionalized Diversity in the UK Film Sector: 'Just Get Something Black Made,'" *Sociological Review* 66, no. 6 (2018): 1111–27; Clive James Nwonka, "White Women, White Men, and Intra-Racial Diversity: A Data-Led Analysis of Gender Representation in the UK Film Industry," *Cultural Sociology* 15, no. 3 (2021): 430–54; Tamsyn Dent, "Devalued Women, Valued Men: Motherhood, Class and Neoliberal Feminism in the Creative Media Industries," *Media, Culture & Society* 42, no. 4 (2019): 537–53; Anne O'Brien and Susan Liddy, "The Price of Motherhood in the Irish Film and Television Industries," *Gender, Work & Organization* 28, no. 6 (2021): 1997–2009; Natalie Wreyford, Helen Kennedy, Jack Newsinger, and Rowan Aust, *Locked Down and Locked Out: The Impacts of the COVID-19 Pandemic on Mothers Working in the UK Television Industry* (Nottingham: University of Nottingham, 2021); and Bridget Conor, Rosalind Gill, and Stephanie Taylor, "Gender and Creative Labour," *Sociological Review*, 63, no. 1 (2015): 1–22.

14 See Atkinson, *From Film Practice to Data Process*; and Erin Hill, *Never Done: A History of Women's Work in Media Production* (Rutgers University Press, 2016).

15 Brooke Erin Duffy, *(Not) Getting Paid to Do What You Love: Gender, Social Media, and Aspirational Work* (New Haven: Yale University Press, 2017), 32.

16 Here, Duffy is drawing on work from David Hesmondhalgh and Sarah Baker, "Sex, Gender and Work Segregation in the Cultural Industries," *Sociological Review* 63, no. 51 (2015): 23–36.

17 Duffy, *(Not) Getting Paid*, 33.

18 See Caitlin Dewey, "The Only Guide to Gamergate You Will Ever Need to Read," *Washington Post*, October 14, 2014, https://www

.washingtonpost.com/news/the-intersect/wp/2014/10/14/the-only
-guide-to-gamergate-you-will-ever-need-to-read/; and Kate Conger,
"Exclusive: Here's the Full 10-Page Anti-Diversity Screed Circulating
at Google [Updated]," Gizmodo, August 5, 2017, https://gizmodo.com/
exclusive-heres-the-full-10-page-anti-diversity-screed-1797564320.

19 Noble, *Algorithms of Oppression*, Kindle, 1226–786.

20 Noble, 1797.

21 Clive Thompson, *Coders: The Making of a New Tribe and the Remaking
of the World* (New York: Penguin Books, 2019), particularly chapter 7.

22 Emily Chang, *Brotopia: Breaking Up the Boys' Club of Silicon Valley* (New
York: Portfolio, 2018).

23 See Chang, particularly chapter 2.

24 Joy Lisi Rankin, *A People's History of Computing in the United States*
(Cambridge: Harvard University Press, 2018), 10.

25 Rankin, 228.

26 See Julia Wright, "Making the Cut: Female Editors and Representation in the Film and Media Industry," UCLA: Center for the Study
of Women, 2009; Kristin Hatch, "Cutting Women: Margaret Booth
and Hollywood's Pioneering Female Film Editors," in Women Film
Pioneers Project (digital resource), ed. Jane Gaines, Radha Vatsal, and
Monica Dall'Asta (New York: Columbia University Libraries, 2013),
https://doi.org/10.7916/d8-t0y9-hv61. Booth was given the title film
editor by the producer Irving Thalberg. Cari Beauchamp, *Without
Lying Down: Frances Marion and the Powerful Women of Early Hollywood* (Berkeley: University of California Press, 1998). For more on
Svilova, see Rachel Pronger, "Elizaveta Svilova: The Woman behind
The Man with a Movie Camera," New East Digital Archive, September 5, 2021, https://www.new-east-archive.org/articles/show/13077/
elizaveta-svilova-the-woman-behind-the-man-with-a-movie-camera.
For more on Shub, see Ilana Shub Sharp, *Esfir Shub: Pioneer of Documentary Filmmaking* (New York: Bloomsbury, 2022).

27 Nathalia Holt, *The Queens of Animation: The Untold Story of the Women
Who Transformed the World of Disney and Made Cinematic History*
(Boston: Little, Brown, 2019).

28 Kathy Kleiman, *Proving Ground: The Untold Story of the Six Women
Who Programmed the World's First Modern Computer* (London:

C. Hurst & Co, 2022); and Mar Hicks, *Programmed Inequality: How Britain Discarded Women Technologists and Lost Its Edge in Computing* (Cambridge, MA: MIT Press, 2017).

29 Thompson, *Coders*, 192–93.

30 Thompson, 196–97.

31 These include Clara Rockmore, Daphne Oram, Bebe Barron, Pauline Oliveros, Delia Derbyshire, Maryanne Amacher, Eliane Radigue, Suzanne Ciani, and Laurie Spiegel.

32 These interviews include the following: Ingrid Kopp, interviews by Sarah Atkinson, 2016 and 2022; Kamal Sinclair, interviews by Vicki Callahan, 2017 and 2022; Liz Rosenthal, interviews by Sarah Atkinson, 2016 and 2022, and interview by Daniel Harley, 2019; Sarah Wolozin, interview by Vicki Callahan, 2016, and interview by Sarah Atkinson, 2022; Illya Szilak, interview by Viola Lasmana, 2016, and interview by Vicki Callahan, 2022; Lina Srivastava, interviews by Vicki Callahan, 2016 and 2022; Nancy Bennett, interviews by Vicki Callahan, 2017 and 2022; Sadah Espii Proctor, interviews by Vicki Callahan, 2017 and 2022; and Debra McGrory, interview by Rose Doherty, 2016, and interview by Sarah Atkinson, 2022. Years for all interviews are cited in the notes, but because the individuals mentioned here were interviewed on more than one occasion, we've clarified the temporal context of their words by additionally noting the specific year of their interviews parenthetically in the text.

33 Judy Malloy, ed., *Women, Art and Technology* (Cambridge, MA: MIT Press, 2003). The book includes contributions from Rebecca Allen, Char Davies, and Lynn Hershman Leeson.

34 Christiane Paul, *Digital Art* (London: Thames & Hudson, 2003). Paul's book includes discussion of Rebecca Allen, Char Davies, Toni Dove, Lynn Hershman Leeson and Tamiko Thiel.

35 Christiane Paul, ed., *A Companion to Digital Art* (Hoboken: Wiley-Blackwell, 2016).

36 Donna Cox, Ellen Sandor, and Janine Fron, eds., *New Media Futures: The Rise of Women in the Digital Arts* (Champaign: University of Illinois Press, 2018).

Chapter 2

1   Rebecca Allen, interview by Sarah Atkinson, March 25, 2022.

2   Allen.

3   See "CBS Dan Rather Interview—1983. Special News Feature: The Computers Are Coming—Man or Machine," Rebecca Allen, 1983, https://rebeccaallen.com/projects/cbs-dan-rather-cbs-interview.

4   Allen, interview by Atkinson, March 25, 2022.

5   Karl Bartos, *The Sound of the Machine: My Life in Kraftwerk and Beyond* (London: Omnibus Press, 2022).

6   Allen, interview by Atkinson, March 25, 2022.

7   Allen.

8   Allen. Emergence is "a real-time 3D software system that supports an active, responsive, networked, virtual world." Rebecca Allen, "The Emergence Project: The Bush Soul," *Leonardo* 38, no. 4 (2005): 314.

9   Cool!, created by DeepStream VR, is one such VR app for pain relief released in 2015.

10   Allen, interview by Atkinson, March 25, 2022.

11   Allen. Brin and Page founded Google in 1996.

12   Allen.

13   Tamiko Thiel, "The Design of the Connection Machine," *Design Issues* 10, no. 1 (1994): 5–18.

14   Tamiko Thiel, interview by Sarah Atkinson, March 15, 2022.

15   Thiel.

16   Thiel.

17   Thiel.

18   Thiel.

19   Thiel. For more on the exhibition, which ran from November 13, 2017, to April 8, 2018, see *Thinking Machines: Art and Design in the Computer Age, 1959–1989*, MoMA, accessed March 15, 2022, https://www.moma.org/calendar/exhibitions/3863.

20   Christiane Paul, *Digital Art*, 2nd ed. (London: Thames & Hudson, 2008); and Char Davies, "Landscapes of Ephemeral Embrace: Immersive Virtual Space as A Medium for Transforming Perception" (PhD diss., Center for Advanced Inquiry in the Interactive Arts, University of Plymouth, UK, 2005).

21   Char Davies, interview by Sarah Atkinson, September 27, 2022.

22 Davies.

23 Davies.

24 Davies.

25 Davies.

26 Davies.

27 Davies.

28 Davies.

29 Davies.

30 Davies.

31 Molly Gottschalk, "Virtual Reality Is the Most Powerful Medium of Our Time," *Artsy*, March 15, 2016, https://www.artsy.net/article/artsy -editorial-virtual-reality-is-the-most-powerful-artistic-medium-of -our-time.

32 "Alejandro González Iñárritu Presents Nonny de La Peña with Field Builder Peabody Award," Peabody Awards, YouTube, March 24, 2022, https://www.youtube.com/watch?v=99IySzyQRhl.

33 Nonny de la Peña, interview by Vicki Callahan, September 26, 2016.

34 De la Peña.

35 De la Peña.

36 De la Peña.

37 De la Peña.

38 Will Mason, "The 'Godmother of VR' Nonny de La Peña on the Future of Immersive Journalism," Upload, January 27, 2015, https:// uploadvr.com/the-mother-of-vr-nonny-de-la-pena-on-the-future-of -immersive-journalism/.

39 De la Peña, interview by Callahan, September 26, 2016.

40 Nonny de la Peña, interview by Vicki Callahan, May 20, 2022. *A Life in Pieces: The Diary and Letters of Stanley Hayami* was available as both VR and 360-degree video (for mobile viewing). The work was created by Nonny de la Peña of Emblematic and Sharon Yamato in collaboration with the Japanese American National Museum. For more information on the project, see *A Life in Pieces: The Diary and Letters of Stanley Hayami*, Japanese American National Museum, accessed May 20, 2022, https://www.janm.org/exhibits/a-life-in-pieces.

41 For more on the Atlanta Race Massacre, see "The 1906 Atlanta Race Massacre," Culture Centers International, accessed May 20, 2022, https://1906atlantaracemassacre.org/index.html (URL unavailable).

42 De la Peña, interview by Callahan, May 20, 2022.

43 For more on Reach, see "Project Reach," Emblematic, accessed May 20, 2022, https://emblematicgroup.com/events/.

Chapter 3

1 Kamal Sinclair, "Challenging the Innovator Stereotype," *Immerse*, December 30, 2017, https://immerse.news/challenging-the-innovator-stereotype-b562a37da008.

2 Christiane Paul, interview by Sarah Atkinson and Vicki Callahan, December 6, 2022.

3 Kamal Sinclair, interview by Vicki Callahan, January 6, 2017.

4 Shari Frilot, interview by Sarah Atkinson, February 17, 2022.

5 Frilot.

6 Sarah Wolozin, interview by Vicki Callahan, December 8, 2016.

7 Sarah Wolozin, interview by Sarah Atkinson, March 7, 2022.

8 Liz Rosenthal, interview by Sarah Atkinson, July 14, 2016.

9 Ingrid Kopp, interview by Sarah Atkinson, July 18, 2016.

10 Sinclair, interview by Callahan, January 6, 2017.

11 Hosted by King's College London, September 2017 and co-convened with Catherine Allen, Helen W. Kennedy, and Sarah Atkinson.

12 Samantha Storr, email interview by Viola Lasmana, July 31, 2017.

13 Madeline Power, interview by Vicki Callahan August 18, 2017.

14 "Producers Code of Credits—Producers Guild of America," Producers Guild of America, accessed February 6, 2019, https://www.producersguild.org/page/code_of_credits (URL unavailable).

15 "Code of Credits—New Media—Producers Guild of America," Producers Guild of America, accessed February 6, 2019, https://www.producersguild.org/page/coc_nm (URL unavailable).

16 Caitlin Burns, interview by Vicki Callahan, September 9, 2016.

17 Burns.

18 Burns.

19 Anonymous, interview by Vicki Callahan, 2016.

20 Emily Bazelon, "A Seat at the Head of the Table: Why Aren't Women Advancing More in Corporate America?," *New York Times Magazine*, February 21, 2019, https://www.nytimes.com/interactive/2019/02/21/magazine/women-corporate-america.html.

21 Jennifer Palais, interview by Vicki Callahan, July 28, 2016.

22 Maureen Fan, interview by Vicki Callahan, September 21, 2017.

23 Fan.

24 Palais, interview by Callahan, September 21, 2017.

25 Jan Libby, interview by Vicki Callahan, July 29, 2016.

26 Niema Jordan, interview by Vicki Callahan, August 17, 2016.

27 Ashley York, interview by Vicki Callahan, November 4, 2016.

28 York.

29 Nancy Bennett, interview by Vicki Callahan, July 27, 2017.

30 *Darfur Is Dying*, Susana Ruiz, accessed June 12, 2024, https://susanaruiz
    .org/takeactiongames-darfurisdying/.

31 Susana Ruiz, interview by Vicki Callahan, November 3, 2016.

32 Illya Szilak, interview by Viola Lasmana, November 17, 2016.

33 Toni B., interview by Vicki Callahan, July 14, 2017.

34 For more, see Browntourage, accessed July 14, 2017, http://
    browntourage.com/#/collabs.

35 Toni B., interview by Callahan, July 14, 2017.

36 For more information on the People's Guide to Tech, see A Peo-
    ple's Guide to Tech, accessed March 29, 2022, https://www
    .peoplesguidetotech.com/about.

37 Mimi Ọnụọha, interview by Sarah Atkinson, March 29, 2022.

38 Danielle Brathwaite-Shirley, interview by Sarah Atkinson, March 30,
    2022.

39 Brathwaite-Shirley.

40 For more, see Code Liberation Front, accessed March 23, 2022, http://
    codeliberation.org.

41 Phoenix Perry, interview by Sarah Atkinson, March 23, 2022.

42 Irene Fubara-Manuel, interview by Sarah Atkinson, April 6, 2022.

43 Taryn Southern, interview by Vicki Callahan, October 14, 2017.

44 Southern.

45 Southern.

46 Power, interview by Callahan, August 18, 2017.

47 Nonny de la Peña, interview by Vicki Callahan, September 26,
    2016.

48 Kate Parsons, interview by Vicki Callahan, July 17, 2017.

49 Erin Reilly, interview by Vicki Callahan, May 18, 2021.

50 Catherine Allen, interview by Daniel Harley, May 20, 2019.

51 For more, see Guild of Future Architects, accessed June 8, 2024, https://futurearchitects.com.

52 Julie Young, "The Invitation Effect: How We Are Using Facebook to Get More Women in Tech." Medium, February 6, 2017, https://medium.com/@juliey4/the-invitation-effect-how-we-are-using-facebook-to-get-more-women-in-tech-58331cc0429a.

53 Young.

54 Young.

55 Jenn Duong, interview by Vicki Callahan, August 17, 2017.

56 Amelia Winger-Bearskin, interview by Sarah Atkinson, February 28, 2022.

57 Anonymous, interview by Daniel Harley, 2019.

58 Jennifer Helene Maher, *Software Evangelism and the Rhetoric of Morality: Coding Justice in a Digital Democracy* (United Kingdom: Routledge, 2015), 1–3.

59 Winger-Bearskin, interview by Atkinson, February 28, 2022.

60 Winger-Bearskin.

61 Martina Welkhoff, interview by Vicki Callahan, January 2, 2018.

62 Denise Restauri, "8 Real Success Tips from Women Building the Future with Virtual Reality," *Forbes*, February 8, 2017, https://www.forbes.com/sites/deniserestauri/2017/02/08/8-real-success-tips-from-women-building-the-future-with-virtual-reality/. For additional information, see Monica Nickelsburg, "Seattle Entrepreneur Launches VR Startup with an Unusual Spin after Selling Her Startup to UW," GeekWire, January 25, 2017, https://www.geekwire.com/2017/seattle-entrepreneur-launches-vr-startup-unusual-spin-selling-startup-uw/.

63 Welkhoff, interview by Callahan, January 2, 2018.

64 Welkhoff.

65 Sadah Espii Proctor, interview by Vicki Callahan, August 24, 2017.

66 Liz Rosenthal, interview by Daniel Harley, May 31, 2019.

67 Sinclair, interview by Callahan, January 6, 2017.

68 Storr, email interview by Lasmana, July 31, 2017.

69 Sinclair, interview by Callahan, January 6, 2017.

70 Frilot, interview by Atkinson, February 17, 2022.

Chapter 4

1 Marsha Kinder, *Playing with Power in Movies, Television, and Video Games: From Muppet Babies to Teenage Mutant Ninja Turtles* (Berkeley: University of California Press, 1991); and Henry Jenkins, *Convergence Culture: Where Old and New Media Collide* (New York University Press, 2006).

2 Caitlin Burns, interview by Vicki Callahan, September 9, 2016. Burns here refers to the Producers Guild of America credit for transmedia producer, which was introduced in 2010. See Sarah Cooper, "Producers Guild Adds Transmedia Producer as Credit," *Screen Daily*, April 7, 2010, https://www.screendaily.com/production/producers-guild-adds-transmedia-producer-as-credit/5012482.article.

3 Jennifer Magee-Cook, interview by Vicki Callahan, December 22, 2016.

4 Kim Plowright, interview by Rose Doherty, July 29, 2016.

5 The experience went on to win the Outstanding Creative Achievement in Interactive Media—User Experience and Visual Design award in the 2015 67th Emmy Awards.

6 Robin Benty, interview by Vicki Callahan, July 26, 2016.

7 Liz Rosenthal, interview by Sarah Atkinson, July 14, 2016.

8 Hazel Grian, interview by Rose Doherty, August 3, 2016.

9 Illya Szilak, interview by Viola Lasmana, November 17, 2016.

10 Carrie Cutforth, interview by Sarah Atkinson, March 16, 2022.

11 Juliana Loh, interview by Sarah Atkinson, March 15, 2022.

12 Mary Feuer, interview by Vicki Callahan, July 26, 2016.

13 Carrie Lozano, interview by Vicki Callahan, August 25, 2016.

14 Jasmine Isdrake, interview by Rose Doherty, July 27, 2016.

15 Ingrid Kopp, interview by Sarah Atkinson, July 18, 2016.

16 May Abdalla, interview by Sarah Atkinson, January 24, 2022.

17 Sarah Wolozin, interview by Vicki Callahan, December 8, 2016.

18 Lina Srivastava, interview by Vicki Callahan, August 19, 2016.

19 Maya Zuckerman, interview by Viola Lasmana, December 15, 2016.

20 Jenni Powell, interview by Vicki Callahan, July 26, 2016.

21 See Universe Creation 101, accessed June 14, 2022, https://www.universecreation101.com/productions/.

22 Liz Miller, interview by Viola Lasmana, November 11, 2016.

23 Mary Feuer, interview by Vicki Callahan, July 26, 2016.

24 Christy Dena, interview by Rose Doherty, August 3, 2016.

25 Sandra Rodriguez, interview by Vicki Callahan, January 21, 2022.

26 Monika Bielskyte, interview by Sarah Atkinson, January 7, 2022.

27 Plowright, interview by Doherty, July 29, 2016.

28 Jennifer Palais, interview by Vicki Callahan, July 28, 2016.

29 Dena, interview.

30 Burns, interview by Callahan, September 9, 2016.

31 Kamal Sinclair, interview by Vicki Callahan, January 6, 2017.

32 Kopp, interview by Atkinson, July 18, 2016.

33 Shari Frilot, interview by Sarah Atkinson, February 17, 2022.

34 Sinclair, interview by Callahan, January 6, 2017.

35 Frilot, interview by Atkinson, February 17, 2022.

36 Sinclair, interview by Callahan, January 6, 2017.

37 Nonny de la Peña, interview by Vicki Callahan, September 26, 2016.

38 For further documentation, see *"Hunger in Los Angeles*—Immersive Journalism," YouTube, January 10, 2013, https://www.youtube .com/watch?v=SSLG8auUZKc;N; https://emblematicgroup.com/ experiences/hunger-in-la/; https://nwn.blogs.com/nwn/2016/09/ nonny-de-la-pena-vr-mentor-palmer-luckey-trump.html.

39 Nonny de la Peña, interview by Vicki Callahan, May 20, 2022.

40 Nonny de la Peña, Peggy Weil, Joan Llobera, et al., "Immersive journalism: Immersive Virtual Reality for the First-Person Experience of News," *Presence* 19, no. 4 (2010): 291–301.

41 Sinclair, interview by Callahan, January 6, 2017.

42 Tamiko Thiel, interview by Sarah Atkinson, March 15, 2022. In 1992 the Silicon Graphics OpenGL standard made it possible to create and design VR on PCs.

43 Char Davies, interview by Sarah Atkinson, September 27, 2022.

44 Davies.

45 Toni Dove, interview by Vicki Callahan, March 17, 2022. Dove here is referring to *Archeology of a Mother Tongue*, a VR murder mystery, created in 1993. For more on this project, see *Archeology of a Mother Tongue*, Toni Dove, accessed March 17, 2022, https://tonidove.com/ archeology/text/.

46 Katerina Cizek, interview by Sarah Atkinson, March 21, 2022. See Cizek, *HIGHRISE—One Millionth Tower*, National Film Board of

Canada, accessed March 21, 2022, https://www.nfb.ca/interactive/highrise_one_millionth_tower_en/.

47 Lily Baldwin, interview by Vicki Callahan, May 27, 2022.

48 Artsy Marie, interview by Sarah Atkinson, May 18, 2022.

49 Valencia James, interview by Sarah Atkinson, March 21, 2022.

50 Debra McGrory, interview by Rose Doherty, July 22, 2016.

51 McGrory.

52 Anonymous, in an interview by Rose Doherty, 2016.

53 Nancy Bennett, interview by Vicki Callahan, July 27, 2017.

54 Anonymous, in an interview by Daniel Harley, 2019.

55 Benty, interview by Vicki Callahan, July 26, 2016.

56 Liz Rosenthal, interview by Daniel Harley, May 31, 2019.

57 Zillah Watson, interview by Daniel Harley, May 17, 2019.

58 Katy Morrison, interview by Vicki Callahan, August 9, 2016.

59 Heidi Boisvert, interview by Vicki Callahan, December 2, 2016.

60 Vicki Lau, interview by Sarah Atkinson, February 7, 2022.

61 Safiya Umoja Noble, Algorithms of Oppression: How Search Engines Reinforce Racism (New York: New York University Press, 2018), 1.

62 Watson, interview by Harley, May 17, 2019.

63 Burns, interview by Callahan, September 9, 2016.

64 Dove, interview by Callahan, March 17, 2022.

65 McGrory, interview by Doherty, July 22, 2016.

66 Anonymous, interview by Daniel Harley, 2019.

67 Anonymous.

68 Carmen Aguilar y Wedge and Ece Tankal, interview by Vicki Callahan, June 1, 2022.

69 Lauren Lee McCarthy, interview by Vicki Callahan, May 20, 2022, refers here to p5.js, https://p5js.org.

70 Phoenix Perry, interview by Sarah Atkinson, March 23, 2022. Perry here refers to the InteractML website, https://interactml.com.

71 Justin Munafo, Meg Diedrick, and Thomas A. Stoffregen, "The Virtual Reality Head-Mounted Display Oculus Rift Induces Motion Sickness and is Sexist in its Effects," Experimental Brain Research 235, no. 3 (2017): 889–901.

72 Sara Lisa Vogl, interview by Sarah Atkinson, March 3, 2022.

73 Nettrice Gaskins, interview by Vicki Callahan, March 5, 2022.

74 Becca Caddy, interview by Daniel Harley, May 29, 2019.

75 Verity McIntosh, interview by Daniel Harley, May 31, 2019.

76 Wolozin, interview by Callahan, December 8, 2016.

77 Frilot, interview by Atkinson, February 17, 2022.

78 Michela Ledwidge, interview by Sarah Atkinson, February 22, 2022.

79 Liz Rosenthal, interview by Sarah Atkinson, January 26, 2022.

80 Rosenthal.

81 Vogl, interview by Atkinson, March 3, 2022.

82 James, interview by Atkinson, March 21, 2022.

83 Artsy Marie, interview by Atkinson, May 18, 2022.

84 Artsy Marie.

85 Sarah Lisa Vogl, interview by Sarah Atkinson, February 3, 2022.

86 Martina Welkhoff, interview by Vicki Callahan, January 2, 2018.

87 Boisvert, interview by Callahan, December 2, 2016.

88 Davies, interview by Atkinson, September 27, 2022.

89 Boisvert, interview by Callahan, December 2, 2016.

90 Watson, interview by Harley, May 17, 2019.

91 Welkhoff, interview by Callahan, January 2, 2018.

Chapter 5

1 Nonny de la Peña, interview by Vicki Callahan, September 26, 2016.

2 Founded in 1967, with Leon Groisser, it later became the MIT Media Lab in 1985.

3 Peggy Weil, interview by Sarah Atkinson, February 23, 2022.

4 Rebecca Allen, interview by Sarah Atkinson, March 25, 2022.

5 Weil, interview by Atkinson, February 23, 2022, *Gone Gitmo* will be discussed in chapter 6.

6 Weil.

7 Weil. Here she refers to Stewart Brand, *The Media Lab: Inventing the Future at MIT* (New York: Penguin, 1987). In the central section of the book is a number of color images, one of them showing the lip-sync interface; there is no credit here, although numerous male practitioners are credited alongside images of projects that they were involved with (146).

8 Allen, interview by Atkinson, March 25, 2022. A version of the advert can be seen in "Canned Food—Sexy Robot (Super Bowl 1985),"

YouTube, December 1, 2020, https://www.youtube.com/watch?v= qwK9BeWxPwQ.

9   Allen.
10 Documentation about the advert can be found here: https:// computeranimationhistory-cgi.jimdofree.com/brilliance-1984/.
11 Allen, interview by Atkinson, March 25, 2022.
12 Mandy Rose, interview by Daniel Harley, May 20, 2019.
13 Char Davies, interview by Sarah Atkinson, September 27, 2022.
14 Davies.
15 Davies.
16 Jennifer Magee-Cook, interview by Vicki Callahan, December 22, 2016.
17 Kaya Jabar, interview by Sarah Atkinson, May 13, 2022.
18 Anonymous, interview by Daniel Harley, 2019.
19 Amelia Winger-Bearskin, interview by Sarah Atkinson, February 28, 2022.
20 Vicki Lau, interview by Sarah Atkinson, February 7, 2022. Lau describes this scenario and others in more detail in her *Why I Do VFX: The Untold Truths about Working in Visual Effects* (independently published, 2021).
21 Liz Rosenthal, interview by Sarah Atkinson, July 14, 2016.
22 Vassiliki Khonsari, interview by Sarah Atkinson, February 8, 2022.
23 Rosenthal, interview by Atkinson, July 14, 2016.
24 Ingrid Kopp, interview by Sarah Atkinson, July 18, 2016.
25 Robin Benty, interview by Vicki Callahan, July 26, 2016.
26 Sara Ticho, interview by Daniel Harley, May 14, 2019.
27 Zillah Watson, interview by Daniel Harley, May 17, 2019.
28 Dee Harvey, interview by Daniel Harley, May 28, 2019.
29 Ingrid Kopp, interview by Sarah Atkinson, January 26, 2022.
30 Martina Welkhoff, interview by Vicki Callahan, January 2, 2018.
31 Lily Baldwin, interview by Vicki Callahan, May 27, 2022.
32 Anonymous, interview by Daniel Harley, 2019.
33 Belén Santa-Olalla, interview by Sarah Atkinson, July 4, 2016.
34 De la Peña, interview by Callahan, September 26, 2016.
35 May Abdalla, interview by Sarah Atkinson, January 24, 2022.
36 Tamara Shogaolu, interview by Sarah Atkinson, May 5, 2022.
37 Isabel Van De Keere, interview by Daniel Harley, May 29, 2019.

38 Neilda Pacquing, interview by Daniel Harley, May 20, 2019.

39 Carmen Aguilar y Wedge and Ece Tankal, interview by Vicki Callahan, June 1, 2022.

40 Debra McGrory, interview by Rose Doherty, July 22, 2016.

41 Heidi Boisvert, interview by Vicki Callahan, December 2, 2016.

42 Joanna Garner, interview by Vicki Callahan, January 3, 2019.

43 Monika Bielskyte, interview by Sarah Atkinson, January 7, 2022.

44 Jabar, interview by Atkinson, May 13, 2022.

45 Winger-Bearskin, interview by Atkinson, February 28, 2022.

46 Liz Rosenthal, interview by Daniel Harley, May 31, 2019.

47 De la Peña, interview by Callahan, September 26, 2016.

48 Taryn Southern, interview by Vicki Callahan, October 14, 2017.

49 Shogaolu, interview by Atkinson, May 5, 2022.

50 Stephanie Dinkins, interview by Sarah Atkinson, July 1, 2022.

51 Welkhoff, interview by Callahan, January 2, 2018.

52 Shogaolu, interview by Atkinson, May 5, 2022

53 Catherine Allen, interview by Daniel Harley, May 20, 2019.

54 Verity McIntosh, interview by Daniel Harley, May 31, 2019.

55 Ticho, interview by Harley, May 14, 2019.

56 Becca Caddy, interview by Daniel Harley, May 29, 2019.

57 Kopp, interview by Atkinson, July 18, 2016.

58 As documented here in relation to a situation that arose with Shutterstock: Helen Kennedy, Sarah Atkinson, and Natalie Wreyford, *The Creative Collaboratory Method: Report and Toolkit* (London: King's College London, 2020): 29.

59 Sarah Jones, interview by Daniel Harley, May 29, 2019, referring to Marija Butkovic, interviewer, "WoW Woman in VR: Sarah Jones, Co-founder of VR Girls UK and Deputy Head of School of Media and Performing Arts at Coventry University," Women of Wearables, February 6, 2017, https://www.womenofwearables.com/new-blog/wow-woman-sarah-jones.

60 Jones, interview by Harley, May 29, 2019.

61 See Catherine Allen, Sarah Atkinson, Grace Boyle, et al., *VWVR: A Vision for Women and Virtual Reality* (London: King's College London, 2018).

62 Pacquing, interview by Harley, May 20, 2019.

63 Anonymous, interview by Daniel Harley, 2019.

64 Shari Frilot, interview by Sarah Atkinson, February 17, 2022.

65 Lynette Wallworth, interview by Vicki Callahan, December 21, 2016.

66 Nicoletta Iacobacci, interview by Simona Spinelli, September 12, 2016, referring to a TEDx Transmedia event held on September 30, 2010, https://www.ted.com/tedx/events/245.

67 Alison Norrington, interview by Sarah Atkinson, March 7, 2022.

68 Carrie Cutforth, interview by Sarah Atkinson, March 16, 2022.

69 Juliana Loh, interview by Sarah Atkinson, March 15, 2022.

70 Nancy Xu, interview by Sarah Atkinson, January 20, 2022, refers to this: https://www.b3media.net/talentlab.

71 Kopp, interview by Atkinson, July 18, 2016.

72 Samantha Gorman, interview by Vicki Callahan, July 24, 2017.

73 Pacquing, interview by Harley, May 20, 2019.

74 Rosenthal, interview by Harley, May 31, 2019. The initiative, founded by Jacqueline Bosnjak, has since been rebranded "Mad Women XR."

75 Anonymous, interview by TK, TK, 201

76 Sarah Lisa Vogl, interview by Sarah Atkinson, February 3, 2022, https://www.wiieurope.org/.

77 Sarah Wolozin, interview by Vicki Callahan, December 8, 2016.

78 Kim Plowright, interview by Rose Doherty, August July 29, 2016.

79 Pacquing, interview by Harley, May 20, 2019.

80 Siobhan O'Flynn, interview by Viola Lasmana, December 22, 2016, speaking about Siobhan O'Flynn, "Transmedia 101," Siobhan O'Flynn: In Medias Unrest, December 2014, http://siobhanoflynn.com/transmedia-101/.

81 Ticho, interview by Harley, May 14, 2019.

82 Allen, interview by Harley, May 20, 2019.

Chapter 6

1 Ingrid Kopp, interview by Sarah Atkinson, July 18, 2016.

2 Sarah Wolozin, interview by Vicki Callahan, December 8, 2016.

3 May Abdalla, interview by Atkinson, January 24, 2022.

4 Catherine Allen, interview by Daniel Harley, May 20, 2019.

5 Mimi Onuoha, interview by Sarah Atkinson, March 29, 2022.

6 Jan Libby, interview by Vicki Callahan, July 29, 2016.

7 Nancy Bennett, interview by Vicki Callahan, July 27, 2017.

8 Michela Ledwidge, interview by Sarah Atkinson, February 22, 2022.

9 Anonymous, interview by Vicki Callahan, 2016.

10 Amelia Winger-Bearskin, interview by Sarah Atkinson, February 28, 2022.

11 Neilda Pacquing, interview by Daniel Harley, May 20, 2019.

12 Dee Harvey, interview by Daniel Harley, May 28, 2019.

13 A New Media Initiative project titled "A New Head Mounted Display System for Use in Artistic Applications of Immersive Virtual Environments."

14 Char Davies, interview by Sarah Atkinson, September 27, 2022.

15 Anonymous, interview by Daniel Harley, 2019.

16 Sandra Rodriguez, interview by Callahan, January 21, 2022.

17 Anonymous, interview by Daniel Harley, 2019.

18 Isabel Van De Keere, interview by Harley, May 29, 2019.

19 Anonymous, interview by Daniel Harley, 2019.

20 Anonymous.

21 Winger-Bearskin, interview by Atkinson, February 28, 2022.

22 Van De Keere, interview by Harley, May 29, 2009.

23 Lina Srivastava, interview by Callahan, August 19, 2016.

24 Helen W. Kennedy, Sarah Atkinson, and Natalie Wreyford, *The Creative Collaboratory Method: Report and Toolkit* (London: King's College London, 2020), 29.

25 Amandine Flachs, interview by Daniel Harley, May 27, 2019. For more on Diversity VC, see https://diversity.vc/about-us/.

26 Vassiliki Khonsari, interview by Sarah Atkinson, February 8, 2022. See "The Ms. Factor: The Power of Female Driven Content," Women and Hollywood, accessed February 8, 2022, https://womenandhollywood .com/activities/partnerships/ms-factor-toolkit/.

27 Martina Welkhoff, interview by Vicki Callahan, January 2, 2018.

28 Tiffany Shlain, interview by Sarah Atkinson, February 28, 2022.

29 Sara Lisa Vogl, interview by Sarah Atkinson, February 3, 2022.

30 Winger-Bearskin, interview by Atkinson, February 28, 2022.

31 Artsy Marie, interview by Sarah Atkinson, May 18, 2022.

32 Onuoha, interview by Atkinson, March 29, 2022.

33 Juliana Loh, interview by Sarah Atkinson, March 15, 2022.

34 Kaya Jabar, interview by Sarah Atkinson, May 13, 2022.

35 Anonymous, interview by Daniel Harley, 2019.

36 Anonymous.

37 Carrie Lozano, interview by Vicki Callahan, August 25, 2016.

38 Nancy Xu, interview by Sarah Atkinson, January 20, 2022.

39 Kamal Sinclair, interview by Vicki Callahan, January 6, 2017.

40 Alex Stolz, Sarah Atkinson, and Helen W. Kennedy, *The Future of Film Report 2021* (London: King's College London, 2021); and Alex Stolz, Sarah Atkinson, and Helen W. Kennedy, *The Future of Film Report 2020* (London: King's College London, 2020).

41 Vicki Lau, interview by Atkinson, February 7, 2022.

42 Jabar, interview by Atkinson, May 13, 2022.

43 Pacquing, interview by Harley, May 20, 2019.

44 Taryn Southern, interview by Vicki Callahan, October 14, 2017.

45 Allen, interview by Harley, 2019.

46 Srivastava, interview by Callahan, August 19, 2016.

47 Jessica Clark, interview by Sarah Atkinson, March 29, 2022.

48 Amy Rose, interview by Sarah Atkinson, January 27, 2022.

49 Anonymous, interview by Rose Doherty, 2016.

50 Abdalla, interview by Atkinson, January 24, 2022.

51 Abdalla.

52 Anonymous, interview by Sarah Atkinson, 2022.

53 Onụọha, interview by Atkinson, March 29, 2022.

54 Katerina Cizek, interview by Sarah Atkinson, March 21, 2022.

55 Jenn Duong, interview by Vicki Callahan, August 17, 2017.

56 Jabar, interview by Atkinson, May 13, 2022.

57 Anonymous, interview by Harley, 2019.

58 Jennifer Palais, interview by Callahan, July 28, 2016.

59 Vogl, interview by Atkinson, February 3, 2022. For more on Somnium Space, see https://somniumspace.com/.

60 Pacquing, interview Harley, May 20, 2019.

61 Southern, interview by Callahan, October 14, 2017.

62 Artsy Marie, interview by Atkinson, May 18, 2022.

63 Artsy Marie.

64 Danielle Brathwaite-Shirley, interview by Atkinson, March 30, 2022.

65 Helen De Michiel, interview by Vicki Callahan, September 23, 2016.

66 Siobhan O'Flynn, interview by Viola Lasmana, December 22, 2016.

67 Stephanie Dinkins, interview by Sarah Atkinson, July 1, 2022.

68 Wolozin, interview by Callahan, December 8, 2016.

69 Libby, interview by Callahan, July 29, 2016.

70 *XR Inclusion: 2020 Annual Report*, XR Inclusion, June 2021, https://xrinclusion.org/report/.

71 The toolkit is found on the website Making a New Reality, https://makinganewreality.org/.

72 For more on the project documentation, see Katerina Cizek and William Uricchio, *Collective Wisdom: Co-Creating Media for Equity and Justice* (Cambridge: MIT Press, 2022), https://wip.mitpress.mit.edu/collectivewisdom.

73 Clark, interview by Atkinson, March 29, 2022. For more, see the Immerse website, https://immerse.news/.

74 For more on the Impact Deck, see Dot Connector Studio, accessed March 29, 2022, http://dotconnectorstudio.com/cards/.

75 Karine Halpern, interview by Simona Spinelli, January 4, 2017. For more, see the Transmedia Ready website, https://transmediaready.com.

76 For more on Women in Immersive Tech Europe, see the WIIT website, https://www.wiiteurope.org/resources. The once publicly accessible directory is no longer available.

77 O'Flynn, interview by Lasmana, December 22, 2016. For more on this resource kit, see Stephen Craven, "Transmedia Multiplatform and Convergent (TMC) Resource Kit," Canada Media Fund, October 17, 2012, https://cmf-fmc.ca/now-next/research-reports/transmedia-multiplatform-and-convergent-tmc-resource-kit/ (URL unavailable).

Chapter 7

1 For an excellent discussion of this challenge, see Christiane Paul, "Introduction: From Digital to Post-Digital—Evolutions of an Art Form," in *A Companion to Digital Art*, ed. Christiane Paul (Hoboken, NJ: Wiley-Blackwell, 2016), 14.

2 Jillian Steinhauer, "Lynn Hershman Leeson: The Artist Is Prescient," *New York Times*, July 8, 2021, sec. Arts, https://www.nytimes.com/2021/07/08/arts/design/hershman-leeson-review-art-museum.html.

3 Lynn Hershman Leeson, interview by Vicki Callahan, June 23, 2022.

4 Hershman Leeson.

5 Christiane Paul, interview by Sarah Atkinson and Vicki Callahan, December 6, 2022.

6 Paul, "Introduction," 9.

7 Katja Kwastek, *Aesthetics of Interaction in Digital Art* (Cambridge, MA: MIT Press, 2015): 43–48.

8 Lauren Lee McCarthy, interview by Vicki Callahan, May 20, 2022.

9 micha cárdenas, interview by Vicki Callahan, April 13, 2022.

10 micha cárdenas, "Becoming Dragon: A Transversal Technology Study," *CTHEORY*, April 29, 2010, https://journals.uvic.ca/index.php/ctheory/article/view/14680/5550.

11 cárdenas, interview by Callahan, April 13, 2022.

12 Hershman Leeson, interview by Callahan, June 23, 2022.

13 Rebecca Allen, interview by Sarah Atkinson, March 25, 2022.

14 Toni Dove, interview by Vicki Callahan, March 17, 2022. For more on the retrospective of Dove's work and *The Dress That Eats Souls*, see Toni Dove, "An Interactive Cinema Installation: *The Dress That Eats Souls*," November 26, 2017, https://tonidove.com/category/the-dress-that-eats-souls/ and Ted Loos, "With 'The Dress That Eats Souls,' Toni Dove Erases Boundaries," October 28, 2017, https://www.nytimes.com/2017/10/28/arts/toni-dove-dress.html.

15 Hito Steyerl, "In Defense of the Poor Image," *e-Flux*, no. 10, November 2009, https://www.e-flux.com/journal/10/61362/in-defense-of-the-poor-image/.

16 Illya Szilak, interview by Viola Lasmana, November 17, 2016.

17 Nancy Bennett, interview by Vicki Callahan, July 6, 2022.

18 May Abdalla, interview by Sarah Atkinson, January 24, 2022.

19 Carmen Aguilar y Wedge and Ece Tankal, interview by Vicki Callahan, June 1, 2022.

20 Stephanie Dinkins, interview by Sarah Atkinson, July 1, 2022.

21 Katy Steinmetz, "The Transgender Tipping Point," *Time*, May 29, 2014, https://time.com/135480/transgender-tipping-point/.

22 cárdenas, interview by Callahan, April 13, 2022.

23 jesikah maria ross, interview by Vicki Callahan, August 15, 2016.

24 For more on Stringfellow's Mojave Project, see "The Mojave Project at LACE, Sept 15–Nov 18, 2018," Kim Stringfellow Projects, accessed January 2019, https://kimstringfellow.com/portfolio_page/mojave-project/.

25 Kim Stringfellow, interview by Viola Lasmana, December 15, 2016.

26 Stringfellow.

27 Sharon Daniel, interview by Viola Lasmana, December 19, 2016.

28 Daniel.

29 Daniel.

30 For more on the *Quipu Project*, visit the website, https://interactive
    .quipu-project.com/#/en/quipu/intro.

31 Rosemarie Lerner and Maria Court, interview by Viola Lasmana, Janu-
    ary 27, 2017.

32 Lerner and Court.

33 Lerner and Court.

34 Lerner and Court.

35 Lina Srivastava, interview by Vicki Callahan, August 19, 2016.

36 Szilak, interview by Lasmana, November 17, 2016.

37 See for example, Maya Zuckerman, "Transformative Media: From
    the Hero's Journey to Our Collective Journey," *Kosmos Journal*
    (Spring/Summer 2016), https://www.kosmosjournal.org/article/
    transformative-media-from-the-heros-journey-to-our-collective
    -journey/.

38 Maya Zuckerman, interview by Viola Lasmana, December 15, 2016.

39 Lily Baldwin, interview by Vicki Callahan, May 27, 2022.

40 Dove, interview by Callahan, March 17, 2022.

41 Dove.

42 Dove.

43 May Adballa, interview by Sarah Atkinson, January 24, 2022.

44 Amy Rose, interview by Sarah Atkinson, January 27, 2022.

45 *Door into the Dark* won the Tribeca Storyscapes award in 2015. For
    more detail on the project, see Amy Rose and May Adballa, *Door into
    the Dark*, Anagram, accessed January 24, 2022, https://weareanagram
    .co.uk/project/door-into-the-dark.

46 Abdalla, interview by Atkinson, January 24, 2022.

47 Lynette Wallworth, interview by Callahan, December 21, 2016.

48 Wallworth.

49 The executive producers for the project initiative of *Un(re)solved* are
    Dawn Porter and Raney Aronson-Rath. For more details on project,
    see *Un(re)solved*, PBS, accessed May 5, 2022, https://www.pbs.org/
    wgbh/frontline/unresolved/.

50 Tamara Shogaolu interview by Sarah Atkinson, May 5, 2022.

51 Nonny De la Peña interview by Vicki Callahan, May 20, 2022.

52 Nonny De la Peña interview by Vicki Callahan, September 26, 2016.

53 De la Peña.

54 De la Peña, interview by Callahan, May 20, 2022.

55 Chris Milk, "How Virtual Reality Can Create the Ultimate Empathy Machine," TED talk, April 22, 2015, https://www.ted.com/talks/chris_milk_how_virtual_reality_can_create_the_ultimate_empathy_machine.

56 Sadah Espii Proctor, interview by Vicki Callahan, August 24, 2017.

57 Lina Srivastava, interview by Vicki Callahan, March 25, 2022.

58 Wallworth, interview by Callahan, December 21, 2016.

59 Wallworth.

60 For more on *Breonna's Garden*, see Black Enterprise Editors, "Breonna's Garden Continues across the Nation with a Homecoming," Black Enterprise, June 2, 2022, https://www.blackenterprise.com/breonnas-garden-continues-across-the-nation-with-a-homecoming/.

61 Carla Borrás, interview by Sarah Atkinson, March 23, 2022.

62 Janet H. Murray, "Not a Film and Not an Empathy Machine," Medium, March 27, 2019, https://immerse.news/not-a-film-and-not-an-empathy-machine-48b63b0eda93.

63 Murray.

64 Murray.

65 De la Peña interview by Callahan, May 20, 2022.

66 Nedra Kline Weinreich, interview by Vicki Callahan, November 21, 2016.

67 Weinreich.

68 Heidi Boisvert, interview by Vicki Callahan, December 2, 2016.

69 cárdenas, interview by Callahan, April 13, 2022.

70 Lee McCarthy, interview by Callahan, May 20, 2022.

71 Anonymous, interview Vicki Callahan, 2022.

72 Lee McCarthy, interview by Vicki Callahan, May 20, 2022.

73 Aguilar y Wedge and Tankal, interview by Callahan, June 1, 2022.

74 Aguilar y Wedge and Tankal.

75 For more on *Shadow Stalker*, see Tess Thacker, "With 'Shadow Stalker,' Lynn Hershman Leeson Tackles Internet Surveillance," *New York Times*, November 8, 2019, Arts, https://www.nytimes.com/2019/11/08/arts/design/Lynn-Hershman-Leeson-Shed-art-technology.html. For more on *Logic Paralyzes the Heart*, see Canada Choate, "Lynn

Hershman Leeson," *Artforum*, April 2022, https://www.artforum.com/ print/202204/lynn-hershman-leeson-discuss-her-venice-project -88118.

76 Hershman Leeson, interview by Callahan, June 23, 2022.

77 Hershman Leeson.

78 Borrás, interview by Atkinson, March 23, 2022.

79 In 2017 Sinclair wrote a series of articles, *Making a New Reality*, based on her research. In 2019 Jessica Clark and Carrie McLaren updated the research and created a toolkit. For more on *Making a New Reality*, see Kamal Sinclair, Jessica Clark, and Carrie McLaren, *Making a New Reality: A Toolkit for Inclusive Media Futures*, Making a New Reality, accessed April 1, 2022, https://makinganewreality.org/.

80 Kamal Sinclair in an interview with Vicki Callahan, April 1, 2022.

81 Baldwin, interview by Callahan, May 27, 2022.

82 Jessica Clark, interview by Sarah Atkinson, March 29, 2022.

Chapter 8

1 *UK VC & Female Founders Report*, British Business Bank, February 4, 2019, https://www.british-business-bank.co.uk/uk-vc-female -founders-report/; Dan Martin, "Less than 2p in Every £1 of UK Equity Funding Went to All-Female Founder Businesses in 2022," Enterprise Nation, February 3, 2023, https://www.enterprisenation .com/learn-something/2p-every-pound-equity-investment-female -founders/; and Camille Kapaun, "The Illusion of Venture Capital for Female Founders," *Forbes*, June 21, 2022, https://www.forbes.com/ sites/columbiabusinessschool/2022/06/21/the-illusion-of-venture -capital-for-female-founders/?sh=5976e11e74c6.

2 Vicki Lau, interview by Sarah Atkinson, February 7, 2022.

3 Neal Stephenson, *Snow Crash: A Novel* (New York: Bantam Books, 1992).

4 Char Davies, interview by Sarah Atkinson, September 27, 2022.

5 Toni Dove, interview by Vicki Callahan, March 17, 2022.

6 Nonny de la Peña, interview by Vicki Callahan, May 20, 2022. De la Peña here refers to a September 14, 2020, episode in the online video series *Deepfakery* by the human rights / media organization Witness, which discusses the feature-length documentary film

Welcome to Chechnya (2020, dir.: David France). The film used "deep-fakes" to protect the identity of LGBTQ activists from the hostile and extremely dangerous conditions of their home country. See "Identity Protection with Deepfakes: 'Welcome to Chechnya' director David France," Witness, YouTube, September 14, 2020, https://www .youtube.com/watch?v=2du6dVL3Nuc.

7   Mark J. P. Wolf, "Worlds Apart: Toward a Canon of Imaginary Worlds," in *Revisiting Imaginary Worlds: A Subcreation Studies Anthology*, ed. Mark J. P. Wolf (New York: Routledge, 2016), 350.

8   Joanna Garner, interview by Vicki Callahan, January 3, 2019.

9   Monika Bielskyte, interview by Sarah Atkinson, January 7, 2022.

10 Jessica Clark, interview by Sarah Atkinson, March 29, 2022.

11 Sarah Lisa Vogl, interview by Sarah Atkinson, March 3, 2022. For more on Parisi, see Tony Parisi, "The Seven Rules of the Metaverse," Medium, October 22, 2021, https://medium.com/meta-verses/the -seven-rules-of-the-metaverse-7d4e06fa864c; and kentbye, #1013: Parisi's Metaverse Manifesto: Unpacking His Seven Rules for the Metaverse, Voices of VR, October 23, 2021, https://voicesofvr.com/ parisis-metaverse-manifesto-unpacking-his-seven-rules-for-the -metaverse/.

Selected Bibliography

Ahmed, Sara. "'You End Up Doing the Document Rather than Doing the Doing': Diversity, Race Equality and the Politics of Documentation." *Ethnic and Racial Studies* 30, no. 4 (2007): 590–609.

Allen, Catherine Allen, Sarah Atkinson, Grace Boyle, Becca Caddy, Amandine Flachs, Dorothea Gibbs, Rebecca Gregory-Clarke, et al. *VWVR: A Vision for Women and Virtual Reality*. London: King's College London, 2018.

Allen, Rebecca. "The Emergence Project: *The Bush Soul*." *Leonardo* 38, no. 4 (2005): 314. http://emergence.design.ucla.edu/.

Alexander, Joanna, and Long, Mark. "Nintendo's New Baby Boy." *VR World*, May/June 1995. Arts Council England (ACE). *Equality, Diversity and the Creative Case: A Data Report, 2019–2020*. Arts Council England, 2021. https://www.artscouncil.org.uk/publication/equality-diversity-and-creative-case-data-report-2019-20.

Atkinson, Sarah A. *Beyond the Screen: Emerging Cinema and Engaging Audiences*. New York: Bloomsbury, 2014.

———. "Film and Audiovisual Media OERs: The Case of SP-ARK: The Sally Potter Film Archive (Topic: OER and Teaching Quality): A HEA/JISC Open Educational Resources Case Study: Pedagogical Development from OER Practice." Paper presented at the Higher Education Academy, London, 2012.

———. *From Film Practice to Data Process: Production Aesthetics and Representational Practices of a Film Industry in Transition*. Edinburgh: Edinburgh University Press, 2018.

———. "Transmedia Critical | The Performative Functions of Dramatic Communities: Conceptualizing Audience Engagements in Transmedia Fiction," *International Journal of Communication* 8 (2014): 2201–19.

———. "Transmedia Film: From Embedded Engagement to Embodied Experience." In *The Routledge Companion to Transmedia Studies*, edited by

Matthew Freeman and Renira Rampazzo Gambarato, 15–24. London: Routledge, 2018.

Bazelon, Emily. "A Seat at the Table: Why Aren't Women Advancing More in Corporate America?" *New York Times Magazine*, February 24, 2019. https://www.nytimes.com/interactive/2019/02/21/magazine/women-corporate-america.html.

Beauchamp, Cari. *Without Lying Down: Frances Marion and the Powerful Women of Early Hollywood*. Berkeley: University of California Press, 1998.

Brand, Stewart. *The Media Lab: Inventing the Future at MIT*. New York: Penguin, 1987.

Callahan, Vicki. "The Future of the Archive: An Interview with Lynn Hershman Leeson." In *Reclaiming the Archive: Feminism and Film History*, edited by Vicki Callahan, 418–29. Detroit: Wayne State University Press, 2010.

———. "Queerskins: Divining a Feminist Phenomenological Method." In *Transmedia Cultures: A Companion*, edited by Simon Bacon, 229–38. Oxford: Peter Lang, 2021.

———. "Where There's Smoke and the Generative Documentary: A Conversation with Lance Weiler." *Afterimage* 49, no. 1 (2022): 14–25.

cárdenas, micha. "Becoming Dragon: A Transversal Technology Study." *CTHEORY*. April 29, 2010. https://journals.uvic.ca/index.php/ctheory/article/view/14680.

Chang, Emily. *Brotopia: Breaking Up the Boys' Club of Silicon Valley*. New York: Portfolio, 2018.

Choate, Canada. "Lynn Hershman Leeson." *Artforum*, April 2022. https://www.artforum.com/print/202204/lynn-hershman-leeson-discuss-her-venice-project-88118.

Cizek, Katerina, and William Uricchio. *Collective Wisdom: Co-Creating Media for Equity and Justice*. Cambridge, MA: MIT Press, 2022.

Cobb, Shelley, and Natalie Wreyford. "'Could You Hire Someone Female or from an Ethnic Minority?' Being Both: Black, Asian and Other Minority Women Working in British Film Production." In *Black Film, British Cinema II*, edited by Clive Nwonka and Anamik Saha, 165–84. London: Goldsmiths Press, 2021.

Conger, Kate. "Exclusive: Here's The Full 10-Page Anti-Diversity Screed Circulating Internally at Google [Updated]." Gizmodo, August 17, 2017. http://gizmodo.com/exclusive-heres-the-full-10-page-anti-diversity-screed-1797564320.

Conor, Bridget, Rosalind Gill, and Stephanie Taylor. "Gender and Creative Labour." *The Sociological Review* 63, no. S1 (2015): 1–22.

Cox, Donna J., Ellen Sandor, and Janine Fron, eds. *New Media Futures: The Rise of Women in the Digital Arts*. Champaign: University of Illinois Press, 2018.

Crawford, Kate. *Atlas of AI: Power, Politics, and the Planetary Costs of Artificial Intelligence*. New Haven: Yale University Press, 2021.

Davies, Char. "Landscapes of Ephemeral Embrace: Immersive Virtual Space as A Medium for Transforming Perception." PhD diss., Centre for Advanced Inquiry in the Interactive Arts, University of Plymouth, UK, 2005.

De la Peña, Nonny, Peggy Weil, Joan Llobera, Bernhard Spanlang, Doron Friedman, Maria V. Sanchez-Vives, and Mel Slater. "Immersive journalism: Immersive virtual reality for the first-person experience of news." *Presence* 19, no. 4 (2010): 291–301.

Dent, Tamsyn. "Devalued Women, Valued Men: Motherhood, Class and Neo-liberal Feminism in the Creative Media Industries." *Media, Culture & Society* 42, no. 4 (2020): 537–53.

Dewey, Caitlin. "The Only Guide to Gamergate You Will Ever Need to Read." *Washington Post*. October 14, 2014. https://www.washingtonpost.com/news/the-intersect/wp/2014/10/14/the-only-guide-to-gamergate-you-will-ever-need-to-read/.

Duffy, Brooke Erin. *(Not) Getting Paid to Do What You Love: Gender, Social Media, and Aspirational Work*. New Haven: Yale University Press, 2017.

Easton, Eliza. *Creative Diversity: The State of Diversity in the UK's Creative Industries and What We Can Do about It*. London: Creative Industries Federation; MOBO Awards. 2015.

Eikhof, Doris Ruth, Jack Newsinger, Daniela Rudloff, Daria Luchinskaya, and Mark Banks. *Workforce Diversity in the UK Screen Sector: Evidence Review*. Leicester: CAMEo Research Institute, 2018. https://www2.bfi.org.uk/sites/bfi.org.uk/files/downloads/bfi-workforce-diversity-in-uk-screen-sector-evidence-review-2018-03.pdf.

Follows, Stephen, Alexis Kreager, and E. Gomes. "Cut Out of the Picture." *A Study of Gender Inequality amongst Film Directors in the UK Film Industry*. London: Directors UK, 2016.

Furness, T. "Helmet-Mounted Displays and Their Aerospace Applications." Paper presented at the National Aerospace Electronics Conference, Dayton, OH, 1969.

Galt, Francis. *Women's Activism behind the Screens: Trade Unions and Gender Inequity in the British Film and Television Industries*. Bristol: Bristol University Press, 2020.

Harley, Daniel Eric. "The Politics of Consumer VR: Framing Contemporary Virtual Reality." PhD diss., York University, Toronto, 2021.

Hatch, Kristen. "Cutting Women: Margaret Booth and Hollywood's Pioneering Female Film Editors." In Women Film Pioneers Project (digital resource), edited by Jane Gaines, Radha Vatsal, and Monica Dall'Asta. New York: Columbia University Libraries, 2013. https://doi.org/10.7916/d8-t0y9-hv61.

Hicks, Mar. *Programmed Inequality: How Britain Discarded Women Technologists and Lost Its Edge in Computing*. Cambridge, MA: MIT Press, 2017.

Hill, Erin. *Never Done: A History of Women's Work in Media Production*. New Brunswick, NJ: Rutgers University Press, 2016.

Holt, Nathalia. *The Queens of Animation: The Untold Story of the Women Who Transformed the World of Disney and Made Cinematic History*. Boston: Little, Brown, 2019.

Hunt, Darnell, and Ana-Christina Ramon. *UCLA Hollywood Diversity Report 2020: A Tale of Two Hollywoods*, pt. 1 *Film*, UCLA College of Social Sciences, February 6, 2020. https://socialsciences.ucla.edu/wp=content/uploads/2020/02/UCLA-Hollywood-Diversity-Report-2020-Film-2-6-2020.pdf (URL unavailable).

Jenkins, Henry. *Convergence Culture: Where Old and New Media Collide*. New York: New York University Press, 2006.

Kennedy, Helen W., Sarah Atkinson, and Natalie Wreyford. *The Creative Collaboratory Method: Report and Toolkit*. London: King's College London, 2020.

Kinder, Marsha. *Playing with Power in Movies, Television, and Video Games: From Muppet Babies to Teenage Mutant Ninja Turtles*. Berkeley: University of California Press, 1991.

Kleiman, Kathy. *Proving Ground: The Untold Story of the Six Women Who Programmed the World's First Modern Computer*. London: C. Hurst, 2022.

Kwastek, Katja. *Aesthetics of Interaction in Digital Art*. Cambridge, MA: MIT Press, 2015.

Maher, Jennifer Helene. *Software Evangelism and the Rhetoric of Morality: Coding Justice in a Digital Democracy*. Routledge Studies in Rhetoric and Communication 25. New York: Routledge, 2016.

Malloy, Judy, ed. *Women, Art and Technology*. Cambridge, MA: MIT Press, 2003.

Milk, Chris. "How Virtual Reality Can Create the Ultimate Empathy Machine," TED talk, April 22, 2015. https://www.ted.com/talks/chris_milk_how _virtual_reality_can_create_the_ultimate_empathy_machine.

Munafo, Justin, Meg Diedrick, and Thomas A. Stoffregen. "The Virtual Reality Head-Mounted Display Oculus Rift Induces Motion Sickness and is Sexist in Its Effects." *Experimental Brain Research* 235, no. 3 (2017): 889–901.

Murray, Janet H. "Not a Film and Not an Empathy Machine." *Medium*, March 27, 2019. https://immerse.news/not-a-film-and-not-an-empathy -machine-48b63b0eda93.

Noble, Safiya Umoja. *Algorithms of Oppression: How Search Engines Reinforce Racism*. New York: New York University Press, 2018. Kindle and print eds.

Nwonka, Clive James. "Diversity and Data: An Ontology of Race and Ethnicity in the British Film Institute's Diversity Standards." *Media, Culture & Society* 43, no. 3 (2021): 460–79.

———. *Race and Ethnicity in the UK Film Industry: An Analysis of the BFI Diversity Standards*. London School of Economics and Political Science, London, 2020.

———. "White Women, White Men, and Intra-Racial Diversity: A Data-Led Analysis of Gender Representation in the UK Film Industry." *Cultural Sociology* 15, no. 3 (2021): 430–54.

Nwonka, Clive James, and Sarita Malik. "Cultural Discourses and Practices of Institutionalised Diversity in the UK Film Sector: 'Just Get Something Black Made.'" *Sociological Review* 66, no. 6 (2018): 1111–27.

O'Brien, Anne, and Susan Liddy. "The Price of Motherhood in the Irish Film and Television Industries." *Gender, Work & Organization* 28, no. 6 (2021): 1997–2009.

Paul, Christiane, ed. *A Companion to Digital Art*. Hoboken: Wiley-Blackwell, 2016.

———. *Digital Art*. 2nd ed. London: Thames & Hudson, 2008. First published 2003.

Pronger, Rachel. "Elizaveta Svilova: The Woman behind *The Man with a Movie Camera*." New East Digital Archive, September 5, 2021. https://www.new -east-archive.org/articles/show/13077/elizaveta-svilova-the-woman-behind -the-man-with-a-movie-camera.

Rankin, Joy Lisi. *A People's History of Computing in the United States*. Cambridge, MA: Harvard University Press, 2018.

Restauri, Denise. "8 Real Success Tips from Women Building the Future with Virtual Reality." *Forbes*. February 8, 2017. https://www.forbes.com/sites/

deniserestauri/2017/02/08/8-real-success-tips-from-women-building-the
-future-with-virtual-reality/.

Shub Sharp, Ilana. *Esfir Shub: Pioneer of Documentary Filmmaking*. New York: Bloomsbury, 2022.

Sinclair, Kamal. "Challenging the Innovator Stereotype." *Immerse*, December 30, 2017. https://immerse.news/challenging-the-innovator-stereotype
-b562a37da008.

——. *Making a New Reality*. Essay series. Immerse.news, 2017–18. https://
makinganewreality.org.

Sinclair, Kamal, Jessica Clark, and Carrie McLaren. *Making a New Reality*. Book and toolkit. Ford Foundation / Sundance Institute, September 7, 2020. https://www.makinganewreality.org/making-a-new-reality-a-toolkit-for
-inclusive-media-futures-a3bdc0e68f20.

Smith, Stacy L., Marc Choueiti, Kevin Yao, Hannah Clark, and Katherine Pieper. *Inclusion in the Director's Chair: Analysis of Director Gender & Race/ Ethnicity across 1,300 Top Films from 2007 to 2019*. Los Angeles: Annenberg Foundation / USC Annenberg Inclusion Initiative, January 2020. https://
assets.uscannenberg.org/docs/aii-inclusion-directors-chair-20200102.pdf.

Smith, Stacy L., Katherine Pieper, and Al-Baab Khan. *Inclusion in the Director's Chair: Analysis of Director Gender & Race/Ethnicity across 1,500 Top Films from 2007 to 2021*. Los Angeles: Annenberg Foundation / USC Annenberg Inclusion Initiative, 2020. http://assets.uscannenberg.org/docs/aii
-inclusion-directors-chair-2022.pdf.

Steinhauer, Jillian. "Lynn Hershman Leeson: The Artist Is Prescient." *New York Times*, July 8, 2021, Arts. https://www.nytimes.com/2021/07/08/arts/
design/hershman-leeson-review-art-museum.html.

Steinmetz, Katy. "The Transgender Tipping Point." *Time*, May 29, 2014. https://time.com/135480/transgender-tipping-point/.

Stephenson, Neal. *Snow Crash: A Novel*. New York: Bantam Books, 1992.

Steyerl, Hito. "In Defense of the Poor Image," *e-Flux* 10 (November 2009). https://www.e-flux.com/journal/10/61362/in-defense-of-the-poor-image/.

Stolz, Alex, Sarah Atkinson, and Helen W. Kennedy. *The Future of Film Report 2020*. London: King's College London, 2020.

——. *The Future of Film Report 2021*. London: King's College London, 2021.

Thacker, Tess. "With 'Shadow Stalker,' Lynn Hershman Leeson Tackles Internet Surveillance." *New York Times*, November 8, 2019, Arts. https://www

.nytimes.com/2019/11/08/arts/design/Lynn-Hershman-Leeson-Shed-art
-technology.html.

Thiel, Tamiko. "The Design of the Connection Machine." *Design Issues* 10, no. 1 (1994): 5–18.

Thompson, Clive. *Coders: The Making of a New Tribe and the Remaking of the World*. New York: Penguin Books, 2019.

Wolf, Mark J. P., ed. *Revisiting Imaginary Worlds: A Subcreation Studies Anthology*. New York: Routledge, 2016.

Women's Media Center. *The Status of Women in U.S. Media 2019*. Women's Media Center, February 21, 2019. https://womensmediacenter.com/reports/the-status-of-women-in-u-s-media-2019.

Wreyford, Natalie, Tamsyn Dent, and Dave O'Brien. *Creative Majority: An APPG for Creative Diversity Report on "What Works" to Support, Encourage and Improve Equality, Diversity and Inclusion in the Creative Sector; A Report for the All Party Parliamentary Group for Creative Diversity*. London: Kings College London, September 2021. https://www.kcl.ac.uk/cultural/projects/creative-majority.

Wreyford, Natalie, Helen W. Kennedy, Jack Newsinger, and Rowan Aust. *Locked Down and Locked Out: The Impacts of the COVID-19 Pandemic on Mothers Working in the UK Television Industry*. Nottingham: University of Nottingham, 2021.

Wright, Julia. "Making the Cut: Female Editors and Representation in the Film and Media Industry." *CSW Update Newsletter*, UCLA Center for the Study of Women, March 1, 2009. https://escholarship.org/uc/item/0pz3k79s.

XR Inclusion: 2020 Annual Report. XR Inclusion, 2020. https://xrinclusion.org/report/.

Young, Julie. "The Invitation Effect: How We Are Using Facebook to Get More Women in Tech." *Medium*, February 6, 2017. https://medium.com/@juliey4/the-invitation-effect-how-we-are-using-facebook-to-get-more-women-in-tech-58331cc0429a.

Zuckerman, Maya. "Transformative Media: From the Hero's Journey to Our Collective Journey." *Kosmos Journal* (Spring/Summer 2016). https://www.kosmosjournal.org/article/transformative-media-from-the-heros-journey-to-our-collective-journey/.

Index

Note: Page numbers appearing in *italics* refer to figures.

Abdalla, May, 96, 134, 153, 170, 189, 203–4, 245, 262, 291n16

accelerator programs, 86, 159, 160, 168

Across the Line (de la Peña, Lichtenstein, and Fitzsimmons), 46, 59, 214

Aguilar y Wedge, Carmen, 112, 137, 190, 221, 245, 293n68

AI. *See* artificial intelligence (AI)

Allen, Catherine, ix, 79, 142, 151, 155, 169, 246

Allen, Dede, 9

Allen, Fran, 10

Allen, Rebecca, 18, 21–28, *28*, 185, 241, 246, 285nn33–34, 286n8; *The Bush Soul*, 25–26, *26*; *Coexistence*, 26–27, *27*; *MyoPhone*, 27–28, *28*; *Swimmer*, *23*, 125

allies, 20, 77, 85, 149, 173

All-Party Parliamentary Group (APPG) for Creative Diversity, 5, 280n10

alternate reality games (ARGs), 94, 95, 97–98, 146, 269

Altspace, 117

Amerika, Mark, 68; *GRAMMATRON*, 69

Anagram, 96, 134, 153, *154*, 170, 189, 203, 241, 245, 255, 262, 302n45

animation, 9, 72, 74, 101, 128, 202; cel, 9; character, 41; computer, 185; facial, 123; female figure in, 21, 125, 126; history of, 126; 3D, 21, 22–25, 125; VR, 62

Annenberg School, USC, 45; Inclusion Initiative, 5; Innovation Lab, 78

Apple computing, 30, 32; Mac computer, 30; Think Different campaign, 30, *31*

AR. *See* augmented reality (AR)

Archeology of a Mother Tongue (Dove), 105, 292n45

Architecture Machine Group (Arch Mac), 122

art: digital, 15, 20, 40, 53, 181–83, 186, 227, 254, 260; generative, 100; net, 69

artificial intelligence (AI), 1–2, 23, 29–30, 36, *37*, 71–72, 81, 83, 202, 264, 267, 269; art and, 100, 123; creativity in, 129; deepfakes and, 36, *37*, 123, 236, 270–71, 304–5n6; face recognition in, 36, *37*; Google and, 30; musical compositions in, 75; Winter and, 30

Ashe '68 (Lichtenstein, Bravo, and Fitzsimmons), 59

Atmos Sphaerae (Thiel), 35–36, 243

Atomic Vacation (Szilak and Tsiboulski), 243

augmented reality (AR), ix, 2, 3, 98, 100, 213, 241, 252, 259, 269; eye wear, 27–28, *28*; geolocative, 34

Awavena (Wallworth), 212–13, 266

B., Tonia, 70–71, 246

Baldwin, Lily, 105–6, *106*, 133, 201, 225–26, 241, 246–47, 293n47; *Through You*, 105–6, *106*, 225

Bay Area, 64–65, 96, 274; Video Coalition (BAVC Media), 58

BBC, 93, 126, 127, 129, 170; interactive / new media department, 127; VR, 110; VR hub, 132

Becoming Dragon (cárdenas), 184, 289n10

Bennett, Nancy, 66–67, 107, 155, 189, 247, 285n32

Benty, Robin, 93–94, 109, 132, 247, 291n6

Beyond Manzanar (Thiel and Houshmand), 32, *34*, 243

bias, 6, 158, 181, 185, 220; mitigation, 87; unconscious, 61, 66, 87, 149

Bielskyte, Monika, 79, 98, 138, 237, 238, 247

BlackTransArchive.com / We Are Here Because of Those That Are Not (Brathwaite-Shirley), 72–73, *73*, 241

blockchain, 161, 163–64, 269–70; crypto mining and, 270; decentralized autonomous organizations (DAOs) and, 270; Ethereum, 270; NFTs and, 163–64; in virtual worlds, 275

Blood Sugar (Daniel), 196, 241

Boisvert, Heidi, 110, 118, 137, 216, 247

Booth, Margaret, 9, 284n26

Borrás, Carla, 213, 223, 248, 303n61

Brathwaite-Shirley, Danielle, 72–73, *73*, 174, 241, 289n38, 299n64; *BlackTransArchive.com / We Are Here Because of Those That Are Not*, 72–73, *73*, 241

Bravo, Janicza, 242

Breathing Machines (Hershman Leeson), 185

Breonna's Garden (Lady Pheønix), 213–14, 242, 303n60

British Film Institute (BFI), 4, 267; Diversity Standards, 5

Browntourage, 70–71, 289n34

Burns, Caitlin, 59–61, 93, 99, 111, 248, 291n2

Bush Soul, The (Allen), 25–26, *26*, 241

Caddy, Becca, 113, 143, 248

cárdenas, micha, 184, 192, *194*, 218, 241, 248–49; *Becoming Dragon*, 184; *Local Autonomy Networks (Autonets)*, 218

Catherine Wheel, The (Tharp), 22, *24*, 243

Chang, Emily, 6–7

Channel 4, 57–58, 93, 132

cinema, 91, 115; early, 2; going, 204; history, 235; interactive, *187*; Limina VR, 112; live, 77; training, 67

Cizek, Katerina, 105, 172, 177, 241, 249, 292n46; *HIGHRISE—One Millionth Tower*, 105, 292–93n46

Clark, Jessica, 2, 79, 169–70, 177–78, 225–26, 238, 249

climate change, 34, 35, 48, 192, 195, 199, 201, 210, 211, 223

Code Liberation Foundation, 73–74

coders, 10, 83; women as, 10

coding, 9–10, 45, 70, 74, 78, 83, 98, 101, 220

—communities, 73–74

—languages: BASIC, 44; CSS, 70; HTML, 32, 70, 276

Coexistence (Allen), 26–27, *27*, 241

Collisions (Wallworth), 211–12, 235

community, 51, 80, 89, 116, 132, 140, 143, 146, 177, 182, 183, 194, 196, 212, 213, 217, 235; builders, 52, 70–74, 89; building, 113, 114, 180, 198, 199, 220, 226, 229; Facebook, 85; groups, 79, 148; initiatives, 163, 178; literary, 70; manager, 64; media, 97, 193; outreach, 197; platforms, 91; storytelling, 193; women-only, 148–51

compilation documentary, 9

computing, 3, 7, 9, 10; design, 21, 29; early, 2, 111, 122; home, 10; programming language, 10; quantum, 30; spatial, 83

Conducttr, vii, 134, 263, 279n5

Connection Machine, 29–32, 33; CM-1, 31; CM-2, 33

Court, Maria Ignacia, 197–98, 220, 249, 302n31

COVID-19, ix, 17, 19, 35, 92, 115, 121, 163, 167, 224, 227, 228, 234

Cox, Donna, 16

Cutforth, Carrie, 94, 146, 150, 249, 291n10

cycles of innovation model, 8, 18, 22, 101, 124, 176, 230, 231

dance, 22, 32; improvisation, 32; narrative, 105, 201; virtual performance, 107, 108

Daniel, Sharon, 195–96, 234, 241, 249–50; Blood Sugar, 196, 241; Public Secrets, 195–96, 234–35

Darfur Is Dying (Ruiz), 67, 68, 203

data: big, 137; driven, 137

Davies, Char, 4, 10, 18, 21, 118, 201, 241, 250, 285nn33–34; Ephémère, 39, 40, 42, 104–5, 241; Osmose, 37, 39–42, 104–5, 241

de la Peña, Nonny, 18, 21, 43–49, 76–77, 250, 287n40, 304n6; as "the godmother of VR," 54; Gone Gitmo (with Weil), 44, 45, 105; Hunger in Los Angeles, 45–46, 47; Out of Exile, 46, 48; Project Syria, 46

De Michiel, Helen, 175, 250

Dena, Christy, 97–98, 250–51, 292n24

developer evangelist, 82–83, 139

digital art, 15–16, 40, 53, 181–82, 183, 185–86, 227; curation, 53; curators, 53

Dinkins, Stephanie, 141, 175, 190, 191, 220, 242, 251, 296n50, 299n67; Not the Only One, 190, 191; When Words Fail, 190, 242

Disney: Imagineering, 122; Nine Old Men, 9; Walt, 9

diversity, 6–7, 49, 55, 57; funding for, 87; gender, ix, 4, 16, 18, 79; initiatives, 5; institutionally led, 19; reporting, 5; VC funding, 162, 298n25

documentary, 64–65, 75, 95, 105, 196, 203–4; genre, 65; storytelling, 92; VR, 76; web, 100

Door into the Dark (Abdalla and Rose), 204, 245, 302n45

Dove, Toni, 105, 111, 186–88, 201–2, 202, 236, 242, 251, 285n34, 292n45, 301n14; Archeology of a Mother Tongue, 105, 292n45; The Dress That Eats Souls, 186, 301n14

Dress That Eats Souls, The (Dove), 186, 301n14

Duffy, Brooke Erin, 6, 283n16

Duong, Jenn, 79, 80, 172, 251

Electric South, 57, 256

electronic audio, 8, 9, 231

electronic music, 8, 9, 10, 231; scene, 10

Electronic Numerical Integrator and Computer, 10

Emblematic Group, 44, 46, 48, 49, 76, 223

Emmy Awards, 94, 105, 247, 249, 261, 266, 267, 291n5

empathy, 210–18, 227; in documentary, 210–11; empathy machine concept, 210, 214–15; versus compassion, 212, 215. *See also* virtual reality (VR)

EmpowHER VR, 136, 260

Em's Theory (Zuckerman), 200, 237, 243, 268

Ephémère (Davies), *39*, 40, 42, 104–5, 241

Espii Proctor, Sadah, 85–86, 210, 251, 285n32

Evolution of Fish (Thiel and /p), 35, 243

experience designer, 63, 70, 113, 136, 149

experience economy, ix, 118, 272

Facebook, viii, 46, 85, 101, 116, 137, 149, 150; groups, 79

Face to Open Doors, A (Anagram), 192, 241

Fan, Maureen, 62–63, 251–52, 289n22

feminized labor, 5, 8, 18, 230

Feuer, Mary, 95, 97, 242, 252

Feynman, Richard, 29, *31*

film, 3, 94, 95–96
—editing, 9
—experimental, 54
—festivals: audiences, 100; Cannes XR Challenge, 85; IDFA, 204; Sundance, 107; Tribeca, 57, 95
—histories, 18
—indie, 76
—industry, ix, 4, 5, 66, 93, 100, 130, 153, 167
—installations, 222
—interactive, 100
—making, 78, 173, 199
—production, 5, 42, 56, 129, 234
—programming, 54, 100
—sector, 230
—silent, 11
—VR, 223

Fisher, Caitlin, 252

Fitzsimmons, Jeff, 242

Fitzsimmons, Keller, 242

Flachs, Amandine, 161, 252, 298n25

force feedback joystick, 25, 26

Foyer, Anthea, 150, 178, 252

Frigo, Renée, 242

Frilot, Shari, 54–55, 88–89, 100–101, 115, 144, 252–53, 288n4

Fron, Janine, 285n36, 309

Frontline (PBS), 46, 206, *207, 208*, 209, 213, 223, 242, 248, 302n49

Fubara-Manuel, Irene, 74, 253

funding, 18, 19–20, 52, 67, 70, 85, 109, 123, 150–65, 179, 218, 219, 220, 228, 232; alternative pathways, 159–65; applications, 169; challenges, 46, 86–87, 232; diversity, 87; military, 123; rounds, 237; targeted, 133; venture capital (VC), 153, 156, 161, 232

futurists, 52, 79–81, 89, 228

games and gaming, 25, 72–73. *See also* alternate reality games (ARGs)
—AAA (Triple-A), 131
—alternate reality games (ARGs), 94, 95, 97–98, 146, 269
—communities, 73–74
—companies: Epic, 121, 147
—design, 74, 95
—diversity in, 98
—first graphic adventure game design, 98
—industry, viii, 93, 126, 131, 143
—interactive, 124, 204
—making, 137, 174
—mobile, 84
—production, 42, 115
—publisher, 60
—serious games, 67
—workforce, 98

Gardens of the Anthropocene (Thiel), 35, 243

Garner, Joanna, 137, 237, 253, 296n42

Gaskins, Nettrice, 113, 253
Girl Icon (Espii Proctor), 210
Goliath (Anagram), 189, 241, 245
Golick, Jill, 150
Gone Gitmo (de la Peña and Weil), *44*, 45, 105, 123, 207, 242
Google: AI, 30; Daydream, 110, 271; founders, *28*; funding, 219; Glass, 28, 271; Manifesto, 6; search, 173, 222, 234; Tilt Brush, 94
Gorman, Samantha, 147, 253
GRAMMATRON (Amerika), 69
Greenland Melting (de la Peña, Upin, Cort, et al.), 46, 223
Grian, Hazel, 94, 253–54, 291n8
Guild of Future Architects, 79, 290n51

hackathon, 85, 160–61, 267
Halpern, Karine, 178, 254, 300n75
haptic: interaction, 21–22, 25–26, *26*, *27*, 241; interfaces, *27*, 113; joystick, 33
Harvey, Dee, 132, 157, 254
head-mounted display (HMD), 37, 38, 41, 45, 104, 111, 119, 157–58, 250, 271, 272, 298n13
health care, viii, 29, 48, 112, 132, 136, 159, 209, 214, 265
Hershman Leeson, Lynn, 180–82, 185, *222*, 222–23, *223*, 242, 254, 279–80n7, 301n12; *Breathing Machines*, 185; *Logic Paralyzes the Heart*, 222, *223*, 303–4n75; *Shadow Stalker*, 222, 303n75
Hicks, Mar, 10
HIGHRISE—One Millionth Tower (Cizek), 105, 292–93n46
Hillis, Danny, 29, 30
Himmelsbach, Sabine, 53
hiring, 59, 62, 63, 130, 220; practices, 63
HMD. *See* head-mounted display (HMD)
Hoffman, Joanna, 30, 32

Hold Vessel I and II (Wallworth), 205, 243
Hollywood, 64, 75, 76; films, 9, 10, 133; franchises, 230; industry, 65; system, 65
Hopper, Grace, 19
House of Electronic Art (HEK), Basel, 53
Houshmand, Zara, 32, *34*, 243
HTC Vive, 111, 276, 277
Hunger in Los Angeles (de la Peña), 45–46, *47*, 101, 209, 214, 241, 250, 292n38
Hyphen-Labs, 112, 137, 190, 245

Iacobacci, Nicoletta, 145, 254, 297n66
Immerse.news, 57, 169, 177, 249, 256
immersive journalism, 44, 45, 103, 209
immersive media, 12, 59, 80, 91, 97, 132, 204
Immersive Rehab, 136, 159, 265
immersive technologies, 21, 120, 136, 138, 163, 234, 238
immersive virtual space, 37–43, 158
inclusive, 1–2, 4, 16, 49, 72, 99, 118, 122, 133–35, 145–46, 177, 199; work culture, 6, 52–54, 219–20, 229, 238–39; workspaces, 52, 66, 76
incubator programs, 86
Indigenous: Australian Martu tribe, 211; people, 164, 197; rights, 205; technologists, 83; values, 83
Industrial Light and Magic, 41
industry conferences, 19, 59, 122, 140, 142, 143, 144, 145, 173, 176; IEEE Conference, 115; Mozilla Hubs, 35; South by Southwest, 213; Storyworld, 146
interaction design, 107, 113, 137
interactive media, 12, 70, 99
In the Land of Babari-an (Thiel), 32, 243

investment. *See* funding
—companies: WXR Fund, 83
—disparity, 88–89, 161
—opportunities, 150
invisible labor, 5, 52, 63–67, 89
Isdrake, Jasmine Idun, 95, 254–55, 291n14

Jabar, Kaya, 128–29, 139, 165, 167–68, 172, 255
James, Valencia, 107, *108*, 116, 242, 255; *Suga'*, 107, *108*, 242
Jaunt VR, viii, 149
Jenkins, Henry, 92
Jennings, Kirsty, 255
Jobs, Steve, 30, 32
Jones, Sarah, 143, 255, 296n59
Jordan, Niema, 64, 255–56, 289n26

Kataoka, Drue, 84
KateModern, 94, 253
Khonsari, Vassiliki, 131, 162, 256
Kinder, Marsha, 92, 291n1, 310
Kleiman, Kathy, 10
Kopp, Ingrid, 57–58, 95, 100, 131–33, 143, 147, 153, 177, 256, 285n32, 288n9
Kraftwerk, 23
Kwastek, Katja, 183

Lady Pheønix, 213, 242; *Breonna's Garden*, 213–14, 242, 303n60
Lau, Vicki, 110, 130, 167, 256, 293n60, 295n20
Lauren (McCarthy), 183, *184*, 241
Ledwidge, Michela, 115, 155, 256
Lend Me Your Face! (Thiel and /p), 36, 243
Lerner, Rosemarie, and Maria Court, 197–98, 220, 256
Levy, Wendy, 58, 256–57
LGBTQ+: communities, 49, 88, 192; youth homelessness, 48

Libby, Jan, 63–64, 95, 155, 176, 242, 257
Lichtenstein, Brad, 76, 242
Life in Pieces, A (de la Peña and Yamato), 48, 287n40
Limina Immersive, 79, 112, 155
LIPSYNC (Weil), 123, *124*, 243
Local Autonomy Networks (Autonets) (cárdenas), 218, 243
Logic Paralyzes the Heart (Hershman Leeson), 222, *223*, 303–4n75
Loh, Juliana, 94, 146, 164, 257
lonelygirl15 (Libby, Powell, Feuer, et al.), 95, 96, 97
Lozano, Carrie, 95, 106, 166, 257
Luckey, Palmer, 46, 88, 101, 140, 273

Magee-Cook, Jennifer, 93, 128, 258
Magic Leap, 109, 234, 272; headset, 109
Maher, Jennifer Helene, 82
Making a New Reality, 2, 53, 86, 170, 177, 224, 281n2, 300n71, 304n79
Malloy, Judy, 15; *Women, Art and Technology*, 15
Manifest.AR, 34, 243
Manovich, Lev, 70
Marie, Artsy, 106, 111, 117, 164, 173, 246, 293n48
McCarthy, Lauren Lee, 113, 183, *184*, 219–20, 242, 258, 293n69
McGrory, Debra, 107, 111, 137, 258, 285n32
McIntosh, Verity, 114, 142, 258
McLaren, Carrie, 2, 177
mentorship, 20, 51, 76, 85, 152, 171, 172, 179, 232
metaverse, ix, 1, 20, 92, 158, 221, 235, 236, 237, 238, 272, 275, 277, 305n11
#MeToo, 3, 4, 87, 90, 127
military: aviation, 3, 272; funding, 123; sectors, 238; testing, 195; training, 3
Milk, Chris, 46, 87, 88, 210, 232, 271, 272
Miller, Elizabeth "Liz," 97, 258–59, 291n22

MIT: Architecture Machine Group (Arch Mac), 122; Co-Creation Studio, 267; digital libraries, 56; Media Lab, 122, 124, 246, 266, 294n2, 294n7; Open Documentary Lab, 55, 149, 153, 267; Project New Media Literacies, 78

mixed reality, ix, 3, 27, 105, 110, 167, 229

mobile games, 84
—apps: Zealyst, 85

Morgan, Nyarri Nyarri, 211–12, 243

Morrison, Katy, 110, 259, 293n58

Morrison, Romi, 71

motion: balance sensors, 37; breath sensors, 37; sensing, 202; tracking, 37, 168

Mozilla Hubs, 35, 115–16, 117, 273

MTV, 23, 67

Murray, Janet, 214–15, 303n62, 311

Museum of Modern Art (MoMA), 30, 34

music videos, 23, 74, 87, 247

MyoPhone (Allen), 27–28, *28*, 242

NASA, vii, 3, 10, 263

networks, 52, 84–85; Seattle Women in Tech, 84

Nintendo, 7; Nintendo 64 console, 25, 273; Virtual Boy console, 7, 11

Noble, Safiya Umoja, 3–4, 6, 111–12

Norrington, Alison, 146, 259, 297n67

Not the Only One (Dinkins), 190, *191*, 242

Nucera, Diana J. (aka Mother Cyborg), 71

Oculus, 80, 104, 121, 138, 158, 273, 276, 277
—Facebook's acquisition, 101, 137
—headset, 46, 111
—Launch Pad, 147
—product lines: Go, 117, 234, 273; Quest, 273; Quest 2, 273

—Rift, viii, *47*, 88, 101–2, 119, 234, 277
—software development kit (SDK), 100, 109, 173
—VR for Good Creators Lab, 85

O'Flynn, Siobhan, 150, 175, 178, 259, 297n80, 300n77

Ọnụọha, Mimi, 71, 155, 164, 171, 220, 259, 297n5

OpenGL, 32, 273, 292n42

open source, 80, 113, 220, 273; blockchain, 271; library, 273; platforms, 116, 275; software, vii, 279n6

Oscar Micheaux Society, 2

Osmose (Davies), 37, 39–42, 104–5, 241

Out of Exile (de la Peña), 46, *48*, 235, 242

Pacquing, Neilda, 136, 144, 148–49, 157, 168, 173, 259–60

Palais, Jennifer, 62–63, 98, 172–73, 260

Parsons, Kate, 77, 79, 87, 260

Paul, Christiane, 15–16, 53, 181–82, *183*, 260

People's Guide to Tech, 71, 220, 289n36

Performance of Your Life (Bennett), 189

Perry, Phoenix, 73–74, 113, 260

Pheønix, Lady, 213, 242

photogrammetry, 46, *69*

PlayStation, 25; Morpheus, 111, 274; VR, viii, 274

Plowright, Kim, 93, 98, 149, 261, 291n4, 292n27

Pokémon Go, 26, 34

Powell, Jenni, 96, 242, 261

Power, Madeline, 59, 76, 261

Producers Guild of America (PGA), 59, 60, 93; guidelines, 59; transmedia producer credit, 93, 167, 291n2

Project Syria (de la Peña), 46, 101, 241

promotion, 62–63, 121; self, 62

Public Secrets (Daniel), 195–96, 234–35

quantum computing, 30
Queerskins (Szilak and Tsiboulski): *Ark*, 69, 200; *A Love Story*, 200; *A Novel*, 68–70, 94, 188, 200, 243
Quipu Project (Lerner and Court), 197–98

Rankin, Joy Lisi, 7
real-time game engine (RTGE), 128–29, 274
Reconstructing Mayakovsky (Szilak, Tsiboulski, and Kirca), 68, 69, 243
redlining, 106, 111, 112
refugee crises: Syria, 48
Reign of Gold (Thiel), 34, 35, 243
Reilly, Erin, 78, 261
Restauri, Denise, 84
Restore/Restory (ross), 193, 242
Reuter, Teresa, 243
Rodriguez, Sandra, 98, 159, 261, 292n25
Rose, Amy, 170, 203–4, 245, 262, 299n48, 302n45
Rose, Mandy, 126–27, 262
Rosenthal, Liz, 56–57, 86, 94, 109, 116, 130–31, 132, 140, 148, 262, 293n56, 294n79
ross, jesikah maria, 193, 242, 262; *Restore/Restory*, 193, 242; *Saving the Sierras*, 193, 242
Ruiz, Susana, 67–68, 68, 70, 203, 242, 262, 289n30; *Darfur Is Dying*, 67, 68, 203
Ryan, Tina Rivers, 53

Sammet, Jean E., 10
Sandor, Ellen, 16, 263, 285n36
Santa-Olalla, Belén, 134, 263
Saving the Sierras (ross), 193, 242
Science Gallery London, 72
Second Life, 44, 45, 105, 184, 209, 274; installation, 44
sensor-based interactivity, 39; biometric response, 100

sensory media, 9, 10, 26
Shadow Stalker (Hershman Leeson), 222, 303n75
SH//FT (Shaping Holistic Inclusion in Future Technology), 79, 80, 172
Shlain, Tiffany, 163, 263, 298n28
Shogaolu, Tamara, 134–35, 140–41, 206, 242, 263, 295n36; *Un(re)solved*, 206
Shub, Esfir, 9, 284n96
Silicon Valley, 6, 7, 82, 83, 109, 147, 161, 274, 275; investment, 109; start-ups, 82
Sinclair, Kamal, 2, 53–54, 58, 86–88, 99, 100, 103, 167, 177, 224, 226, 238, 263–64, 281n2
Sin Sol / No Sun (cárdenas), 192, 243
Sisters with Transistors, 10
Sleepy Hollow VR experience, 93, 291n5
social media, 59, 64, 71, 85, 132, 149, 150, 172–73, 195, 216
—platforms: Snapchat, 97, 168; Tumblr, 71
soft skills, 18, 58
Sony, 25, 93, 121, 128, 274
Southern, Taryn, 74–76, 140, 168, 173, 264, 289n43
spatial computing, 83, 116
spatialized sound, 37
Spielberg, Steven, 103, 265
Sponge Space Trash Takeover (Thiel), 35, 243
Srivastava, Lina, 96, 161, 169, 199, 211, 220, 264, 285n32
Starbright World, 32, 103–4
Steyerl, Hito, 186, 188
Storr, Samantha, 59, 87–88, 264
Stringfellow, Kim, 194–95, 197, 301n24
Suga' (James), 107, 108, 242
Sundance Film Festival, 47, 100, 103, 107, 115, 121, 148; board, 143; Institute, 99; New Frontier Lab, 1, 2, 54–55, 99, 145; New Frontier program, 46, 87, 99, 209

Svilova, Elizaveta, 9, 284n26
Swimmer (Allen), *23*, 125, 241
Szilak, Illya, 68–70, 94, 188, 200, 264, 285n32; *Ark*, *69*, 200; *Atomic Vacation*, 68, 243; *A Love Story*, 200; *A Novel*, 69, 188, 200; *Queerskins*, 68, 94, 188, 243, 200; *Reconstructing Mayakovsky*, 68, 69, 243

Tankal, Ece, 112, 137, 190, 221
Taylor, Breonna, 213–14, 242, 303n60
Taylor, Jessica, 265
TED talk, 46, 210
television, 3, 74, 91, 192, 229; documentary, 66; production, 5, 129, 234
Tharp, Twyla, 22, 243; *The Catherine Wheel*, 22, *24*
Thiel, Tamiko, 7, 18, 20, *31*, *32*, *33*, 265, 285n34, 286n14, 292n42; *Atmos Sphaerae*, 35–36, 243; *Beyond Manzanar*, 32; *Evolution of Fish*, 35, *36*, 242; *Gardens of the Anthropocene*, 35, 243; *In the Land of Babari-an*, 32, 243; *Reign of Gold*, 34, *35*, 243; *Sponge Space Trash Takeover*, 35, 243; *Unexpected Growth*, 35, 243; *Virtuelle Mauer / ReConstructing the Wall*, 32–33, 243; *We AR in MoMA*, 34, 243
Thinking Machines Corporation, 29, 30
Thompson, Clive, 10
3D
    —animation, 21, *24*, 24–25, 125
    —artist, 166
    —authoring software, 37, 40, 42, 286n8
    —computer games, 104, 275
    —graphics, 274
    —immersive space creation, 43
    —modeling, 22, 125, 144, 174, 274

    —real-time creativity, 32
    —software types: Alias, 40; Softimage 3D, 40–41, 127–28; Unity Engine, 174, 275; Wavefront, 40
    —touch, 271
    —virtual worlds, 32, 33, 103, 115, 274
    —visualization software, 107
    —web applications, 105
360-degree, 105, 133, 134, 143, 212; video, 48, 59, 77, 211, 241, 242, 275, 287n40; VR, 36, 223, 243; workshops, 77
Through You (Baldwin), 105–6, *106*, 225
Ticho, Sarah, 132, 143, 150, 265
transmedia, 2–3, 18, 59, 60, 65, 68, 92–100, 119, 175, 182, 193, 199, 229–30, *231*; campaigns, 167; database, vii; design, 58; experiences, 93; format, 67; franchises, 60, 93; industry, viii, 96; narrative strategy, 188; producer, 167, 291n2; production, 12, 107; professionals, 150; publications, 279–80n7; Ready (platform), 178, 300n75; storytelling, 92, 134, 137, 146, 217, 269; storyworlds, 60, 93; studies, vii, 92; women in, vii
Tribeca Film Festival (TFI), 48, 49, 57, 95, 121, 141, 148, 302n45; New Media Fund, 57
Truong, Huy, *68*
Tsiboulski, Cyril, 69, 200, 243

Unconstitutional (de la Peña), 45, 209, 241
Unexpected Growth (Thiel), 35, 243
Un(re)solved (Frontline), 206, *207*, *208*, 242, 248, 302n49
Unseld, Saschka, *106*, 201, 241
Uricchio, William, 55, 177

USC, vii, 26, 45, 46, 101, 209;
Annenberg School, 45; iMAP
(Media Arts and Practice PhD
program), 68; Interactive Media
and Games division, 70

Van De Keere, Isabel, 136, 159, 161, 265
Venice Biennale, 34; Film Festival, 122,
148; Immersive, 56, 94; Production
Bridge Market, 57
Virgin Interactive, 24, 126
virtual production, 32, 42, 115, 167–68,
276; producer, 147, 166–67;
sector, 128–29, 147; studios, 165;
supervisor, 165; technologies, 32,
234
virtual reality (VR), viii, 1, 2, 3, 9, 25,
45, 57, 100–103, 137, 167, 212, 213;
accessibility, 85, 86, 110, 111–15,
117, 120; animation, 62; art, 84,
104; cinema, 112; commercial, 18;
consumer, 10–11; definition, 276;
documentary, 76; embodied, 21, 43,
112, 182, 201, 202, 209, 214; empathy
and, 210–15 (see also empathy); first
wave, 103–5, 119; game engine, 116;
head-mounted display (HMD),
45, 104, 119, 157–58; health care,
136; installations, 68; live events,
84; mobile, 21, 47, 86; modeling
language, 32, 276; music videos,
87; narrative, 105, 110; nausea, 104,
113, 114; pain distraction, 26, 286n9;
platforms, 91, 276, 277; social VR,
19, 92; training, 136; walk-around,
101; web-based, 115, 116
virtual world, 32, 117, 286n8
—art works, 32–33, 33, 103
—children's, 32, 103
—creation, 11, 19, 21, 29, 32, 43, 92,
108, 119, 229

—platforms: Second Life, 32, 274;
Starbright World, 32, 103;
Worlds Chat, 32, 277
Virtuelle Mauer / ReConstructing the
Wall (Thiel), 32–33, 243
Vision for Women in Virtual Reality
(VWVR), ix, 151, 280n10
Visual Effects (VFX), 41, 42, 167, 270,
276; artist, 110, 130; companies, 165;
industry, 130, 147; supervisor, 130
Vogl, Sara Lisa, 113, 116–17, 149, 163, 173,
178, 238, 265, 293n72
volumetric: capture, 277; imagery, 46;
performance, 116; streaming, 107;
video, 69
volunteer labor, 20, 177, 178
VR. See virtual reality (VR)

Wallworth, Lynette, 145, 204–5, 206,
211–15, 220, 227, 243, 266, 297n65;
Awavena, 212–13, 266; Collisions,
211–12, 235; Hold Vessel I and II,
205, 243
Wampum Codes, 83
Watson, Zillah, 110, 119, 132, 266,
293n57
We AR in MoMA (Thiel and Manifest.
AR), 34, 243
Webby Awards, 69, 163
WebGL, 105, 277; documentary, 105
web series, 94, 95, 150
Weil, Peggy, 44, 45, 105, 122–26, 207,
209, 242–43, 266, 294n3, 294n7;
Gone Gitmo (with de la Peña), 44,
45, 105; LIPSYNC, 123, 124, 125, 243
Weinreich, Nedra Kline, 216, 266,
303n66
Welkhoff, Martina, 83–84, 118–19, 133,
141, 162, 266–67, 290n61
When Words Fail (Dinkins), 190, 242
Whitney Museum of American Art,
53, 181
Williams, Roberta, 98

Winger-Bearskin, Amelia, 81–83, 129, 139, 156, 160–61, 163, 171, 267, 290n56

Wolozin, Sarah, 55–56, 114, 149, 153, 176–77, 267, 285n32, 288n6

Women, Art and Technology (Malloy), 15

Women and Film History International, 2

Women Film Pioneers project, 2, 11, 281n3, 284n26

Women in VR: Facebook group, 79–80, 87, 149, 150, 172; groups, 78, 79–80

women's health care, 48, 214

Women's Media Center, 5, 282n9

Wood, Marni, 225

working culture(s), viii, 19, 128–32, 151, 232; alternative, 19, 121–22

worldbuilder, 174; VR, 94

worldbuilding, 96, 123, 137, 146, 229, 237, 238, 277

WXR Fund, 83, 84, 87, 118, 133, 162

Xu, Nancy, 147, 166, 267, 297n70

Yamato, Sharon, 242, 267

Yard, Itzel, 236

York, Ashley, 65–66, *68*, 267

Young, Julie, 79–80, 85, 290n52

YouTube, 55, 74–75, 116, 169

Zuckerman, Maya, 96, 200, 243, 268, 291n19